Managing Airports

30.00
SJ
2/02

Managing Airports
An international perspective

Anne Graham

OXFORD   AUCKLAND   BOSTON   JOHANNESBURG   MELBOURNE   NEW DELHI

Butterworth-Heinemann
Linacre House, Jordan Hill, Oxford OX2 8DP
225 Wildwood Avenue, Woburn, MA 01801-2041
A division of Reed Educational and Professional Publishing Ltd

 A member of the Reed Elsevier plc group

First published 2001

© Anne Graham 2001

British Library Cataloguing in Publication Data
Graham, Anne
    Managing airports: an international perspective
    1.   Airports – Management
    I.   Title
    387.7'36

ISBN 0 7506 4823 6

For information on all Butterworth-Heinemann
publications visit our website at www.bh.com

Composition by Scribe Design, Gillingham, Kent
Printed and bound in Great Britain

Contents

Figures

Tables

Preface

In most of the published literature the airport industry has received relatively little attention and has traditionally been very much overshadowed by the airline sector. Attitudes towards airports have changed dramatically as their role has shifted from that of public utility to that of a dynamic, commercially oriented business. Airport operators are no longer just operating within the scope of their national boundaries, and the whole industry is becoming global. At the same time there is a growing recognition of the need to balance the wider economic benefits that airport expansion can bring with the increased environmental costs.

The aim of this book is to provide a comprehensive appreciation of the key management issues facing modern-day airport operators. Airports are now complex businesses requiring a range of business competencies and skills. The emphasis here is on the economic, commercial and planning areas at a strategic level, rather than on the detailed operational and technical aspects. An international approach has been adopted reflecting the increasingly international nature of the industry. The book uses material from a wide range of airports and has a very practical focus. While most of the case studies are from the developed world, which has witnessed the fastest pace of change, they nevertheless have relevance to airport operators throughout the world.

The book provides an overview of all the key management challenges facing airports. By necessity the scope has to be very far-reaching and so it cannot offer an in-depth treatment of every issue. Instead it is intended that the book should enable the reader to acquire a broad and up-to-date insight into the workings of the industry which will meet the needs of anyone who wishes to work, or is already working, in the airport sector.

Acknowledgements

I am indebted to many individuals and organizations for helping this book come to fruition. I would like to begin by thanking my colleagues at the University of Westminster for their continual support and encouragement. I am particularly grateful to Dr Nigel Dennis for his guidance and constructive advice, as well as tolerance and patience, as I struggled to write the book with numerous other deadlines approaching.

I have spent over fifteen years undertaking research into airports and teaching about airport-related topics. This book draws heavily upon these experiences. During this time I have been very fortunate in meeting a large number of industry professionals who have provided me with invaluable insights into the management of airports. I have also benefited enormously from discussions with my own students, and with participants from airport management training programmes organized by the University. Thanks are due to all these people. Special thanks must go to Professor Rigas Doganis who was largely responsible for introducing me to the world of airports and who has remained supportive of my airport work ever since.

So many people have helped me over the years that it is difficult to name them all. I particularly want to express my appreciation to the following individuals who have always willingly given up their valuable time to contribute on our industry seminars: Sigi Gangl from Vienna Airport, Stan Maiden and Mike Toms from BAA plc, John Riordan from the Bank of Ireland International Finance, Stan Abrahams formerly from the UK Civil Aviation Authority, Nigel Mason from York Consulting, Edward Clayton from Hochtief Airport, Hartmut-Ruediger Simon and Rolf Ewald from Dusseldorf Airport, Professor Brian Graham from the University of Ulster, Jan Veldhuis from the Netherlands Civil Aviation Department and John Twigg from Manchester Airport. I have learned much from their presentations and informal discussions.

Amongst the many other airport experts who have helped with this book I must give a special thanks to Wendy O'Connor. Over the years at ACI-Europe she spent much time and effort replying to my endless questions and searching out relevant documents. Thanks are also due to Natalie Marchioro at ACI-

Europe. I wish to express my gratitude to Ian Stockman and Dr Romano Pagliari at Cranfield University who have always been most supportive and helpful in sharing their knowledge and expertise and very willing to provide research material. I am grateful as well to Dr Ian Humphreys at Loughborough University. Special mention must go to Jason Vallint, with whom I spent long hours debating about the WLU concept, and Peter Mackenzie-Williams, both of the Transport Research Laboratory. I also very much appreciate the help given by Patrick Alexander from Southampton Airport, Trevor Eady from Norwich Airport, Ivo Favotto from Arthur Andersen, Dr Brigitte Bolech from Vienna Airport and Hans-Arthur Vogel from Frankfurt airport. I am very much indebted to many other airport financial professionals, too numerous to mention individually, who have tirelessly responded to my frequent requests for data over the years. In addition, I must thank all the staff at Butterworth-Heinemann. I am a novice at book writing and they have given me much helpful advice and assistance.

Finally, I must thank my family and friends for putting up with the disruption to their lives while I have been writing this book. I owe a special debt of gratitude to Sandra Bollard, for always being their to look after my children when I tried to juggle writing and family life, and to the Daswani family for their help and encouragement. I am very appreciative of the support from my mother Barbara Miller, who has shown a keen interest in my work and has provided an invaluable press-cutting service, and from the rest of the Miller family. My children, Lorna, Callum and Ewan, have been very patient with my preoccupation with this book – although they still do not understand why anyone would want to write or read about airports! Above all, without the support and encouragement of my long-suffering husband, Robert, this book would never have been finished. With good humour he has tolerated my unreasonable behaviour and I am very much indebted to him.

Abbreviations

ACCC	Australian Competition and Consumer Commission
ACI	Airports Council International
ACSA	Airports Company South Africa
AdP	Aeroports de Paris
AEA	Association of European Airlines
AENA	Aeropuertos Espanoles y Navegacion Aerea
AGI	Airports Group International
AIA	Athens International Airport SA
AIP	Airport Improvement Program
ANSconf	Conference on the Economics of Airports and Air Navigation Services
APU	airport throughput unit
ARI	Aer Rianta International
ASAS	airport surface access strategy
ATC	air traffic control
ATF	airport transport forum
ATM	air transport movement
BA	British Airways
BCIA	Beijing Capital International Airport
BOOT	build–own–operate–transfer
BOT	build–operate–transfer
BRT	build–rent–transfer
BT	build–transfer
CAA	Civil Aviation Authority
Capex	capital expenditure
CDG	Charles de Gaulle
CIPFA	Chartered Institute of Public Finance and Accountancy
CO_2	carbon dioxide
CPH	Copenhagen Airport A/S
CRI	Centre for Regulated Industries
dB	decibel
DCMF	design–construct–manage–finance
DDF	Dubai Duty Free

EBIT	earnings before interest and tax
EBITDA	earnings before interest, tax, depreciation and amortization
EIA	environmental impact assessment
EIS	environmental impact statement
EMAS	Eco Management and Audit Scheme
ENEA	Establishing a Network for European Airports
ETRF	European Travel Research Foundation
EU	European Union
EV	enterprise value
FAA	Federal Aviation Administration
FAC	Federal Airports Corporation
GA	general aviation
GDP	gross domestic product
IATA	International Air Transport Association
ICAO	International Civil Aviation Organization
IDFC	International Duty Free Confederation
IPO	initial public offering
ISO	International Standards Organization
LAX	Los Angeles International
LTO	landing and take-off
MA	Manchester Airport plc
MAW	maximum authorized weight
MCT	minimum connect time
MII	majority in interest
MIS	management information system
mppa	million passengers per annum
MTOW	maximum take-off weight
NO_x	nitrogen oxide
OAG	Official Airline Guide
PFC	passenger facility charge
PIATCO	Philippine International Air Terminals Co.
PNR	preferred noise route
POS	passenger opinion survey
ppa	passengers per annum
QSM	quality of survey monitor
ROCE	return on capital employed
ROR	rate of return
ROT	rehabilitate–own–transfer
SLA	service level agreement
SPA	strategic partnership agreement
TDENL	total-day-evening-night-level
TFP	total factor productivity
TJ	Tera Joule
TQM	total quality management
VAT	value added tax
WLU	work load unit
YVRAS	Vancouver Airport Services

1

Introduction

Airports are an essential part of the air transport system. They provide all the infrastructure needed to enable passengers and freight to transfer from surface to air modes of transport and to allow airlines to take off and land. The basic airport infrastructure consists of runways, taxiways, apron space, gates, passenger and freight terminals, and ground transport interchanges. Airports bring together a wide range of facilities and services in order to be able to fulfil their role within the air transport industry. These services include air traffic control, security, fire and rescue in the airfield. Handling facilities are provided so that passengers, their baggage and freight can be successfully transferred between aircraft and terminals, and processed within the terminal. Airports also offer a wide variety of commercial facilities ranging from shops and restaurants to hotels, conference services and business parks.

As well as playing a crucial role within the air transport sector, airports have a strategic importance to the regions they serve. In a number of countries they are increasingly becoming integrated within the overall transport system by establishing links to high-speed rail and key road networks. Airports can bring greater wealth, provide substantial employment opportunities and encourage economic development – and can be a lifeline to isolated communities. However, they do have a very significant effect, both on the environment in which they are located and on the quality of life of residents living nearby. Growing awareness of general environmental issues has heightened the environmental concerns about airports.

The focus of this book is on management issues facing airport operators. These operators vary considerably in their ownership, management structure and style, degree of autonomy and funding. Typically the actual airport operators themselves only provide a small proportion of an airport's facilities and services. The rest of these activities will be undertaken by airlines, handling agents, government bodies, concessionaires and other specialist organizations. The way in which operators choose to provide the diverse range of airport facilities can have a major impact on their economic and operational performance and on their relationship with their customers.

Each airport operator will thus have a unique identity – but all have to assume overall control and responsibility at the airport. Each will be faced with the challenging task of co-ordinating all the services to enable the airport system to work efficiently. The providers of services are just some of the airport stakeholders which operators need to consider. Others include shareholders, airport users, employees, local residents, environmental lobbyists and government bodies. A complex situation exists with many of these groups having different interests and possibly holding conflicting views about the strategic role of the airport. All the stakeholder relationships will be important but, clearly, the development of a good relationship with the airlines will be critical, as ultimately this will largely determine the air services on offer at the airport.

Globally the airport industry is dominated by North America and Europe (Figures 1.1, 1.2 and 1.3). According to the Airports Council International (ACI), North American airports handled 1386 million passengers in 1999, which represented 47 per cent of the total 3003 million passengers. There were 912 million passengers in Europe, accounting for a further 30 per cent of the total traffic. As regards cargo, North America is again the largest market with 27 million tonnes of the global 61 million tonnes – again with a market share

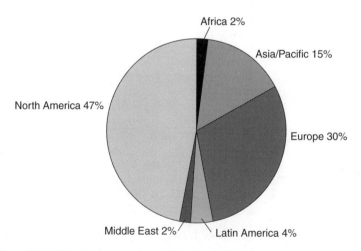

Figure 1.1 Airport passengers by world region, 1999
Source: ACI.

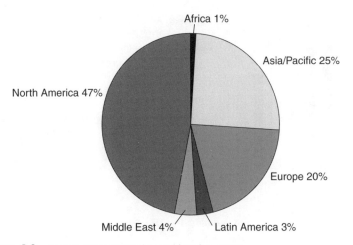

Figure 1.2 Airport cargo tonnes by world region, 1999
Source: ACI.

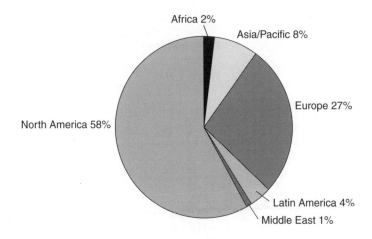

Figure 1.3 Airport aircraft movement by world region, 1999
Source: ACI.

of 47 per cent. Asian/Pacific airports have the second highest volume of cargo with a global share of 25 per cent, reflecting the importance of this area in the global economy. North America has a larger share of the total 58 million aircraft movements (58 per cent) since the average size of aircraft tends to be smaller due to competitive pressures and the dominance of domestic traffic.

The importance of the North American region is reflected in the individual traffic figures of the various airports. For example out of the twenty largest global airports, fourteen are US airports in terms of passenger numbers, ten with cargo and seventeen when air transport movements are being considered (Figures 1.4, 1.5 and 1.6). However, when just international traffic is being

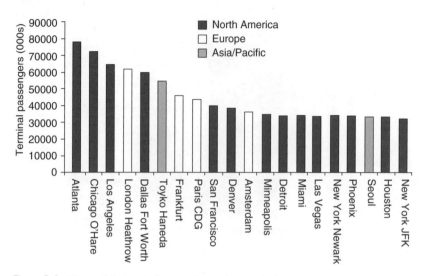

Figure 1.4 The world's twenty largest airports by terminal passengers, 1999
Sources: ACI and BAA plc.

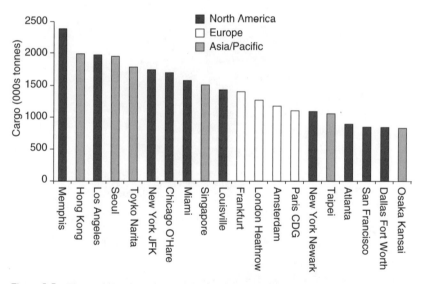

Figure 1.5 The world's twenty largest airports by cargo tonnes, 1999
Sources: ACI and BAA plc.

examined, the European region's significance becomes much more important (Figure 1.7).

Heathrow has the most international traffic, while Atlanta, Chicago and Los Angeles have the largest passenger throughput. The largest passenger airport in Asia is Toyko Haneda, which is dominated by domestic traffic. Not all the

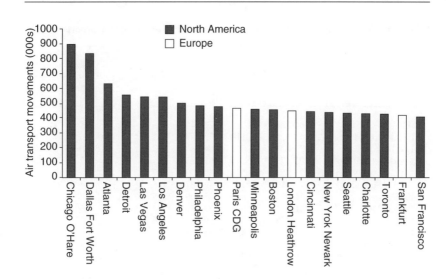

Figure 1.6 The world's twenty largest airports by air transport movements, 1999
Sources: ACI and BAA plc.

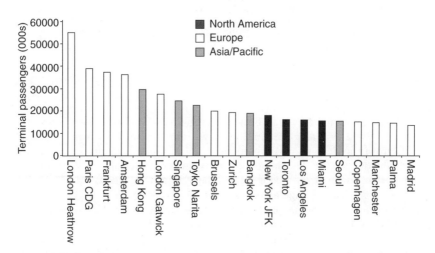

Figure 1.7 The world's twenty largest airports by international terminal passengers, 1999
Sources: ACI and BAA plc.

major cargo airports coincide with the major passenger airports. Memphis is the world's largest cargo airport because Federal Express is based here. Similarly UPS has its base at Louisville. The cargo market is more widespread with six of the important cargo airports situated in Asia. The larger than average aircraft size in Asia means than none of the busiest airports in terms of movements are situated in this region. All the twenty busiest airports, whether measured in passengers, cargo or movements are in North America, Europe or Asia/Pacific, with none in any other global region.

Table 1.1 Growth in passenger numbers at the world's twenty largest airports

	1980	1990	1999	% average annual change, 1990/1980	% average annual change, 1999/1990
1 Atlanta	40 180	48 015	77 744	1.8	5.5
2 Chicago O'Hare	44 425	60 118	72 157	3.1	2.0
3 Los Angeles	33 038	45 810	64 280	3.3	3.8
4 London Heathrow	27 472	42 647	61 975	4.5	4.2
5 Dallas Fort Worth	21 951	48 515	60 000	8.3	2.4
6 Toyko Haneda	20 810	40 188	54 307	6.8	3.4
7 Frankfurt	16 873	28 862	45 400	5.5	5.2
8 Paris CDG	10 091	22 506	43 439	8.4	7.6
9 San Francisco	21 338	30 388	39 586	3.6	3.0
10 Denver	20 849	27 433	38 034	2.8	3.7
11 Amsterdam	9 401	16 178	36 425	5.6	9.4
12 Minneapolis/St Paul	9 252	20 381	34 216	8.2	5.9
13 Detroit	9 883	21 942	33 968	8.3	5.0
14 Miami	20 505	25 837	33 899	2.3	3.1
15 Las Vegas	10 302	18 833	33 669	6.2	6.7
16 New York Newark	9 223	22 255	33 623	9.2	4.7
17 Phoenix	6 586	21 718	33 554	12.7	5.0
18 Seoul	n/a	16 821	33 284	n/a	7.9
19 Houston	10 695	17 438	33 051	5.0	7.4
20 New York JFK	26 796	29 787	31 701	1.1	0.7
Average				5.6	4.8

Sources: ACI and BAA plc.

The aviation industry has been growing virtually continuously since the Second World War and continues to grow – albeit at lower growth rates now. This growth in demand and subsequent need for additional airport capacity is undoubtedly one of the major influences on the airport business. Table 1.1 shows the growth at the major international airports of the world for the last twenty years. The average annual growth was 5.6 per cent in the 1980 and 4.8 per cent in 1990s. Some of the US airports, particularly those not to have benefited substantially from US deregulation, such as New York JFK and Miami, have experienced relatively low growth rates. Within Europe, Paris and Amsterdam airports have grown faster than both London Heathrow and Frankfurt.

The growth in demand for air transport has had very significant economic and environmental consequences for both the airline and airport industries. Moreover, since the 1970s there have been major regulatory and structural developments, which have affected dramatically the way in which the two industries operate. Initially most change was experienced within the airline sector as a consequence of airline deregulation, privatization and globalization trends. The pace of change was slower in the airport industry, but now this sector, too, is developing into a fundamentally different business.

The trend towards airline deregulation began in 1978 with the deregulation of the US domestic market. Many more markets subsequently have been liberalized or deregulated. In some places this has been the result of the adoption of more liberal bilateral air service agreements, as has occurred on a number of the North Atlantic and Pacific routes. In the European Union (EU), deregulation has been achieved with a multilateral policy which has evolved over a number of years with the introduction of the three deregulation packages, in 1987, 1990 and 1993. The 1993 package, which did not become fully operational until 1997, was the most significant package and has had the most far-reaching impact.

At the same time, airline ownership patterns have changed. Most airlines, with the notable exception of those in the USA, traditionally were state owned and often subsidized by their government owners. However, this situation has substantially changed as an increasing number of governments have opted for partial or totally private sector airline ownership, primarily to reduce the burden on public sector expenditure and to encourage greater operating efficiency.

The other most significant development within the airline industry, partly due to deregulation and privatization trends, is the globalization of the industry and the emergence of transnational airlines. Five major alliance groupings, namely Star, Oneworld, 'Wings', Sky Team and Qualiflyer, have emerged with global networks. These are dominating the airline business – accounting for two-thirds of all traffic. Moreover, many other airlines are aligning themselves to these groupings with code-sharing, franchising or other co-operative arrangements.

The airports have now found themselves being caught up in this environment of change. Radical restructuring has occurred, which in many ways mirrors that which has fundamentally changed the airline industry. Three key developments have been witnessed within the airport sector:

1 *Airport commercialization.* The transformation of an airport from a public utility to a commercial enterprise and the adoption of a more businesslike management philosophy.
2 *Airport privatization.* The transfer of the management of an airport, and in many cases the ownership as well, to the private sector by a variety of methods. These include share flotations, the adoption of strategic partnerships or the introduction of private management contracts.
3 *Airport globalization.* The emergence of a few global airport companies who are operating at an increasing number of airports around the world. Some of these global players are traditional airport operators whereas others are new to airport management.

This book discusses the implications of the development of the airport sector, which is moving from an industry characterized by public sector ownership and national requirements, into a new era of airport management which is dominated by the private sector and global players. Airports are now complex enterprises that require a wide range of business competencies and skills – just as with any other industry. Airports can no longer see their role simply as providers of infrastructure but, instead, as providing facilities to meet the needs of their users.

Chapter 2 describes the privatization and globalization processes that are taking place. These developments are having a major impact on both economic performance and service provision. This is considered in Chapters 3 and 4. The sweeping changes, occurring concurrently within both the airline and airport industries mean that the traditional airline–airport relationship has been irreversibly changed. Chapter 5 looks at this, focusing primarily on airport charging and slots issues.

A major consequence of airport commercialization and privatization trends is that airport operators are devoting much more time and effort to building up the non-aeronautical or commercial areas of the business. Chapter 6 looks in detail at this area of operation. Airport competition, hardly considered to be a relevant issue by many airports just a few years ago, is also becoming increasingly important. Marketing, which for so long has been a basic business competence in most other industries but ignored by many airports, is now a firmly accepted management practice at airports. Chapter 7 considers airport marketing.

The remaining chapters of the book take a broader view of the airport business and consider the role that airports play on the environment and surrounding community. This role needs to be clearly understood if future growth in the airport industry is to continue. Chapter 8 discusses the economic impacts of airports and how airports can act as a catalyst for business and tourism development. Chapter 9 goes on to consider the environmental impacts and ways in which airports are attempting to minimize the adverse effects. The concept of sustainability and environmental capacity is introduced. Finally, the key issues of each chapter are brought in Chapter 10 in order to make predictions for the coming years and to assess the future prospects for the industry.

2

The changing nature of airports

It is the aim of this chapter to discuss the development of the airport sector as it moves from an industry characterized by public sector ownership and national requirements into a new era of airport management which is beginning to be dominated by the private sector and global players. The impact of such fundamental changes will be assessed from the point of view of the airport industry itself, the airlines and the passengers.

Virtually all airports traditionally were owned by the public sector. European airports serving major cities such as Paris, London, Dublin, Stockholm, Copenhagen, Madrid and Geneva were all owned by national governments, as were many other airports outside Europe such as those in Tokyo, Singapore, Bangkok, Sydney and Johannesburg. Elsewhere local governments, either at a regional or municipal level, were the airport owners. This was the situation with most US airports. Regional airports in the UK also followed this pattern. Manchester airport, for example, was owned by a consortium of local authorities with 55 per cent ownership resting with Manchester City Council and the remaining 45 per cent split evenly among eight councils of other nearby towns. In Germany, Düsseldorf airport was jointly owned by the governments of North Rhine Westfalia state and the city of Düsseldorf, while the joint owners of Hanover airport were the governments of the state of Lower Saxony and the city of Hanover.

With a number of airports, there may have been both local and national government interest. For example, Frankfurt airport was jointly owned by the state of Hesse (45 per cent), the city of Frankfurt (29 per cent) and the federal government (26 per cent). Similarly, Amsterdam was owned by the national government (76 per cent) and the municipalities of Amsterdam (22 per cent) and Rotterdam (2 per cent). Vienna airport was another example, owned by the republic of Austria (50 per cent), the province of Lower Austria (25 per cent) and the city of Vienna (25 per cent). Basel-Mulhouse or EuroAirport, situated on the border between Switzerland and France, was a rather unique airport being jointly owned by the national governments of both Switzerland and France.

It is only in the 1990s that there has been a significance presence of privately, or partially privately, owned airports. The only privately owned airports traditionally, tended to be the very small general aviation or aeroclub airports and so the influence of the private sector on the airport industry was very limited. Thus public ownership – either at a local and/or national level – used to be the norm. However, the way in which the government owners chose to operate or manage the airports varied quite significantly and had a major impact on the airport's degree of independence and autonomy. The strictest form of control existed when the airport was operated directly by a government department, typically the Civil Aviation Authority (CAA), Ministry of Transport or, in a few cases, the military. This was the common practice for airports in areas such as Asia, the Middle East, Africa and South America. In Canada, the state department Transport Canada directly operated the 150 commercial Canadian airports. Within Europe, Greece was a good example of a country where airports were effectively run by the CAA.

In other cases, semiautonomous bodies or companies, but still under public ownership, operated the airports. In some instances, these organizations managed more than one airport, as was the situation in Europe with the British Airports Authority (BAA) and Aer Rianta Irish Airports. There were also airport authorities or companies that operated just one major airport. This was the case at Amsterdam airport and many of the German airports. In the USA, airport authorities also existed for some of the airports, such as the Minneapolis-Saint Paul Metropolitan Airports Commission. In a few cases there were multipurpose transport authorities, such as the Port Authority of New York and New Jersey or Massport in Boston, which operated other transport facilities as well as airports.

There were also a few examples of airports being operated on a concession basis for central government. At the larger Italian airports (e.g. Venice, Milan), companies with public (usually local) shareholdings and perhaps some private shareholdings as well held the operating concession for a long-term period, such as sixty years at Milan airport. The concession could cover management of the total airport and handling services (e.g. Milan, Turin) or just some of the services such as terminal management and handling (e.g. Palermo). At French regional airports also, the concessions were given to the local chambers of commerce with the national government retaining some control over the airfield facilities. At Zürich airport, the Zürich Airport Authority, which was owned by the Canton of Zürich, was responsible for the planning and overall operation of the airport and the airfield infrastructure, while a mixed public-private company, FIG, managed and constructed the terminal infrastructure.

Moves towards commercialization

Attitudes towards these publicly owned, and often strictly controlled, airports was historically that of a public utility with public service obligations (Doganis, 1992). As a consequence commercial and financial management practices were not given top priority. In the 1970s and 1980s, however, as the air transport industry grew and matured, and as the first steps towards airline privatization and deregulation took place, views about airport management began to change. Many airports gradually started to be considered much more as commercial enterprises and a more businesslike management philosophy was adopted. Thus 'commercialization' of the airport industry began to take place. The pace of change varied considerably in different parts of the world, with Europe gener-ally leading the way. By contrast airports in areas such as those in Africa and South America generally held on to more traditional attitudes towards airports and experienced less change.

Moves towards commercialization were reflected in a number of different interrelated developments. First, various airports loosened their links with their government owners. This was achieved with the establishment of more independent airport authorities or, in some cases, by corporatization, which involved the setting up of an airport company with public sector shareholders. Such developments generally gave the airports more commercial and opera-tional freedom, and sometimes opened the door to private sector investment and partnerships.

There had always been a number of airports, such as Amsterdam and Frank-furt, which had been run by airport corporations or companies. However, changing attitudes in the 1970s and 1980s led to many more airport authorities and companies being established. For example, in 1972 the International Airports Authority of India was established to manage the country's four inter-national airports, while in 1986 the domestic airports came under the control of the National Airports Authority. These two authorities merged in 1995. In Indonesia, two organizations – Angkasa Pura I and II, in charge of the airports in the east and west of the country respectively – became public enterprises in 1987 and limited liability companies in 1993. Other examples include the Polish Airport State Enterprise established in 1987, the Federal Airport Corporation of Australia set up 1988 and Aeropuertos Espanoles y Navegacion Aerea (AENA) in Spain and the Kenya Airports Authority, both formed in 1991. In some cases, such as with Copenhagen airport (1991) or the South African airports (1994), the establishment of an airport corporation was primarily undertaken as an interim step towards airport privatization.

Canada is an interesting example where the management of many of the country's major airports, previously under the direct central control of Trans-port Canada, was passed over by way of long-term leases to individual non-profit-making authorities in the 1990s. The aim behind this was to improve efficiency and integrate each airport more closely with the local economy. The first airport authorities were set up for Montreal's two airports, Vancouver, Calgary and Edmonton in 1992. By 2000, control of over 100 Canadian airports had been transferred to local organizations (Caves and Gosling, 1999).

Greater attention began to be placed on the commercial aspects of running an airport such as financial management, non-aeronautical revenue generation and airport marketing. The operational aspects of the airport traditionally had overshadowed other areas and most airport directors and senior management were operational specialists. However, the commercial functions of an airport gradually were recognized as being equally important and, as a result, the resources and staff numbers employed in these areas were expanded. Relatively underused practices, such as the benchmarking of financial performance and quality management techniques, also began to be accepted – albeit rather slowly at the start – by a growing number of airports as essential management tools. In some airports the typical functional organization structure with different departments for finance, operations, administration and so on was replaced with departments or business units more focused on customers' needs, such as airline or passenger services.

One of the most visible indications of moves towards commercialization and an increased focus on treating the airport as a business was greater reliance being placed on non-aeronautical or commercial revenues. Aeronautical revenues, such as landing and passenger fees from the airlines, had been traditionally by far the most important source. For a number of airports, notably in Europe, non-aeronautical sources overtook aeronautical sources as being the most important revenue. For instance, this occurred at Amsterdam airport in 1984. This development was primarily the result of greater space being allocated to retail and other non-aeronautical facilities, the quality being improved and the range of commercial activities being expanded.

The airport industry historically had played a rather passive role towards marketing and only responded to customer needs when necessary. A more businesslike approach to airport management, coupled with a more commercially driven and competitive airline industry, encouraged airports to take a much more active and proactive role. In the UK, for example, many of the airports set up marketing departments, started to use pricing tactics and promotional campaigns to attract new customers, and began to undertake market research (Humphreys, 1999).

In the past, because of government controls, it was sometimes very difficult to obtain financial accounts that gave a true indication of an airport's financial and economic performance. Often an airport would adopt public accounting practices specific to the country and would use public sector rather than more standard commercial procedures. This meant that comparisons with other organizations could not easily be made. Moreover, some of the airports were not considered as a separate accounting unit. This meant that the airport's costs and revenues were treated as just one item within the government department's overall financial accounts and rarely were they matched together to assess the profitability of the airport. In certain cases no separate balance sheet existed for the airport.

An increasing number of airports started adopting more commercial accounting practices in the 1970s and 1980s. This was often the direct result of the loosening of government links with the establishment of an airport authority or corporation. For instance in the UK in 1987, all the major regional airports became public limited companies. This meant that the airports adopted commercial private sector accounting procedures. One example of this was that for the first time they showed depreciation as a measure of cost of capital. Similarly when Geneva airport became an independent authority in 1994 it began to show a balance sheet and asset values in its annual accounts, which had previously been omitted.

Why privatization?

While the 1970s and 1980s were dominated by airport commercialization, the 1990s were the decade when airport privatization became a reality. But what is meant by 'airport privatization'? It can have various meanings. In its broadest sense, it is usually associated with the transfer of the management of an airport, and in many cases the ownership as well, to the private sector.

The theoretical arguments for and against privatization of publicly owned organizations, particularly when a share flotation is being considered, are well known. They have been fiercely debated over the years and are well documented (e.g. see Beesley, 1997; Jackson and Price, 1994). Privatization will reduce the need for public sector investment and free access to commercial markets. It will reduce government control and may increase an organization's ability to diversify. It may bring about improved efficiency, greater competition and wider share ownership. On the other hand, it may create a private monopoly and give insufficient consideration to externalities such as controlling environmental impacts and maintaining social justice. Less favourable employment conditions may be adopted.

There have been a number of developments in the 1980s and 1990s which occurred within the air transport industry which have specifically strengthened the case for airport privatization in some countries (ICAO, 2000a); Croes, 1997; Freathy and O'Connell, 1998). First, the demand for air transport has continued to grow and is predicted to grow well into the future. In some markets, notably Europe and North America, deregulation has encouraged growth. The current airport capacity cannot cope with this growth. Whether all this demand can or should be provided for is debatable, but what is certain is that some additional infrastructure will have to be built. Within this context, airport privatization has been seen as a way of injecting additional finance into the airport system to pay for future investment. Moreover, one of the major traditional sources of airport financing, namely public sector funds, has become increasingly scarce in the modern-day global economic climate as governments have striven to reduce their public sector spending or to shift their focus onto non-revenue-earning activities which appear to be more worthy, such as health and education.

From one viewpoint, airport privatization can be seen as just an evolutionary stage of airport development. Airports have evolved from public sector utilities to commercial enterprises and privatization can be considered as commercialization taken to its limits. Increased commercialization has brought about healthy profits and market-oriented management. Airports have shown that they have the proven ability to meet private sector requirements – albeit from a rather protected position in many cases. At the same time, the changes within the airline industry have inevitably had a major impact on the airport sector. The transformation from a predominately publicly owned and state-controlled airline industry to a global business with much more commercial freedom has forced many airports to have a much more customer-focused outlook when coping with their airline customers.

The increasing number of airport privatizations which are taking place throughout the world demonstrate the growing acceptance of this process as a method of tackling some of the challenges which many airports face in the twenty-first century. However, airport ownership and control is always likely to be a controversial area. For many countries, transferring airports which are considered to be national or regional assets to the private sector remains a politically sensitive policy. The inherently monopolistic position of many airports will also continue to be of concern to politicians and airport users. The fear is that priority will be given to shareholders or investors and that user and community needs will be neglected. To some opponents, the privatization of airports, which is in effect the air transport 'infrastructure', does not make sense. Unlike the situation with the airlines, that is, air transport 'operators', where competition can more easily be encouraged, airports have a greater tendency to be natural monopolies which cannot be duplicated. Views about privatization vary considerably in different regions of the world, in different countries and even between local and central government bodies in individual countries. As a result, commercialization does by no means always have to lead to privatization and there are a number of examples of airports, such as Manchester in the UK, which are run on a very commercial basis but have no desire to become totally private organizations.

The evolution of the airport business at Vienna airport

Vienna airport authority was created in 1954 when the airport handled just 64 000 passengers annually. The shareholders were the federal republic of Austria (50 per cent), the city of Vienna (25 per cent) and province of Lower Austria (25 per cent). In the next two decades the airport embarked on major expansion projects of the runway, passenger terminal and cargo facilities and by 1978 was handling 2.8 million passengers. During this time the authority was being run very much as a public utility, making losses and receiving subsidies from the public sector owners (Gangl, 1995).

Between 1978 and 1985 the airport authority went through a major organizational restructuring which meant that the airport began to be considered much more as a business enterprise. A new functional organization structure with main departments of airport traffic operation, financial/accounting, planning and construction, maintenance and infrastructure services and administration was set up. New planning and management procedures were introduced and the airport began to proactively market itself to airlines. As a result the airport made a profit for the first time in 1979 and has remained in profit ever since. By 1985 the airport was handling 3.9 million passengers and had begun to pay dividends to its three public sector shareholders.

In the late 1980s, further commercialization took place with the replacement of the functional organization structure with a new system which allowed the airport authority to respond more effectively to its customers. It set up business units or customer divisions separately for airlines and passengers, and supported these with service divisions (such as construction, maintenance and technical service, safety and security, and finance and accounting) and central offices (such as legal affairs, communications and environment, human resources). The business units were required to make profits while the service units were there to provide services in the most cost-effective manner. Management practices with greater emphasis on private sector practices in the area of business and strategic planning and cost control were introduced. A comprehensive management information system (MIS) was launched, and training programmes focused on customer orientation and effective business practices, were set up. Attention was also given to developing the non-aeronautical side of the business, such as retail and catering, marketing and service quality provision (Gangl, 1998).

In 1990 it became apparent that a capital expenditure programme of AS8 billion was needed to extend the airport's annual capacity from 6 to 12 million passengers. Eighty per cent of this capital was available through cash flow and retained profits but other sources were needed for the remaining 20 per cent. Budget constraints meant that increasing the equity of the public shareholders was out of the question. The realistic options were either raising the money through loans/bonds or raising equity on the capital markets. At that time Austrian interest rates for medium and long-term loans as well as bonds were high. On the other hand, the Vienna stock market, like most others throughout the world, was in a poor trading situation. Eventually the airport decided on a share flotation for 1992. This was primarily because it did not want the large loan servicing costs right through until the next capacity expansion, which was planned in 2000, and then further debt requirements.

In order to be floated on the stock exchange, the airport authority had to implement a number of very significant changes. This included changing the corporate status from a limited liability company to a joint stock company, and increasing the share capital by 50 per cent. Business appraisals for valuing the company were undertaken and consultations held with capital market analysts. Employee share-acquisition programmes and investor relations programmes were set up and sales support undertaken through marketing, advertising and road shows in areas such as Austria, the UK, Germany, Switzerland, Japan and Taiwan. The airport also had to ensure that it developed a private sector and market-oriented management approach with an appropriate corporate culture and image – a process which had begun in the 1980s and was further developed during the privatization process (Gangl, 1994). The organizational structure was further refined to be more customer focused, with aviation units (airside services, airline and terminal services, and handling services) and non-aviation units (consumer services, technical services, land development and real estate) both being supported by central services.

In spite of the poor stock market conditions the flotation or initial public offering (IPO) took place in June 1992 and was oversubscribed three times in Austria and five times internationally. The sale brought in AS1.8 billion, which was used by the airport company to partly finance its expansion plans. The success of the flotation meant that the Austrian government opted to sell half its remaining

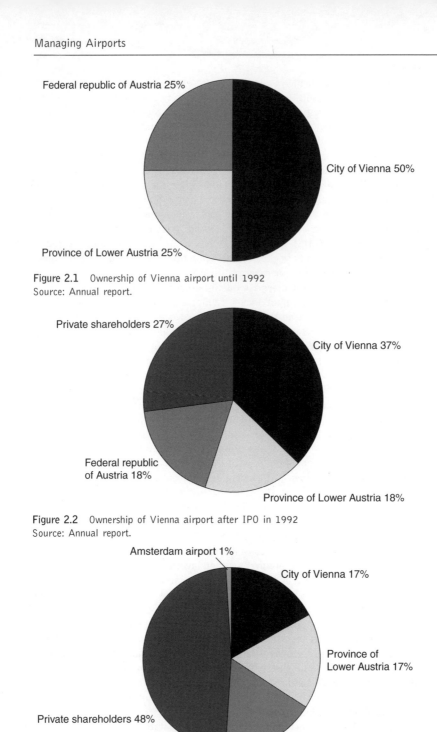

Figure 2.1 Ownership of Vienna airport until 1992
Source: Annual report.

Figure 2.2 Ownership of Vienna airport after IPO in 1992
Source: Annual report.

Figure 2.3 Ownership of Vienna airport after secondary offering in 1995
Source: Annual report.

36.5 per cent stake in the airport in a secondary offering in 1995 – this time retaining the AS2.2 billion proceeds itself. This gave private shareholders 47 per cent of the airport. In 2001 the public shareholding in the company was reduced to 40 per cent. In 1995, Amsterdam airport also bought 1 per cent of the airport with the aim of establishing a strategic alliance to encourage commercial and technical co-operation. This arrangement was terminated in 1998 (Figures 2.1, 2.2 and 2.3).

Since the first year of profits in 1978, passenger numbers have increased by an average annual growth of 6.9 per cent (Figure 2.4). In 1999, the airport handled 11.2 million passengers. During the same period revenues have grown by 9.5 per annum (Figure 2.5). Since 1991 when new accounting procedures were adopted profit before interest and tax has increased from AS409 million in 1991 to AS1157 million in 1999 – an annual average growth of 13.9 per cent. The airport has not, however, performed as well as the other privatized

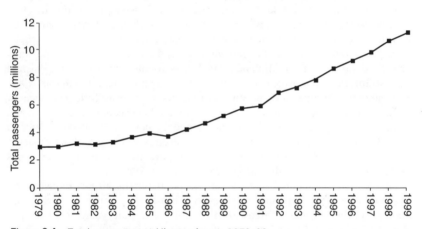

Figure 2.4 Total passengers at Vienna airport, 1979–99
Source: Annual reports.

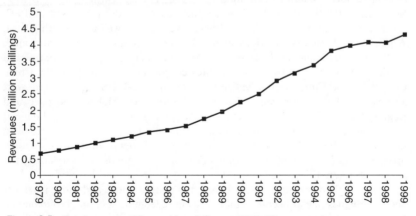

Figure 2.5 Total revenues: Vienna Airport Group, 1979–99
Source: Annual reports.

airports on the stock exchange and as a result one of the tasks set for a new management which was introduced in 1999 was to improve investor relations. Like many major airports in Europe, the airport has been keen to become involved in international projects. For example, it was active in the privatization bidding process of Berlin airport and some Australian airports, and had a 5 per cent interest in a consortium which was involved with building and operating a new international terminal and car park at Istanbul airport. This facility opened in 2000.

The privatization timetable

The first major airport privatization took place in the UK in 1987. This was the total flotation of shares of BAA plc, which at that time owned three London airports (Heathrow, Gatwick and Stansted) and four Scottish airports (Aberdeen, Edinburgh, Glasgow and Prestwick). This successful privatization opened up the debate at many other airports as to whether they too should be privatized. However, in the next few years only a handful of airports actually were privatized. In the UK this included Liverpool airport which was partially privatized in 1990, East Midlands which was totally privatized in 1993 and Belfast International which was subject to a management buyout in 1994. Elsewhere in Europe and in other continents there was little evidence of definite moves towards privatization, with the notable exceptions of Vienna and Copenhagen airport. As previously mentioned, 27 per cent of shares in Vienna airport were floated in 1992 followed by a secondary offering of a further 21 per cent in 1996. Similarly at Copenhagen airport there were share flotations of 25 per cent in 1994 and a further 24 per cent in 1995.

The year 1996 appeared to be a turning point for the airport industry and the following few years saw airport privatization becoming a much more popular option in many areas of the world. In that year, for instance, Bournemouth and Cardiff airports were privatized in the UK and private involvement in the new Athens airport at Spata was agreed. Airports as diverse as Düsseldorf, Sandford Orlando, Naples, Rome, Birmingham, Bristol, Melbourne, Brisbane and Perth were partially or totally privatized in 1997. Further privatizations took place in 1998 in Australia as well as in South Africa, Argentina and other destinations such as Luton, Stockholm Skavsta, Auckland, Wellington and Hanover. In 1999 and 2000 a number of airports in central and southern America countries, such as Mexico, the Dominican Republic, Chile, Costa Rica and Cuba, were privatized, as were the small US airports of Stewart and Niagara Falls. There were also share flotations for Malaysia Airports and Beijing Capital International Airport. The first partially privately financed Indian airport was opened in Cochin, Kerala in southern India, having been financed 35 per cent from local government, 35 per cent from individual investors and 30 per cent from companies supplying goods and services at the airport (Barker, 1999).

As the pace to privatize has gathered momentum, more and more investors and companies have become interested in becoming potential purchasers. Inevitably this has meant that in some cases purchase prices have been inflated and that some buyers are thought to have overpaid for their airport acquisitions.

This is of particular concern to airlines that fear charges will have to be raised to compensate for the high purchase cost. The long-term viability of the airports in question in this privatized form may also be in doubt and it could be that certain airports may be reoffered to investors. Analysts typically will consider the price of the airport (enterprise value (EV)) in relation to profit (earnings before interest, tax, depreciation and amortization (EBITDA) or earnings before interest and tax (EBIT)) when deciding whether to invest. For earlier privatizations such as BAA plc, Vienna and Copenhagen the EV/EBITDA multiples were in the region of five to ten. For later privatizations multiples of up to fifteen have been achieved in countries such as Mexico, South Africa and Argentina. The EV/EBITDA multiples were particularly high, up to 20 in some cases, for the Australian airport sales. This was due to a combination of factors such as an excessive number of bidders and the attractiveness of the airports on offer with regard to their traffic and commercial potential, the relatively low investment needs and the economic and political stability of the country (Aviation Strategy, 2000; Bennett, 1999; Deutsche Bank, 1999).

By the end of 2000, there was some evidence that the popularity of airports as investment opportunities was dwindling slightly in reaction to uncertainties over regulation constraints, environmental restrictions and, within Europe, the loss of intra-EU duty- and tax-free revenues. A number of the regional UK airports owned by National Express and other bus companies were sold. However, all evidence points to the continuation of this privatization trend well into the twenty-first century. An International Civil Aviation Organization (ICAO) survey of eighty-two countries covering 303 airports found that privatization through sales, leasing or concession arrangements was expected to grow significantly in the future (ICAO, 2000b). Numerous countries, many with very different political and economic systems, were actively considering some type of privatization option as the 1990s came to an end. These included European countries such as Portugal, Spain, Italy (especially Milan airport), Germany (particularly the airports of Frankfurt, Stuttgart, Cologne/Bonn, Munich and Berlin – where a buyer had been chosen in 1999 but was subsequently disallowed because of irregularities in the bidding process), the Czech Republic, Ireland (the Aer Rianta company), Malta, Cyprus and the Netherlands (Amsterdam airport). Privatization was also being considered for a number of South American countries such as Mexico (Mexico City), Venezuela, Brazil, Panama and Peru, and in Asian countries such as Thailand, Indonesia, Korea, and Japan. Sydney airport is planned to be privatized in 2001. Privatization has begun in China and further progress is envisaged. India has been considering the leasing out of its main international gateways for some time but has been hit by political delays. Muscat airport in Oman is also set to be the first privatized airport in the Middle East.

Types of privatization

Airports are generally seen as attractive organizations to investors, for a number of reasons. First, the airport industry has strong growth potential. Many of the airports, particularly the major ones, face limited competition, both from other airports and other modes of transport. There are very high barriers to entry within the industry due to the large capital investment needed and the difficulties in finding appropriate, convenient locations where airport development is allowed. Risks clearly exist as well, such as political interference in the form of airport regulation and control over airport development and the changing nature of the airline industry with developments such as deregulation and greater collaboration through alliances.

As airport privatization has become more popular, the types of privatization models which have been adopted have become increasingly diverse. They broadly fall into five categories:

1 Share flotation.
2 Trade sale.
3 Concession.
4 Project finance privatization.
5 Management contract.

The selection of the most appropriate type of privatization involves a complex decision-making process which will ultimately depend on the government's objectives in seeking privatization. For example, is the type of privatization required to lessen the burden on public sector finances, generate funds from the airport sale, increase share ownership or encourage greater efficiency, competition or management expertise within the airport sector? In reaching a decision, factors such as the extent of control which the government wishes to maintain, the quality and expertise of the current airport operators, further investment requirements and the financial robustness of the airports under consideration all have to be taken into account.

Share flotation

The first option is a share flotation with the airport company's share capital being issued and subsequently traded on the stock market. By the end of the 1990s, the only 100 per cent share flotation which had taken place was with BAA plc in 1987. Other partially floated airport companies include Vienna airport (Flughafen Wien AG), Copenhagen Airports A/S, Zürich, Auckland Airport, Malaysia Airports (an organization owning thirty-seven airports in the country) and Beijing Capital International Airport (BCIA) (Table 2.1). The BCIA flotation is interesting as it the first airport where a share flotation has been combined with a trade sale to a strategic partner, namely Aeroport de Paris (AdP). AdP bought 10 per cent of the airport, ABN Amro Ventures bought another 8 per cent, and institutional and retail investors a further 17 per cent – leaving the Chinese government with a 65 per cent share (Beechener, 2000).

With a share flotation the government owner will give up total or partial ownership, while transferring the economic risks and effective control to the new shareholders. Generally the stock markets have viewed purchases of shares in airport companies in a favourable light, with positive factors such as strong growth prospects, limited competition because of high barriers to entry and minimal threats of substitutes, and potential commercial opportunities influencing their views.

Table 2.1 Airport privatization through share flotations

Airport	Date	Type of sale
UK: BAA	1987	100% IPO
Austria: Vienna	1992	27% IPO
	1995	21% Secondary offering
Denmark: Copenhagen	1994	25% IPO
	1996	24% Secondary offering
Italy: Rome	1997	45.5% IPO
New Zealand: Auckland	1998	51.6% IPO
Malaysia: Malaysia Airports	1999	18% IPO
China: BCIA	2000	35% IPO and trade sale
Switzerland: Zürich	2000	22% IPO and 28% Secondary offering

Source: Compiled by author from various sources.

Total or partial privatization of this type will totally eliminate or certainly reduce the need for state involvement in the financing of airport investment. The proceeds from such a privatization could be used for funding future investment at the airport, as with the IPO of 27 per cent at Vienna airport, or can go directly to the government, as with BAA plc. Even when total privatization takes place, a degree of government influence can theoretically be maintained by issuing a golden share to the government so that in extreme cases national interests can be protected. To prevent domination by any individual shareholder, limits can be placed on the maximum shareholding. For instance, for BAA airports this limit is 15 per cent and the government has a golden share – although the legality of this has been challenged by the European Commission.

In order to be floated on the stock market, the airport company will be required to have a track record of minimum profits to make the airport attractive enough to investors. Airports not performing well clearly would find it hard to be successfully privatized in this way. Fully developed capital markets also need to be in existence, which may not be the situation in certain areas of, for example, South America and Africa. The airport company will have to get used to daily scrutiny of its financial performance by its shareholders and other investors and, as a consequence, may find it hard not to become preoccupied with the share price. However, issuing shares to employees may give them an incentive and make them feel move involved in the affairs of the airport company.

Trade sale

With this option, some or all of the airport will be sold to a trade partner or consortium of investors. All the trade sales which took place in the 1990s involved strategic partners rather than just passive investors. This meant that the management and technological expertise of the partners as well as financial capabilities were taken into account when agreeing on a sale.

The first significant trade sale was in 1990 when 76 per cent of Liverpool airport, previously owned by local government, was sold to British Aerospace (Table 2.2). Subsequently a number of other UK airports, such as East Midlands, Cardiff, Bournemouth and Southend have been totally sold off to a trade partner. In the case of Birmingham, Newcastle and Humberside airports, a strategic partner has been brought in through a partial sale. Elsewhere in Europe, Hanover, Düsseldorf and Naples airports have also been partially privatized through a trade sale. Aeroports de Paris has a 25 per cent share of

Table 2.2   Airport privatization through trade sales

Airport	Date	Share of airport sold (%)	Buyer
UK: Liverpool	1990	76	British Aerospace
UK: Prestwick	1992	100	British Aerospace
UK: East Midlands	1993	100	National Express
UK: Southend	1994	100	Regional Airports Ltd
UK: Cardiff	1995	100	TBI
UK: Bournemouth	1995	100	National Express
UK: Belfast International	1996	100	TBI
UK: Birmingham	1997	51	Aer Rianta/Natwest Ventures (40%); other investors (11%)
UK: Bristol	1997	51	Firstbus
UK: Liverpool	1997	76	Peel Holdings
UK: Kent International	1997	100	Wiggins
Germany: Düsseldorf	1997	50	Hochtief and Aer Rianta consortium
Italy: Naples	1997	70	BAA
Australia[1]: Brisbane, Melbourne, Perth	1997	100	Various
Sanford Orlando	1997	100	TBI
Skavsta Stockholm	1998	90	TBI
ACSA	1998	20	ADRI South Africa consortium (Aeroporti di Roma has 69% share)
Germany: Hanover	1998	30	Frankfurt airport
New Zealand: Wellington	1998	66	Infratil
Australia[1] :15 remaining major Australian airports (except Sydney)	1998	100	Various
UK: Humberside	1999	83	Manchester airport
USA: Stewart International[2]	1999	100	National Express
Belgium: Liège	1999	25	AdP
USA: Niagara Falls[2]	2000	100	Cintro
Spain: Ciudad Real Airport	2000	65	Various including TBI (20%)
Italy: Rome	2000	51	Leonardo consortium
Italy: Turin	2000	41	Benetton Group consortium
Germany: Hamburg	2000	36	Hochtief and Aer Rianta consortium
UK: Newcastle	2001	49	Copenhagen airport

Notes: [1] Most of the Australian airports have been sold on a fifty-year lease with an option for a further forty-nine years.
[2] Ninety-nine year lease.
Source: Compiled by author from various sources.

Liège airport in Belgium, which it wants to develop as an alternative venue for freight activities. Outside Europe, 20 per cent of the Airports Company South Africa (ACSA) has been sold to a strategic partner. The ACSA owns and manages nine South African airports including the three major international airports of Johannesburg, Durban and Cape Town. Two-thirds of Wellington airport in New Zealand has been sold through a trade sale. Airports which have been leased on long-term arrangements to strategic partners or consortia can also be included in this category – as effectively all control will be transferred from the publicly owned airport to the trade partner. The most notable example here is the Australian airports, the majority of which have been sold on long-term leases (fifty years with a further possible option of forty-nine years) to different consortia.

In many of these cases, the strategic partner is an established airport operator or the purchasing consortium will contain a member with airport management experience. For example, BAA plc is the strategic partner in the Naples airport sale and Aeroporti di Roma belongs to the consortium which bought part of the ACSA. With most of the Australian airport sales, there was an airport interest within the successful consortia. Many of the participating airports in these airport privatizations are not actually privatized airports themselves which leads to further complications in the definition of a 'private' airport. For example, Aer Rianta Irish Airports, which is a public corporation, has been successfully involved in the partial privatization of Birmingham, Hamburg and Düsseldorf airports. Similarly the publicly owned Amsterdam airport has a number of interests in other airports around the world. Both these airports, though, do have plans to be privatized in the early 2000s.

Concession

With this type of arrangement an airport management company or consortium will purchase a concession or lease to operate the 'privatized' airport for a defined period of time, commonly between twenty and thirty years. Financial terms and the types of lease will vary but typically this option will involve an initial payment and a guaranteed level of investment and/or payment of an annual fee. One of the earliest concession arrangements were agreed in 1997 for the three main airports of Bolivia, namely La Paz, Santa Cruz and Cochabamba. Airports Group International, an airport management company, was awarded the thirty-year concession during which time it guaranteed to upgrade the three airports and pay an annual fee of 21 per cent of gross revenues. Another example is the thirty-year concession for the thirty-three Argentinian airports, which was awarded to the consortium, Aeroportuertos Argentinos 2000, which has among its partners, SEA, the Milan airport company, and Ogden, the airport services company. The consortium has agreed to pay an annual US$171 million a year for the first five years of the agreement. After that time, the concession fee will be related to traffic growth. The consortium has also agreed to invest US$2.1 billion at the airports in the thirty years, with over US$800 million being spent in the first five years, primarily at the two Buenos Aires airports (Gray, 1998).

Generally with this type of arrangement, the concessionaire will take full economic risk and will be responsible for all operations and future investment. Since the privatized airport will only be handed over for a fixed period of time, the government owner will have a greater degree of control than with an outright sale. This has proved more politically acceptable in some countries, for example, in South America where a number of concession arrangements were negotiated in the late 1990s. Here traffic growth is predicted to be high but in many cases the infrastructure is inadequate and the governments are unwilling or unable to invest in the airports (Ricover, 1999). At Luton airport in the UK, a consortium originally consisting of Barclays Investment, Bechtel Enterprises and AGI (which was subsequently bought by TBI in 1999) was given the thirty-year concession to run the airport in 1998. A concessionaire-type arrangement was chosen, rather than a flotation or trade sale, since the local government owners had promised not to relinquish total control of this publicly owned asset to private hands. This arrangement involves paying an initial annual concession fee of US$19 million which will increase as passenger traffic grows (Communique Airport Business, 1998).

The situation is rather different in Mexico where the country's fifty-eight airports have been divided into four groups, namely the North-Central Group, the Pacific Group, the Southeast Group and the Mexico City Group. Concession contracts have been awarded or are planned for each group for an initial fifteen-year period with an underlying fifty-year agreement. There is or will be a strategic partner with each group, and it is planned that there will be a subsequent flotation of remaining government shares as well. In 1998 15 per cent of the Southeast Group (which includes the airports of Cancun and Merida) was sold to a consortium which included Copenhagen airport and the construction company, Cintra. In 1999 15 per cent of the Pacific Group of twelve airports was sold to a consortium with AENA, the Spanish airport group, as a key partner. In 2000 an identical share of the North Central Group was sold to an AdP consortium. Other countries which have concession agreements for their airports include the Dominican Republic, Chile, Uruquay, Costa Rica, Peru and Tanzania (Table 2.3).

Project finance privatization

With this option, a company will usually build or redevelop and then operate an airport or specific facility, such as a terminal, for a certain length of time. At the end of this period, ownership will revert back to the government owners. Generally such an arrangement will require no upfront payment but the operating company will bear all the costs of building or redeveloping the facility. When it is built, the company will have to cover the operating costs but will also retain all revenues until the facility is handed back. Thus the airport company will take full economic risk for investment and operations. There are a number of project finance privatization methods with the most popular being build–operate–transfer (BOT) when, as the name suggests, the company will build the facility, operate it for a certain length of time and then transfer ownership back to the government. Other similar models include build–transfer (BT), build–rent–transfer

(BRT) or design–construct–manage–finance (DCMF). Other options may actually involve the ownership of the facility such as build–own–operate-transfer (BOOT) or rehabilitate–own–transfer (ROT) projects. All these methods, however, are often referred to by the generic term BOT (Ashford, 1999).

This type of arrangement is often used when relatively large investments are needed for totally new airports or perhaps for new passenger terminals or other major facilities. One of the first major projects of this type was Terminal 3 at Toronto's Lester B. Pearson International Airport which was developed as a BOT project by Huang and Danczkay and Lockheed Air Terminals (Ashford and Moore, 1999). Airports Group International/TBI now have a management contract for this terminal The Eurohub at Birmingham airport was build under a BOT-type arrangement by a company comprising Birmingham airport (25 per cent), British Airways (21.4 per cent), local authorities (14.3 per cent), National Car Parks (21.4 per cent), Forte (6 per cent) and John Laing Holdings (11.9 per cent) (Lambert, 1995). This terminal is now a fully owned and managed facility of Birmingham International Airport plc. Elsewhere the international terminals at airports such as Budapest and New York JFK are all being developed through BOT projects (Table 2.4).

The new Athens airport at Spata was built under a thirty-year BOT arrangement. The Greek government holds 55 per cent of the shares in the new company, Athens International Airport SA (AIA). The remaining share 45 per cent share belongs to an international consortium, which is being led by the German construction company, Hochtief, and Frankfurt airport. The airport named 'Eleftherios Venizelos' will have a capacity of 16 million passengers when it opens in 2001 and will have cost US$2.1 billion (Communique Airport Business, 2000).

Table 2.4   Airport privatization through project finance

Airport	Date	Length of agreement (years)	Contractor
Canada: Toronto Terminal 3	1987	Terminated	Lockheed consortium
UK: Birmingham Eurohub	1989	Terminated	Various including Birmingham airport, British Airways, National Car Parks
Greece: Athens	1996	30	55% Greek state, 45% Hochtief consortium
Hungary: Budapest International Terminal	1997	12	Aeroport de Montreal Consortium
Philippines: Manila International Terminal	1999	25	Frankfurt airport consortium
USA: New York JFK International Arrivals Terminal	1997	20	Schiphol consortium

Source: Compiled by author from various sources.

Table 2.3 Airport privatization through concession agreements

Airport	Date	Length of concession (years)	Concessionaire
Columbia: Cartagena	1996	15	Amsterdam airport consortium
Columbia: Barranquilla	1997	15	AENA consortium
Columbia: Cartagena	1998	15	AENA consortium
Bolivia: La Paz, Santa Cruz, Cochabamba	1997	25	AGI
UK: Luton	1998	30	AGI/Bechtel/Barclays consortium
Mexico: South East Group	1998	15[1]	Copenhagen airport consortium
Mexico: Pacific Group	1999	15[1]	AENA consortium
Argentinian Airport System	1998	33	Aeropuertos Argentina 2000 consortium (including SEA Milan and Ogden)
Tanzania: Kilimanjaro International Airport	1998	25	Mott Macdonald consortium with minority government share
Dominican Republic: 4 airports including Santo Domingo	1999	20	Vancouver Airport Services (YVRAS) and Odgen consortium
Chile: Terminal at Santiago International Airport	1999	15	YVRAS consortium
Uruguay: Montevideo	1999	25	YVRAS consortium
Costa Rica: San Jose	1999	20	TBI
Columbia: Cali	2000	20	AENA consortium
Mexico: North-Central Group	2000	15[1]	AdP consortium
Peru: Lima	2000	20	Frankfurt airport/Bechtel consortium

Notes: AGI was bought by TBI in 1999.
[1] Fifteen-year contract but underlying fifty-year concession.
Source: Compiled by author from various sources.

Another example of a BOT project is the international passenger Terminal 3 at Ninoy Aquino International Airport in Manila. This is the first project finance model of its kind in the Asia/Pacific region. The consortium which is involved with this project, the Philippine International Air Terminals Co. (PIATCO) is being led by Frankfurt airport. Lufthansa is involved through a joint venture project and there is also investment from Japan. It is a twenty-five year project which is due to open in 2002. The new terminal will have a design capacity of 13 million passengers, more than double the present terminal, and will cost around $US 500 million (Frankfurt Airport, 2000a).

Management contract

The least radical privatization option is a management contract when owner-ship remains with the government and the contractors take responsibility for the day-to-day operation of the airport. The contractor will pay an annual management fee, usually related to the performance of the airport. Investment will normally remain the responsibility of the government owner and so the overall economic risk will be shared between the owner and the management company. For the government owner this may be politically more acceptable, whereas for the contractor such an arrangement may be attractive in countries where greater financial exposure, through a trade sale for example, may be seen as too great a risk.

Within Europe, the terminal of Brussels airport was under a management contract to a private company, the Brussels Airport Terminal Company, from 1987. In 1998, however, this company merged with the public company operating the rest of the airport to become the Brussels International Airport Company. More common is for European airports to have management contracts in other areas of the world. For example, AdP has management contracts in Cameroon and Madagascar, Bordeaux airport has contracts in Togo and Mauritania, and Marseilles airport has an involvement with the airports in Gabon and Côte d'Ivoire (Carre, 1999). The Spanish airport company, AENA, has management contracts for Cayo Coco airport in Cuba and three major airports in Columbia. Elsewhere, Vancouver Airport Services (YVRAS) has contracts with the main Bermuda airport, the Cook Islands and the Turks and Caicos Islands, while AGI (now TBI) has management contracts at some US airports such as Burbeck and Albany. Such arrangements can cover all airport operations or just one aspect, such as retail. BAA plc, for instance, has general management contracts at Indianapolis and Harrisburg airports in the USA, in Mauritius and with a number of small Chinese airports. It has retail contracts with Pittsburgh, Boston, New York Newark and New York JFK in the USA. Aer Rianta, the Irish operator has retail contracts at various airports including Greece, Cyprus, Russia, Bahrain, Pakistan, Kuwait, Beirut, Syria, Qatar and Canada.

Competition issues

The amount of influence that a government can exert over a private airport clearly depends upon the type of privatization model chosen. A government may hold on to a considerable amount of control if a management or private finance contract is chosen, while very little state influence may remain after an airport company has been floated on the stock market or sold to a strategic partner. In these latter cases it is often feared that the privatized airport will become a private monopoly and will not always operate with the best interests of the airport users in mind. Therefore economic regulation has been introduced at a number of airports when the privatization process has taken place. This has occurred, for example, at BAA plc London airports, Vienna airport, and some of the Australian and South American airports. Chapter 5 explains in detail the type of regulation introduced and the rationale behind it.

There is also another competition issue which has to be taken into account if a group of airports rather than a single individual airport is being considered for privatization: should the airports be sold off together as a group or should they be split up into different companies? This is particularly an issue when the airport group or system may contain a few large international airports which are profitable and a number of smaller regional or local airports which are loss makers. This was the case with the Australian airports and also in a number of South American countries prior to privatization.

If the airport group is sold as a single entity, and if generally this group as a whole has a good financial track record, a higher sale price may be achieved – primarily because of the lack of perceived competition from other airport operators. In addition, any unprofitable parts of the airport system (usually the smaller airports) will not have to remain under public ownership and raising capital on the commercial money markets for future investments may be easier for a larger company. However, selling off airports in this manner may inhibit competition, although the extent of competition which exists between airports in a group is always debatable. Airlines tend to be suspicious of airport groups, fearful that they will be paying charges at one airport which will finance the development of another airport, typically in some remote area which they do not use (IATA, 2000b). In response, airports often argue that they are making best use of resources and expertise by operating as an airport group.

After a long debate in the UK, BAA plc, owning London Heathrow, Gatwick and Stansted airports in the South East and Aberdeen, Edinburgh, Glasgow and Prestwick airports in Scotland, was sold off as a single entity in 1987. This was an interesting example as BAA plc airports in London were in many ways in direct competition with each other. Critics of BAA plc privatization argue that the group sale has given BAA plc much less incentive to provide any extra capacity than would have been the case with individual airport sales. Unsurprisingly, the sale proceeds from the group privatization was much higher than would have been achieved otherwise. Interestingly, a few years after BAA plc privatization, Belfast International airport wanted to buy the neighbouring Belfast City airport but was prohibited from doing so by the government as it was seen as anti-competitive.

In Australia the government decided on individual privatizations for the major international airports but with packages of some of the smaller ones. Restrictions were imposed to stop the same operator from having overall control at a number of airports. In South America, all thirty-three Argentinian airports are covered under the same concession agreements, while in Mexico the airports have been divided into four different groups. This debate is also relevant for Aer Rianta, the Irish airport company, which owns three airports – Dublin, Shannon and Cork – and is likely to be privatized in the early 2000s. In India, reaching an agreement to lease out the four major airports on long-term agreements has been a long and difficult process since these airports provide the bulk of the profits of the whole Indian airport network.

The UK: paving the way for airport privatization

The UK is worthy of special attention when privatization is being considered, not only because the first major airport privatization took place in this country, but also because subsequent privatizations have been quite varied in nature. Airport privatization came about because of a major piece of legislation, the Airports Act, which was introduced in 1986. The first part of the Act was concerned with the then government-owned BAA which operated seven UK airports, namely London Heathrow, London Gatwick, London Stansted and the four Scottish airports of Aberdeen, Edinburgh, Glasgow and Prestwick. The Act made provision for BAA plc to become a private company through a subsequent 100 per cent share flotation in 1997. This reflected the overall aim of the conservative Thatcher government of the time to privatize nationalized industries such as utilities and communications, and to increase share ownership among the UK population.

The second part of the Act required all airports with a turnover of more that £1 million in two of the previous three years to become companies. Prior to this these airports had been run directly by their local government owners. Sixteen airports were covered by this part of the Act, ranging from Manchester airport, owned by a consortium of local authorities which at that time had a throughput of 9 million passengers, to Southend airport, owned by Southend Borough Council and handling just over 100 000 passengers. The shareholders of these airport companies were initially to be the local government owners but the shares could then be sold off to private investors if desired by the public sector owners. This was the Conservative government's ultimate aim. The Act also introduced economic regulation at these airports which is discussed in Chapter 5 (UK Government, 1986).

BAA plc was floated in 1987 with £1.2 billion going to the government. This gave BAA plc the freedom to borrow from commercial markets and diversify into areas of operations such as hotels, property management and hospital shops, which it did in its first few years of operation (Doganis, 1992). BAA plc has subsequently dramatically expanded the retail part of its business and has become a global player in airport management by having interests in airports in as diverse areas as Australia, Italy, the USA, Mauritius and China. Meanwhile the new situation at the regional airports had also given them considerable more opportunity to commercialize their activities. As a result the share of non-aeronautical revenue has increased at the majority of these airports and more resources have been devoted to commercial activities such as marketing (Humphreys, 1999).

The most significant impact of the Airports Act has been the change in ownership patterns which have emerged (Table 2.5). By the early 1990s, the regional airports were finding it increasingly difficult to obtain permission to borrow funds for investment and, in 1993, the government announced that there would be no further spending allocation for airports. The only alternative for airports that wished to invest was privatization, which an increasing number of airports had no choice but to adopt. Political pressures from a Conservative central government, which was very much ideologically attracted to the transfer of public service to the private sector whenever possible, undoubtedly played a major role.

Table 2.5   Ownership patterns at main[1] UK airports, 2001

Airport	Present ownership	Private interest (%)	Privatization date
Aberdeen	BAA	100	1987
Belfast International	TBI	100	1994
Birmingham International	Local authorities/Aer Rianta/Nat West Ventures/ Employees/other investors	51	1997
Bournemouth International	Manchester airport	100	1995
Bristol International	Cintra/Macquarie Bank	100	1997
Cardiff International	TBI	100	1995
East Midlands	Manchester airport	100	1993
Edinburgh	BAA	100	1987
Exeter and Devon	Local authorities	0	n/a
Glasgow	BAA	100	1987
Highlands and Islands Airports[2]	Highlands and Islands Airport Ltd	0	n/a
Humberside International	Local authorities/ Manchester airport	83[3]	1999
Leeds-Bradford International	Local authorities	0	n/a
Liverpool	Local authorities/Peel Holdings	76	1990
London Gatwick	BAA	100	1987
London Heathrow	BAA	100	1987
London Luton	TBI/Bechtel	100[4]	1998
London Stansted	BAA	100	1987
Manchester	Local authorities	0	n/a
Newcastle International	Copenhagen airport	49	2001
Norwich	Local authorities	0	n/a
Prestwick	Infratil	100	1987
Southampton International	BAA	100	1961
Teeside International	Local authorities	0	n/a

Notes: the table shows the most recent owner, not necessarily the first private sector owner.
n/a = not applicable.
[1] All airports with more than 100 000 annual passengers.
[2] Nine airports including Inverness and Sumburgh with over 100 000 passengers.
[3] Eighty-three per cent share is held by Manchester airport which is under local authority ownership. Manchester airport also owns East Midlands and Bournemouth airport.
[4] The private investors have a thirty-year concession contract. Ownership remains with the local authorities.
Source: Compiled by author from various sources.

Various airports have chosen full privatization through a trade sale to a strategic partner, such as East Midlands, Cardiff and Bournemouth. Southend airport has also been totally privatized but in this case the sale was undertaken to ensure the survival of the airport rather than to give access to finance for expansion as with many of the other airports (Humphreys, 1999). As long as the airports have over 50 per cent private sector ownership then by UK law they can have access to commercial markets. Thus some airports such as Newcastle and Liverpool have opted for a partially privatized approach which gives them access to finance but also enables some local public control to be maintained. Birmingham airport is an interesting example which initially overcame funding difficulties by establishing a joint venture company to build the additional Eurohub terminal with a BOT project without a change in overall ownership. This solved the short-term problem of funding but subsequent traffic growth meant that there was once again pressure for additional investment and this time the airport opted for a partial privatization.

Some local authority airport owners have remained strongly opposed to privatization moves – arguing that the airport should remain in public sector hands to maintain its role as a regional public asset. Manchester is one such airport and financed the whole of its second runway project from retained profits. Its public sector status, however, means that it has not been free to expand internationally on equal terms with competing private airports. It was involved with the successful consortium in the sale of Adelaide/Parafield and Coolangetta airports in Australia but because of its status could only act on a consultancy basis with no equity share involved. From April 1999, however, this situation changed with legislation introduced to allow for the larger profitable regional airports which were still in local governments hands (Manchester, Newcastle, Leeds-Bradford and Norwich) to be able to borrow money on the open market (DETR, 1998). This enabled Manchester to purchase 83 per cent of the nearby Humberside airport soon afterwards.

There are also a small number of other airports in the UK which have had a different history. The newly developed London City, Belfast City and Sheffield City airports have always been in private hands. Belfast International was privatized by means of a management buyout in 1994 and was subsequently sold to TBI in 1996. Most of the smaller regional airports in the UK remain under public sector ownership. Highlands and Islands Airports Ltd, a state-owned company, operates nine airports in Scotland with the help of a government subsidy.

Looking back to 1986 before the Airports Act, it may be seen that a number of airports, such as Exeter, Humberside, Liverpool, London Stansted, Norwich and Prestwick, recorded a loss before depreciation and interest (results after depreciation charges were not available) (Table 2.6). By 1998 all airports were in a profitable situation. If depreciation was taken into account, however, Humberside and Liverpool still made losses. Traffic has grown substantially at all these airports over these years. The smallest average traffic growth of 3 per cent was recorded at Belfast International airport whereas growth in excess of 10 per cent annum was experienced for Birmingham, Bristol, Humberside, Liverpool and Stansted airports. Some of the privatized airports have performed better than those remaining in public sector ownership, while others have not. Thus it is difficult at this relatively early stage to draw any conclusions as to whether privatization, in addition to providing a new investment opportunity, has indeed improved efficiency.

Table 2.6   Traffic and profitability growth at main¹ UK airports, 1987–99

Airport	Total passengers (000s)		Profit before depreciation, interest and tax (£000s)		Profit before interest and tax (£000s)
	1986/7	1998/9	1986/7	1998/9	1998/9
Aberdeen	1 452	2 638	1 500	11 927	10 091
Belfast International	1 882	2 712	3 935	15 880	14 986
Birmingham International	1 725	6 816	6 781	38 187	28 798
Bournemouth International	137	359	164	1 404	725
Bristol International	436	1 879	1 131	11 323	9 788
Cardiff International	436	1 283	689	8 197	7 340
East Midlands	941	2 145	3 637	14 543	11 666
Edinburgh	1 756	4 650	2 800	18 529	14 698
Exeter and Devon	105	258	–59	880	169
Glasgow	3 200	6 643	5 500	33 300	24 685
Highlands and Islands	n/a	947	n/a	857	–521
Humberside International	118	439	–34	871	–251
Leeds-Bradford International	508	1 417	2 134	6 361	4 233
Liverpool	263	936	–2 053	508	–440
London Gatwick	16 751	29 710	53 200	159 100	127 800
London Heathrow	32 092	61 348	119 000	407 300	323 000
London Luton	1635	4 405	4 003	10 722	9 250
London Stansted	577	7 567	–1 800	31 592	17 388
Manchester	7 596	17 721	18 715²	115 115	64 189
Newcastle International	1 165	3 051	3 526	18 721	12 883
Norwich	191	329	–56	1 178	445
Prestwick	330	651	–500	2 600	2 319
Southampton International	267	767	n/a	3 591	2 156
Teeside International	297	674	135	1 661	798

Notes: ¹ All airports with more than 100 000 annual passengers.
² 1985/6 data.
Source: Chartered Institute of Public Finance and Accountancy (CIPFA), Centre for Regulated Industries (CRI) and annual accounts.

Australia: a phased privatization process

Between 1988 and 1997, most of Australia's airports were operated by the state-owned Federal Airports Corporation (FAC). At the beginning of 1997 the FAC operated twenty-two airports and handled over 60 million passengers annually. The FAC corporate office undertook various central services and imposed a common charging policy on its airports. Discussions relating to the privatization of the FAC began in the early 1990s with a firm decision to privatize being made in 1996. Considerable attention was given to whether the airports should be sold off as a system (as had happened with BAA plc which was the only other airport group at that time that had been privatized) or to whether they should be sold off individually. Issues relating to the national interest, efficiency and competition were fiercely debated. Political factors played a key role, particularly as government forecasts had shown that separate sales would generate more income (Knibb, 1999). Eventually it was decided that the airports would be leased off individually on long-term fifty-year leases, with a further option for forty-nine years.

In phase 1 of the privatization process, three airports, namely Melbourne, Brisbane and Perth, were sold in 1997. After Sydney, these three airports were the most profitable airports in the FAC system and they handled the most traffic (Figures 2.6 and 2.7). It was the government's intention to bring competition and diversity into the airport system and so there were strict cross-ownership limits associated with the airport sales. Potential buyers had to have a majority Australian interest and airport management experience. As in the UK, the privatized airports are price regulated. In addition they are required to undertake quality of service monitoring and to provide

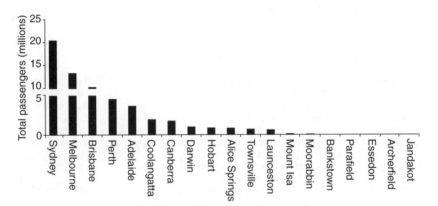

Figure 2.6 Traffic at Australian airports, 1996/7
Source: Annual accounts.

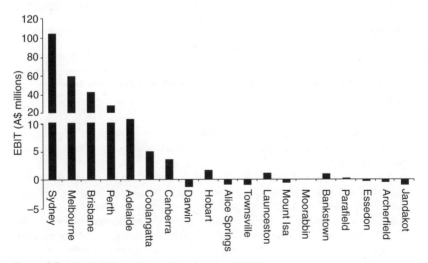

Figure 2.7 Profitability at Australian airports, 1996/7
Source: Annual accounts.

Table 2.7 Privatization details of Australian airports

Airport	Ownership	Privatization date: sale price (A$ million)
Brisbane	Brisbane Airport Corporation Ltd (Schiphol Group, Commonwealth Investments, Port of Brisbane and others)	July 1997: 1397
Melbourne	Australia Pacific Airports Pty Ltd (BAA, AMP, Deutsche Asset Management and Hastings Fund)	July 1997: 1307
Perth	Westralia Airports Corporation Ltd (AGI, Hastings Fund, Infratil)	July 1997: 639
Adelaide/Parafield	Adelaide Airport Ltd, Parafield Airport Ltd (Unisuper, Macquarie Bank, John Laing, Serco and others)	May 1998: 365
Alice Springs/ Darwin/Tennant Creek	Northern Territories Airports Ltd (AGI/Infratil)	May 1998: 110
Archerfield	Archerfield Airport Corporation Ltd (Miengrove Pty)	May 1998: 3
Canberra	Capital Airports Group (local company)	May 1998: 66
Colangatta	Gold Coast Airport Ltd (Unisuper, Macquarie Bank, Serco and others)	May 1998: 104
Hobart	Hobart International Airport Corporation (AGI, Hobart Ports, Hambros)	May 1998: 36
Jandakot	Jandakot Airport Holdings (property investors and former FAC employees)	June 1998: 7
Launceston	Australia Pacific Airports Pty Ltd (BAA, AMP, Deutsche Asset Management and Hastings Fund)	May 1998: 17
Moorabbin	Metropolitan Airport Consortium (property investors and former FAC employees)	May 1998: 8
Townsville/Mount Isa	Australian Airports Ltd (former FAC chief executive officer and financial investors)	May 1998: 16
Sydney/Bankstown /Camden, Hoxton Park/Essendon	Sydney Airports Corporation Ltd	Transferred from FAC; yet to be privatized

Source: Compiled by author from the individual airports' regulation reports and other sources.

evidence of this to the regulator. They also have to provide development guarantees by preparing five-yearly master plans and pledging a certain sum for investment.

A number of airport companies were interested in operating the Australian airports including BAA plc, Manchester, Vienna, Amsterdam, Aer Rianta, National Express and AGI. In the end BAA plc, Amsterdam and AGI were each partners in winning consortia (Table 2.7). As previously mentioned, the EV/EBITDA multiples were particularly high for the Australian airports, which was not only due to the fact there were a large number of binders, but also because high growth was being forecast and the infrastructure needs were relatively small.

It was decided that a further group of airports would be privatized in 1998. These 'phase 2' airports included Adelaide which was the largest airport with just under 4 million passengers and general aviation airports such as Archerfield, Parafield and Jandakot. Whereas the phase 1 airports had been relatively independent profitable entities, over half of these smaller airports were making losses and were much more reliant on the services of the FAC corporate office. Considerable preparation was therefore involved in getting the airports reading to be stand-alone entities (FAC, 1997). In spite of the fact that these airports were smaller and not in such a healthy position, again there was considerable interest in the sales and relatively high purchase prices were paid. Some airport companies which were involved with the phase 1 airports, such as BAA plc and AGI, gained further airports under this phase 2 privatization. Former FAC employees also gained interest in a number of airports such as Jandakot, Moorabbin, Townsville and Mount Isa. Cross-ownership restrictions prevented certain neighbouring airports coming under single ownership.

Sydney Kingsford airport and the general aviation airports in the Sydney basin (Bankstown, Camden and Hoxton Park) were excluded from these two phases of privatization because of unresolved issues related to noise control at Sydney Kingsford airport and continuing controversy over if, when and where a second Sydney airport would be built (Ballantyne, 1997). In 1998 a separate state-owned entity, Sydney Airports Corporation, was established to run the four Sydney airports and Elldeson, the general aviation airport in Victoria which had been withdrawn from the privatization process. In 2000 plans to develop a second Sydney airport were shelved for at least a decade clearing the way for privatization in 2001.

US airports: the slow pace towards privatization

Since the USA has always possessed a private airline industry, it is often assumed that the airport industry must be primarily driven by private sector considerations as well. This is not the case. Nearly all US airports remain under local public ownership – with the pace towards privatization being much slower than in many other parts of the world.

There are two key factors which make US airports unique when possible privatization is being considered. First, US airports enter into legally binding contracts with their airline customers, known as airport use agreements, which detail the charging and conditions for the use of both airfield and terminal facilities. The airports, in reality, operate very closely with the airlines and the airlines have a considerable amount of influence as regards future developments at the airports. Airline approval would be needed, therefore, if privatization were to take place. Second, the airports are funded through a mixture of private and public funds. Most airports, and all the major ones, already have access to the commercial bond markets, with airports being seen as a popular investment particularly because of their tax-exempt status due to their public ownership. Funding is also available from passenger facility charges (PFCs) which are generated by the passengers at individual airport, and from grants from the Airport Improvement

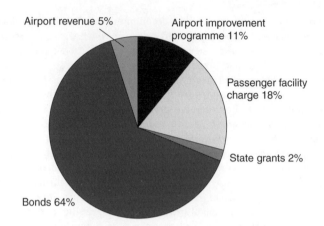

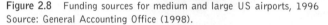

Figure 2.8 Funding sources for medium and large US airports, 1996
Source: General Accounting Office (1998).

Program (AIP) which comes from the federal government's Aviation Trust Fund, financed primarily by a national passenger tax. At major airports tax-exempt commercial bonds make up the bulk of the investment funds (Figure 2.8).

There is a growing concern that in the future there will not be enough funds to meet investment needs – estimated to be in the region of US$3 billion (General Accounting Office, 1999). The major criticism of the federal grants is that they are subject to congressional spending procedures and that the amount of funds available is not enough. The PFC and AIP were raised in value in 2000 but shortfalls in investment funds are still thought to exist. Inevitably, as elsewhere where airport funding has become an issue, privatization has been considered as an option. In the USA, though, it is not an easy process. In 1995, the privatization of John Wayne Airport in California's Orange County was discussed as part of the solution to the county's bankruptcy (Poole, 1995). However the likelihood of litigation by the airlines – who argued that federal law prohibited the use of airport revenues (including sale proceeds) for non-airport purposes (so-called 'revenue diversion') – led to the conclusion that airport privatization was not feasible. This issue, namely the inability of airport owners to reap the financial benefits from the airports, is seen as one of the key obstacles to airport privatization in the USA. Also many local politicians, who hold very powerful positions, do not wish give up control of their airports. Various other issues would have to be resolved if such privatization were to take place. For example, would private airports survive if they could not use trust fund, PFC or tax-exempt debt financing? Would they have to pay back the federal grants? At many of the airports, the use agreements with the airlines could mean that the airports could only be privatized as the agreements expire or that privatization would have to be limited within the bounds of the agreement.

There has been some, albeit rather limited, moves towards airport privatization with the introduction of the airport privatization pilot programme in October 1996. This makes provision for five airports to be exempt from some of the legal requirements that impede their sale to private entities (General Accounting Office, 1996b). For example, the restrictions on prohibiting revenues to be used for non-aeronautical reasons have been waived. Such privatizations need approval of the majority of airlines using the airport. Under the scheme there must be a general aviation (GA) airport and only one large hub airport. General aviation airports may be leased or sold but larger airports can only be leased. By 2000, two airports had been approved under the scheme. First, was Stewart International Airport, in New York, which was leased for ninety-nine years to National Express. Second, the Spanish construction company Ferrovial, with its wholly owned subsidiary, Cintra, which already had interests in a number of South American airports, obtained the ninety-nine year lease for Niagara Falls airport. Three other airports, namely Brown Field, Aguadilla in Puerto Rico and Lakefront outside of New Orleans had also expressed an interest to privatize (McCormick, 2000a).

By 2000, there were some indications that the Federal Aviation Authority might be prepared to accept more airport privatization – although full privatization at major airports still seemed fairly remote (McCormick, 2000b). However, greater private participation has been achieved with the adoption of management contracts and project finance schemes at some airports. Airports Group International had some management contracts before the 1990s, but mostly at small airports with the exception of the international terminal at Atlanta airport. However, in 1995 BAA plc won the ten-year management contract for Indianapolis airport, which was an airport of considerable size with a throughput of 6.7 million passengers. Under the scheme, BAA plc was not to receive any fixed management fee but would share in the savings it generated. The company guaranteed average annual savings of more than US$3 million (US$32 million over a ten-year agreement) and would not be paid any fees until after it produced average annual savings of nearly US$6 million (US$58 million over a ten-year agreement). BAA plc expected to save the airport $100 million during the ten-year contract by increasing non-aviation revenue and reducing expenditure from energy supply, equipment and payroll costs. The airport board would continue to set policy enforce agreements and control rates and charges (Ott, 1998).

BAA plc also acquired the management contract for Harrisburg International Airport in 1998 and has retail management contracts at Pittsburgh, Newark, JFK and Boston. There is even a suggestion that BAA plc may take over the general management of New York's JFK and La Guardia airports. In another development in 1997, the financing, construction and operation of the international arrivals building at New York JFK airport was handed over to a private consortium (which includes Amsterdam Schiphol airport) for twenty years. This is the first such project in the USA. BAA plc, Schiphol, and TBI therefore appear to be ready if further US privatization options arise.

The globalization of the airport industry

Privatization has enabled a number of airport companies to expand beyond previously well-defined national barriers. As further opportunities for privatization occur, this will accelerate the pace of globalization of the industry. This expansion has occurred not only with well-established airport companies such as BAA plc and Amsterdam Schiphol, but also with a number of non-airport companies whose previous experience in running airports was rather limited or non-existent (Bennett, 1999; Schneiderbauer, Feldman and Horrex, 1998).

Traditional airport companies

There are a number of airport operators who are well established in providing services for other airports. For example, BAA plc, AdP, Aer Rianta and the airports of Amsterdam and Frankfurt have always been very active in providing consultancy services and running management contracts for certain activities at some airports. Aeroport de Paris has built a reputation in the management of engineering and construction projects in countries such as China, Vietnam, Cyprus, the Philippines, Indonesia and the Lebanon. Frankfurt airport has been involved with ground-handling contracts and baggage systems in as diverse areas as Spain, the USA and Kenya. Aer Rianta has mostly specialized in retail contracts.

The opportunities for international expansion have increased substantially with airport privatization. BAA plc, for example, now has airport interests in countries such as Italy, the USA, Australia, Mauritius and China. Similarly Amsterdam Schiphol has involvement in other airports in the Netherlands, Australia and the USA. Other European airports or airport groups with international interests include Rome, Milan, Copenhagen, Frankfurt, Paris, Vienna, Manchester, AENA (Spain) and Aer Rianta (Ireland). Some of these airports, such as Rome, Milan, Frankfurt and Manchester, also have involvement in other airports in their own country. Most of these European airports have ambitious plans to expand their external operations. For example, Frankfurt airport has set a business target for 2005 which aims for 50 per cent sales to be generated by external business (Frankfurt Airport, 2000b). Outside Europe, international airport companies are less involved, with the exception of some Canadian airports such as Vancouver with interests in a number of South American airports and to a lesser extent Montreal and Singapore. With most global industries, US companies tend to play a major role. However, because of the unique situation of US airports, unusually, there is little competition from US companies.

The Schiphol Group: from Amsterdam airport to a global airport company

The Schiphol Group is a publicly owned company. The shares are held by the state of the Netherlands (76 per cent), the city of Amsterdam (22 per cent) and the city of Rotterdam (2 per cent). Since 1958 the company has operated as an independent, self-sufficient business. In 1999 it handled 37 million passengers and 1.2 million tonnes of freight, which made it the fourth largest European airport in terms of passengers and freight (Schiphol Group, 2000). In the last ten years its passenger traffic has grown by an average annual increase of 9 per

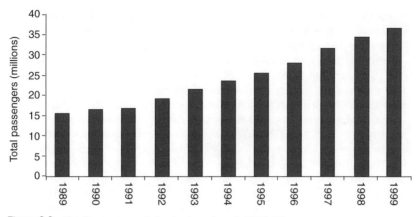

Figure 2.9 Total passengers at Amsterdam airport, 1989–99
Source: Annual reports.

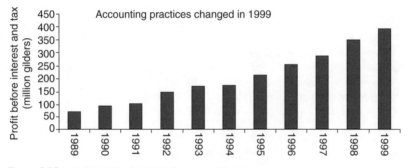

Figure 2.10 Profitability: Schiphol Group, 1989–99
Source: Annual accounts.

cent, while its profit figures before tax and interest have increased by 19 per cent (Figures 2.9 and 2.10).

Up until 1991, Schiphol's international involvement was confined to providing training and education at other airports. In this year it made the decision to expand by offering more general airport consultancy and managing commercial airport operations. One of its first management contracts was in Curacao, which was agreed in 1993. By the mid-1990s it had considerable consultancy experience particularly in the developing areas of South East Asia in countries such as Indonesia, Malaysia, the Philippines, China, and in the CIS in countries such as Russia, Lithuania and Georgia. It also had management contracts with other airports such as Cartagena in Columbia and St Maarten. Further expansion meant that by the end of 1999 it had active consultancy and management projects being undertaken in a wide range of countries including the USA, South Africa, the Gambia, St Maarten, Curaçao, Egypt, Portugal, France, Greece, Bulgaria, Russia, Lithuania, Malaysia, Thailand, China and the Philippines.

Since 1990, the Schiphol Group has also been pursuing a policy of acquiring equity shares and other interests in both domestic and international airports. The first domestic airport to come under Schiphol's control was Rotterdam airport in 1990, which is being developed into an airport offering short-haul scheduled flights for the business community. In 1993 Lelystad was bought with the aim of making it into as a business airport for general aviation. Then, in 1998, Schiphol acquired a 51 per cent shareholding in the regional airport of Eindhoven where it plans to attract scheduled European airlines to the airport, to optimize feeder flights with Amsterdam and to develop charter traffic.

Schiphol's first international involvement came in 1997 when it took a 40 per cent share in the JFKIAT company which was selected to provide a new international arrivals terminal at New York JFK airport. This BOT project was due to be completed by 2001 and then the JFKIAT consortium, whose other partners are a property developer LCOR (40 per cent) and the American financial institution Lehman Brothers (20 per cent) will operate the facility until 2015. Since 1997, Schiphol has had a 13 per cent shareholding in the Brisbane Airport Corporation, the consortium chosen to run Brisbane airport. Schiphol has also been involved in a number of unsuccessful bids, for example in South Africa, Mexico and Stewart in the USA.

The airport company has been adapting its organizational structure to reflect this increasing involvement in other airports. Separate business units, namely Schiphol Project Consult and Schiphol International were set up for the consultancy and international undertakings. In 1998 these units became independent, limited liability companies. In 1999 the name of the airport company was also changed to reflect the increasing diversity of activities. The overall company name became Schiphol Group, rather than Amsterdam Airport Schiphol which

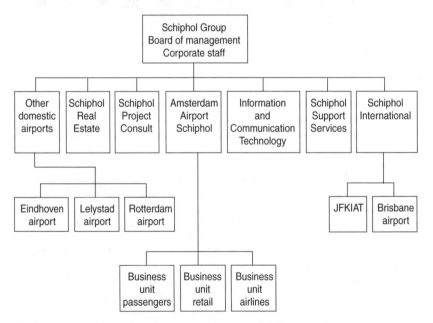

Figure 2.11 Organizational structure within the Schiphol Group, 1999
Source: Annual report.

is now just one organization within the structure. In addition there are the three independent subsidiaries – Schiphol Project Consult, Schiphol International and Schiphol Real Estate, called the domestic airports and the two support units – Schiphol Support Services and Information and Communication Technology (Figure 2.11).

It is the Schiphol Group's stated mission to be a leading international airport operator. It aims to do this by reinforcing Amsterdam Airport Schiphol's international competitive position particularly by developing its concept of an 'AirportCity' which provides services twenty-four hours a day in the form of shops and catering, hotels and recreation, and information, communication and business activities. It wants to market this concept internationally. It is particularly keen to develop alliances with other airports to optimize management skills and knowledge (Schiphol Group, 2000). In 1995 it became the first airport company to take a shareholding in another company, 1 per cent in Vienna airport, with the aim of sharing expertise, for example in the areas of retail performance, cost efficiency and property development. It has been working with Brussels International Airport Company to develop a new flight information system and with other information technology projects. In 1999, it put in a bid jointly with BAA plc for 49 per cent of the shares of Soekarno-Hatta airport, in Jakarta in Indonesia. In the same year, it formed the Pantares alliance with Frankfurt airport (Fraport) and started looking at co-operation in areas such as information-technology, handling and cargo, retail, property development and international activities. The airports consider that synergies in airport operations and combined financial strength will help in the acquisition of further international airports (Schiphol Group, 1999a). In 2000 Fraport purchased 0.8 per cent of Brisbane airport. Also in this year a consortium of financial and industrial organizations was formed with both the Schiphol Group and Fraport having a 1 per cent shareholding. This consortium, called Establishing a Network for European Airports (ENEA) expressed interest in gaining a share in the Aeroporti di Roma company, but was subsequently unsuccessful.

One of the reasons for why the Schiphol group has a strategy of expanding overseas and entering into alliances is its relatively small home market. Moreover, there is uncertainty about long-term growth at Amsterdam airport, although a government decision at the end of 1999 confirmed that the airport would be allowed to expand at a controlled pace (Schiphol Group, 1999b). The other key issue for the group is its public ownership. The group has stated that privatization is a prerequisite for remaining competitive in the international scene, as continued state ownership reduces its flexibility and limits its ability to co-operate with other airports and have access to capital markets. The government has stated that in principle it is in favour of privatization and by the year 2000 the company had already begun to prepare for privatization by talking about economic regulation with its airline customers (Schiphol Group, 2000).

New airport operators

The other organizations which have taken advantage of the privatization trend to become airport management companies are quite varied. They include property developers such as TBI (which took over AGI in 1999) which has interests in airports in the UK, Sweden, Spain, Australia and North America. Other UK companies include Peel Holdings which has a majority share in Liverpool airport and has plans to develop Finningley airport in the North of the UK, and Wiggins which owns the Manston airport in the UK, and manages a further three small airports in Nashville (USA), Odense (Denmark) and Pilsen (Czech Republic). The utility and property company, Infratil, has involvement with Prestwick, Perth and Wellington airports. There are also construction companies such as Hochtief which has interests in Athens and Düsseldorf airports, Cintra which has involvements in the Mexican airports, Bristol and Niagara Falls airport, and Bechtel which has an interest in Luton airport. Then there is Ogden the airport service provider, which is a partner in the Argentinian concession. Finally, there are transport companies, most notably National Express which had interests in East Midlands, Bournemouth and Stewart International until 2001 when it sold its UK airports to concentrate on other transport activities. United Kingdom transport operators Firstgroup and Stagecoach also each owned and sold a UK airport. In many cases these companies will have teamed up with international financial investors such as Lehman Brothers and Barclays International (as have the traditional airport operators) to form consortia to run airports.

There has been considerable discussion as to whether airlines could buy and operate airports. In the USA, airlines already partially or totally lease terminals and in Australia the domestic terminals are leased to the domestic carriers. This means that the airlines get exclusive rights to parts of the terminal and/or they may receive substantial discounts on usage. Elsewhere, however, such practice is rare. An unusual example is the Birmingham Eurohub which was partially financed by British Airways (BA). The only recent developments have been the terminal facilities developed exclusively for BA at Manchester airport and Lufthansa's agreement to become a joint venture partner with Munich airport in developing the second terminal. If an individual airline or alliance grouping wanted to buy a substantial share of an airport to obtain more control and develop a stronger brand presence, there would be a number of regulatory and competition issues which would need to be considered. Low-cost carriers have also expressed an interest in running their own facilities in order to keep the service simple and keep down costs. EasyJet, which has developed services out of London Luton airport, unsuccessfully tried to buy the airport when it was up for sale. Ryanair, based at Dublin airport has also proposed building its own low cost terminal.

TBI: from property management to global airport operations

TBI began life as a Wales-based property company, Thomas Bailey Investment. It was listed on the stock exchange in 1994. It first became involved with airports when it bought Cardiff International, an airport handling around 1 million passengers, in April 1995 from the local government owners. It subsequently went on to buy Belfast International Airport, which was handling around 2 million passengers, in August 1996 from the management owners. Its first airport acquisition outside of the UK was in 1997 when it purchased Orlando Sanford International, the third busiest international airport in Florida, handling just under 1 million passengers. At all three airports it embarked on major capital investment programmes.

Further expansion into the airport business occurred in June 1998, when TBI acquired 90 per cent of Stockholm Skavsta airport in Sweden. Skavsta airport is a small airport about 100 km south of Stockholm. TBI initially paid US$27.5 million for the airport with a further US$6.5 million to be paid when certain goals are achieved. These goals relate to passenger and freight throughout, namely US$2.5 million when passengers numbers exceed 600 000, US$2.5 million when freight exceeds 71 120 tonnes and US$1.25 million when both goals are achieved (Graham, 1998). In 1998 there were 213 000 passengers, flying mostly on low-cost carriers and charter, and 25 000 tonnes of freight (ACI Europe, 1999). TBI has subsequently developed new terminal facilities allowing the airport to handle 1 million passengers annually and is lobbying for the airport to achieve 'Stockholm Second Airport' status.

Two major changes occurred in 1999 to the company's focus and operations in line with the company's declared strategic objective of becoming an established airports group with a substantial international presence. In June 1999 it took the decision to concentrate on its airport business and so disposed of all its £190 million property interests except the Cardiff Hilton Hotel. This meant that its stock market classification was changed from property to transport.

Then in September 1999, it acquired Airports Group International (AGI) for £86 million (TBI, 2000). Airports Group International was a large private airport operating company backed by the US financier George Soros, Lockheed Martin, Bechtel and GE Capital. Airports Group International had involvement with twenty-nine airports worldwide when it was acquired by TBI. It had equity shares in a number of Australian airports (Darwin, Alice Springs, Tennant Creek, Perth and Hobart) and equity interests in a concession contract for La Paz, Santa Cruz and Cochabamba airports in Bolivian airports. In North America it had management contracts for Terminal 3 at Toronto Pearson International airport, for the international concourse at Atlanta Hartsfield and for the small airports of Burbank airport in California and Albany airport, New York. At a number of other US airports it had contracts for handling and other airport services. Finally AGI had a 25 per cent equity share in the concession consortium which was managing Luton airport. Acquiring AGI changed TBI into a company which had controlling equity shares at seven airports, non-controlling equity shares at another six and contracts to manage or to provide services at another twenty-four locations (TBI, 2000).

TBI has subsequently gone on to expand its business further. At around the same time as the AGI acquisition, approval was given to TBI for a thirty-year management contract to operate Orlando Sanford airport's domestic terminal. This involved TBI paying US$10 million towards the US$25 million cost of the terminal expansion to handle up to 3 million passengers – US$7.5 million paid upfront and the rest in annual payments. The annual payments are matched by Federal Aviation Authority and Florida Department of Transportation funding (Orlando Sanford Airport Authority, 1999).

In November 1999, a twenty-year management contract was agreed for Juan Santamaria International Airport in Costa Rica which served around 2 million

Table 2.8   TBI's expansion into the airport business 1995–2000

Date	Development
1995	Acquisition of Cardiff International airport
1996	Acquisition of Belfast International airport
1997	Acquisition of Orlando Sanford International airport (long leasehold interest)
1998	Acquisition of 90% share of Stockholm Skavsta airport
1999	Disposal of entire property business (except Cardiff Hilton Hotel)
	Purchase of Airports Group International (AGI) acquiring airport interests in Australia, Bolivia, USA, Canada and Luton
	Acquisition of management contract for domestic terminal at Orlando Sanford airport
	Acquisition of 82% share of Consorcio AGI which has management contract for Juan Santamaria International airport in Costa Rica
2000	20% equity involvement in Aeropuerto de Ciudad Real company which has BOT contract at airport

Source: Compiled by author from various sources.

passengers. TBI owns 82 per cent of the equity in management company, Consorcio AGI, and has guaranteed to implement the master plan which will increase the capacity of the airport to around 4 million passengers at a cost of around US$20 million (TBI, 1999). In 2000 TBI took a 20 per cent equity stake in a company involved in a thirty-year BOT project to develop and operate an airport on a greenfield site near the city of Ciudad Real in South-Central Spain.

TBI has grown very rapidly from a property company with interest in a couple of small airports to a major global airport company in less than five years. Its turnover and profit before interest and tax has increased by 40 and 30 per cent respectively per annum (Figure 2.12). In 1996/7 when it began to enter into the airport business its profit from airports was £10 million compared with £15 million from the property business. By 1997/8, however, £21 million profits came from airports while £17 million came from property. The gap widened in 1998/9 with £24 million from airport profit and only £14 million from property. The disposal of the property business in 1999 meant that subsequently nearly all profits in that year were airport related. Profits were not as high as expected in 2000 primarily because of poor performance of Sanford and Skavsta airports.

Skills needed to become a global airport player

For a traditional airport company to become a global player, it is clearly not just a question of transferring the core skills and competencies which have already been gained through airport management in the home country to the new airport. To be successful these core skills will have to be adapted for an airport perhaps in another part of the world, which may operate within a different competitive environment and regulatory regime. This may be hard to achieve for some of the large state-owned European airport operators, which have always held a rather privileged, quasi-monopolistic position by serving the

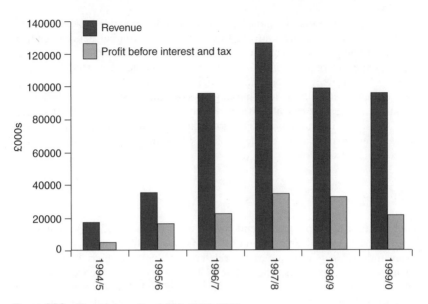

Figure 2.12   Financial results of TBI, 1994–2000
Source: Annual reports.

capital city of the country, In addition, there are a number of new areas of expertise which must be acquired if the airport operator is to become a success-ful international organization (Schneiderbauer, Feldman and Horrex, 1998; Gangl, 2001).

The core competencies in traditional airport operations are familiar to any airport manager. They include overall management of the airfield and termi-nal areas, surface access planning and co-ordination, security and safety opera-tions, facility and utility management, and master planning. In addition, in this modern age of airport management, skills in running the airport as a business as well as operational expertise are equally as important. These include skills in the management and development of retail and other commercial facilities, cost control and optimizing organization and productivity, marketing expertise in meeting the needs of airlines, passenger and other customers, and compe-tence in quality management techniques.

If the airport company is to compete within the global airport industry, it will need to be competent in bid and project management. This means that it will need to have skills in investment evaluation and business planning, consortia formulation and management, and bid preparation and negotiation. Once the airport company has bought or acquired effective control of the 'privatized' airport it then has to demonstrate additional skills to those just associated with the core competencies of airport operations and commercial management. It must be able to achieve success and add value at the new airport, which may involve identifying new opportunities and marketing and developing new business. In order to take advantage of these new opportunities it will also have to have expertise in change management and global business skills.

Many of the airports that have been privatized, for example in Australia and South America, are being controlled by various consortia partners rather than individual companies. In some cases, the tender authorities may stipulate the type of expertise required in the consortia. For example, in Australia previous aviation management experience was required and in Mexico a major local partner was essential. In any bidding process there is always considerable debate as to the best mix of partners. Nichols, Koll and Stevins (1999) suggest that an airport operator plus an engineering company to control the master project management and a financing partner to structure project financing may be the optimal solution.

Why go global?

Globalization is a dominant trend within the world's economy bringing cost savings, marketing advantages and technological development opportunities to many industries – including travel-related businesses such as hotels, travel agents and tour operators. The airline industry is a high-profile example of an industry which has been developing alliance and globalization strategies for a number of years. For airlines, there are many perceived advantages of such a development such as marketing strength, network spread and product integration, brand loyalty and reduction in costs.

For airport companies the motivation for globalization is somewhat less well defined. There certainly do not seem to be such obvious synergies in controlling a global group of airports as there are with airlines, particularly when the airports are operating in different regulatory environments. There is no guarantee that successful management practices at one airport will work in a similar manner at another airport.

There are, of course, some quite persuasive general arguments for encouraging any business to aim for a global or worldwide presence. Benefits can include higher returns and increased shareholder value. Also risks may be reduced by going global, thereby placing less relevance on any one national economy and lessening exposure to downturns in individual economies.

Specifically for airports there may be distinct advantages in expanding internationally if their own core infrastructure (e.g. terminal or runway) is physically or environmentally constrained, as is the situation with the London, Frankfurt and Amsterdam airports. Financial growth in the home market may be hindered by a regulatory system which may limit the amount of revenue generated from aeronautical sources, as is the case with BAA plc. The abolition of EU duty- and tax-free sales in 1999 has also made commercial opportunities outside the EU more attractive. In addition, international expansion can provide the much needed finance for development in the home market and may safeguard the success of the core business.

Globalization can be seen as a natural progression for airport companies that have gone through the processes of commercialization and then privatization. Once privatization has proved to be successful, it seems quite logical that the commercially minded airports might next seek to acquire other interests to expand and add value to their company. It is not, however, just the privatized or partially privatized airports (such as those of BAA plc, Copenhagen and

Vienna) which are seeking to become international companies. There are also companies such as AdP, Milan and AENA, which are not responsible to private shareholders, but are just as keen to acquire other airports. The motivation for such expansion is less clear – though it is true that such airports, too, are increasingly under greater pressure to perform well and many are expected eventually to be privatized. Perhaps for some airports there may be an element of fear of being left behind in the race to globalize. This factor may be partly responsible for increasing the competition at the bidding stage at a number of airports in the late 1990s, and in some cases inflating the prices being paid.

One of the major general benefits that international or global companies have is that they may be able to reduce costs through bulk buying and joint purchasing in some areas. This could be the situation of the airport industry although the savings would probably not be very substantial. For example, cost reductions could be achieved with joint purchasing of equipment such as ramp buses and fire engines, and through negotiation of more favourable insurance policies. Costs could also be saved by having a single head office and through centralizing many functions such as accounting and information technology. Joint training programmes could be arranged and there may be cost advantages through combined marketing. Standard commercial contracts could be agreed with core partners at the airports. In addition, the advantages of being 'big' may help the airport company keep up to date with technology developments and the latest airport management tools and techniques around the world.

As with any expansion, there are also many risks. Too high a price may be paid, particularly if the bidding process is highly competitive. There may be some fundamental flaw in the business plan which has been put together. There are also political risks, which are particularly relevant to the airport industry given the industry's high political profile. Even if a government has relinquished all effective control of an airport to a private operator, a change in the air transport regulatory system or the introduction of more stringent environmental legislation could have a fundamental impact on the way in which the airport operates.

Airport alliances and co-operation

The main driving force behind the globalization of airport networks has been airport privatization which has enabled a growing number of airports to be purchased outright or at least managed on a long-term basis by an external airport operator. In the future, airport globalization also looks likely to occur as a result of greater co-operation between airport operators or through the establishment of airport alliances. This seems inevitable, particularly in the light of increased competition in the airline industry and more advanced globalization strategies. This has meant that airports themselves face increased competition and are under greater pressure to reduce costs, improve quality and add value to their organizations – all of which, theoretically, can be helped by airport co-operation. In some cases this may be just a question of developing informal links, which already exist for information exchange or marketing support, to a cover a broader scope of activities. Unlike airline co-operation, which is primarily driven by a need to expand networks and increase market accessibility, airport co-operation is likely to be encouraged by a desire to benefit from shared knowledge, expertise and financial resources.

The Schiphol–Fraport alliance, which was agreed in late 1999 was the first major alliance agreement witnessed by the airport industry. As with other industries, alliances can enable the transfer of knowledge, skills and technology which can produce synergies and economies of scale. Co-operating in international projects can share both the risk and investment needed. However, as with all collaborations, particularly involving partners from different countries, conflicts can also arise through incompatible vision, a lack of common strategy or objectives, or inherent cultural and business differences. Schiphol and Fraport believed that there was scope for co-operation because the two airports were both European hubs but serving different airlines alliances, they had complementary competencies, they were at similar levels of globalization and they shared the same strategic approach. They identified seven areas where co-operation seemed possible (Endler, 2000; Verboom, 2000):

1 *Aviation ground services*: ground and cargo handling logistic systems; bidding for international projects.
2 *Retail and passengers*: retail business at home and international airports; e-business and intermodal strategies.
3 *Facility management*: purchasing, project management and technical services; standardization of equipment and technology.
4 *Real estate*: site development at home and other airports, marketing, bidding for international projects.
5 *Information technology*: system and equipment standardization; product and technology development; marketing.
6 *International projects*: privatization projects; project management; financial risk sharing.
7 *Other*: marketing, research, training and recruitment, environmental issues.

Since this 'Pantares' alliance was formed Fraport has taken a share in Brisbane airport, a joint venture has been formed for retail operations and the alliance has been chosen to manage a new logistics centre at Hong Kong airport. Rome has joined the alliance. Other co-operation examples include Auckland and Singapore airport. A number of airports have also joined together to form the 'world airports' alliance to develop e-business opportunities.

Impact of airport globalization on users

Passengers

One of the major advantages of globalization for airlines and other companies is the advantage of being able to sell one common product or one global brand to the customer. For international or global airport companies, branding involves the use of similar signposting, colour schemes and interior design for the entire airport. Examples of this have existed for many years with national airport groups. For example, BAA plc has traditionally used a common and constant brand image for its seven UK airports. The merits of branding within the airport industry, are, however very questionable. Most passengers, particularly leisure passengers who travel infrequently, would probably not be aware of any common branding and would find it very difficult to define any distinguishing features of a certain airport brand. Branding could make passengers feel more familiar with the airport services and facilities they use, but it will not be until the global airport companies have established a much stronger presence that a 'global brand' will be recognizable by most passengers. From the airport operator's point of view, however, there may be some advantage in aiming to provide a common brand image in that a well defined level of quality of service can be defined and guaranteed for all airports.

Airlines

As with most industry privatizations there has been concern from users, particularly the airlines, that prices will rise once privatization has occurred and profit maximization becomes the key business driving force and motivation. In the UK, for example, airport charge increases at Belfast International airport (owned by TBI) and Luton airport (operated as a concession by TBI and other partners) have been bitterly opposed – notably by British Midland at Belfast and easyJet at Luton. Chapter 5 describes how, in some cases, regulation has been introduced to control charges – but this may not always be satisfactory to users if, for example, not all relevant prices are regulated. For instance, with the Argentinian airports the airlines have claimed that there have been unreasonable increases in charges in the non-regulated areas such baggage handling, check-in desks and other office space, while the direct airside charges, such as landing and passenger fees, have remained fixed by regulation (Gill, 1998).

On the other hand, there may also be benefits to an individual airline or airline alliance in operating out of more than one airport which is owned by a global airport company. For example, standard contracts may be agreed for the whole airport network, quantity discounts on charging may be negotiated and there may be common agreements on the use of gates and other facilities. Moreover, the availability of new sources of funding may enable the quality of airport facilities to be improved which will generally be welcomed by the airlines – as long as it does not push up airport charges. The transfer of skills in the management and development of retail and other commercial facilities may increase non-aeronautical revenue and may reduce the airport's reliance on aeronautical sources. The airline industry body, the International Air Transport Association (IATA), has acknowledged that airport globalization may bring beneficial economies of scale due to, for example, joint purchasing and shared development costs of new systems. It is in favour of such developments if the resultant lower costs bring lower charges. However, IATA has also expressed concerns that globalization could lead to management attention and funds being diverted away from core airports. An additional fear is that sophisticated systems not really necessary for certain smaller airports may be adopted merely because they are available (IATA, 2000b).

In conclusion, airport privatization and moves towards globalization have been two of the most important changes occurring within the airport industry in recent years. By the end of 2000 the popularity of airports as investment opportunities seemed to be dwindling slightly in reaction to a number of uncertainties, and it seemed likely that the high prices which had been paid for some airports would not be repeated in the future. Nevertheless all indications were that many more privatizations were planned for the early years of the twenty-first century in numerous countries, many with very different political and economic systems.

References and further reading

ACI Europe (1999). *Airport Traffic Report*. ACI Europe.

Ashford, N. (1999). Experiences with airport privatization. In *Airport 2000: Trends for the New Millennium* (N. Ashford, ed.), Sovereign.

Ashford, N. and Moore, C. (1999). *Airport Finance*. 2nd edn, Loughborough Airport Consultancy.

Aviation Strategy (1999a). Airport privatization – no stopping the juggernaut. *Aviation Strategy*, January, 10–13.

Aviation Strategy (1999b). Airport privatization: competition for management project intensifies. *Aviation Strategy*, October, 14–17.

Aviation Strategy (2000). How to sell an airport. *Aviation Strategy*, March, 8–9.

Ballantyne, T. (1997). Sydney syndrome. *Airline Business*, October, 58–61.

Barker, J. (1999). Private interest in India. *Jane's Airport Review*, May, 36.

Beechener, J. (2000). Beijing rides market downturn. *Jane's Airport Review*, June, 8–9.

Beesley, M. E. (1997). *Privatization, Regulation and Deregulation*. 2nd edn, Routledge.

Bennett, P. (1999). Taking on the world. *Airline Business*, December, 46–58.

Carre, A.-D. (1999). Possible forms of state intervention. Institute of Air Transport Airport Management symposium, Senegal, November.

Caves, R. and Gosling, G. (1999). *Strategic Airport Planning*. Elsevier.

Collet, F. (1999). Changes in airport management, worldwide and in Africa. Institute of Air Transport Airport Management symposium, Senegal, November.

Communique Airport Business (1998). Our best deal ever – AGI and London Luton. November/December, 28.

Communique Airport Business (2000). *Athens International Airport: Pre-opening Special Report*, Summer.

Croes, H. (1997). Airport privatization: cleared to take off. *Aerlines*, Winter, 28–30.

Department of the Environment, Transport and the Regions (DETR) (1998). *A New Deal for Transport*. HMSO.

Deutsche Bank (1999). *European Airports: Privatization Ahead*. Deutsche Bank.

Doganis, R. (1992). *The Airport Business*. Routledge.

Endler, J. (2000). Global alliances and privatization. Tenth ACI Europe Annual Assembly, Rome, June.

Federal Airports Corporation (FAC) (1997). *Annual Report 1997*. FAC.

Frankfurt Airport (2000a). Flying into the 21st century: the Frankfurt airport authority is major partner in Terminal 3 project Manila International airport. Press release, 28 June.

Frankfurt Airport (2000b). *Annual Report 1999*. Frankfurt Airport.

Freathy, P. and O'Connell, F. (1998). *European Airport Retailing*. Macmillan.

Gangl, S. (1994). Financing a partially-privatized airport. Airports as Business Enterprises Conference, April.

Gangl, S. (1995). Going to market – Vienna Airport's share flotation. In *Sources of Finance for Airport Development in Europe*, (J. Amkreutz, ed.), ACI Europe.

Gangl, S. (1998). Experiences of privatization. University of Westminster/ Cranfield University Airport Economics and Finance Symposium, London, March.

Gangl, S. (2001). The globalization of airport companies. University of Westminster/Cranfield University Airport Economics and Finance Symposium, March.

General Accounting Office (GAO) (1996a). *Funding Sources for Airport Development*. GAO.

General Accounting Office (GAO) (1996b). *Airport Privatization: Issues Related to the Sale or Lease of US Commercial Airports*. GAO.

General Accounting Office (GAO) (1998). *Funding of Airport Development*. GAO.

General Accounting Office (GAO) (1999). *Annual funding as Much as $3 Billion Less than Planned Development*. GAO.

Gill, T. (1998). Stampede to market. *Airline Business*, April, 50–3

Graham, E. (1998). TBI buys Stockholm-Skavsta in Sweden's first privatization. *ACI Europe Communique*, October, 8.

Gray, S. (1998). SEA consortium prepares $2.1 billion Argentinian plan. *ACI. Europe Communique*, August/September, 7.

Hanlon, J. P. (1999). *Global Airlines*. 2nd edn, Butterworth-Heinemann.

Humphreys, I. (1999). Privatization and commercialization changes in UK airport ownership patterns. *Journal of Transport Geography*, 7, 121–34.

International Air Transport Association (IATA) (2000a). *World Air Transport Statistics*, 6/44, IATA.

International Air Transport Association (IATA) (2000b). Airport networks and airport cross ownership. *ANSConf Working Paper No 18*, ICAO.

International Civil Aviation Organization (ICAO) (2000a). Privatization in the provision of airports and air navigation services. *ANSConf Working Paper No 6*, ICAO.

International Civil Aviation Organization (ICAO) (2000b). Organisational aspects of the provision of airports and air navigation services. *ANSConf Working Paper No 18*, ICAO.

Jackson, P. M and Price, C. P. (eds) (1994). *Privatization and Regulation*. Longman.

Jane's Airport Review (2000). Stockholm's third airport. *Jane's Airport Review*, March, 14.

Knibb, D. (1999). Australia's road to privatization. *Airline Business*, August, 40–1.

Lambert, R. (1995). Birmingham's public-private finance partnership. In *Sources of Finance for Airport Development in Europe* (J. Amkreutz, ed.), ACI Europe.

McCormick, C. (2000a). Private partners. *Airports International*, March, 36–41.

51

McCormick, C. (2000b). US privatisation program to expand? *Airports International*, September, 9.

Nichols, W. K., Koll, E. and Stevins, A. (1999). Airport internationalisation: the time is now, *Airports International*, June, 16–20.

Orlando Sanford Airport Authority (1999). Sanford Airport Authority approves deal – TBI US to Operate Orlando Sanford airport's domestic terminal. Press release, 30 August.

Ott, J. (1998). Indianapolis serves as a privatization testbed. *Aviation Week and Space Technology*, 14 December, 52.

Poole, R. W. (1995). *How to Privatize Orange County's Airports*. Policy study 194, Reason Foundation.

Ricover, A. (1999). Airport privatization of Latin American airports. In *Airport 2000: Trends for the New Millennium* (N. Ashford, ed.), Sovereign.

Schiphol Group (1999a). Schiphol Group and FAG seek close co-operation. Press release, 21 December.

Schiphol Group (1999b). Dutch government gives go-ahead for further growth. Press release, 17 December.

Schiphol Group (2000). *Annual Report 1999*. Schiphol Group.

Schneiderbauer D., Feldman D. and Horrex, M. (1998). *Global Airport Management: Strategic Challenges in an Emerging Industry*. Mercer Management Consulting.

TBI (1999). *Interim Report 1999*. TBI.

TBI (2000). *Annual Report 1999*. TBI.

UK Government (1986). *Airports Act 1986*. HMSO.

Verboom, P. (2000). Schiphol Group: creating airportcities. Tenth ACI Europe Annual Assembly, Rome, June.

3

Airport economics and performance benchmarking

A profitable industry?

This chapter considers the economics of the airport industry. The modern-day commercial and business pressures being placed on most airports mean that a thorough understanding of the economics of airports is now, more than ever before, a fundamental prerequisite for all airport managers. The chapter begins by looking at profit levels within the industry and describing the revenue and cost structures. It then goes on to discuss some of the key factors which influence the economics of airports. This leads to a discussion of how economic performance can be measured and whether it is possible to produce a single efficiency measure for each airport.

Table 3.1 shows the net profit after tax at thirty of the largest airports or airport groups in the world in 1999. All the airports were profitable except for the Japanese airports. However, a broader assessment of overall profitability can be obtained from the ACI which produces the most comprehensive global economic surveys. The 1999 survey covered 526 airports which collectively handled over 1.9 billion passengers, or about two-thirds of all ACI members traffic in 1998 (ACI,

2000). The survey identified trends in airport economics by geographical region but some distortions may have arisen because of the composition of the sample used. This seemed to be particularly the case with the African and Latin America/Caribbean regions where the influence of the strong financial performance of a few large airports may have resulted in the presentation of an overly optimistic situation for these two regions.

The general profitable situation, as illustrated in Table 3.1, is not evident throughout the airport industry, particularly with smaller airports and those in developing areas. Overall the ACI survey found that in 1998 below 40 per cent of all the airports produced a net profit after depreciation, interest and tax. Profits before these cost items (in international accounting terms known as EBITDA) were achieved by 69 per cent of the airports. The advantage of this second measure is that the comparability problems between the airports, due

Table 3.1 **Profitability for thirty major airport operators, 1999**

Airport operator	Passengers at major airports (million)[1]	Net profit after tax (US$ million)
1 AENA Spanish Airports	128.1	148.8
2 BAA	117.4	206.7
3 Port Authority of New York and New Jersey	89.6	253.2
4 Aeroports de Paris	68.9	111.0
5 Los Angeles World Airports	64.3	170.6
6 Dallas-Fort Worth Airport	60.0	148.3
7 Frankfurt Airport	45.8	75.1
8 Detroit Metro Wayne County	43.8	34.0
9 San Francisco	40.4	27.5
10 Schiphol Group	36.8	135.8
11 Washington Airports Authority	34.7	15.8
12 Korea International Airports Authority	33.4	39.6
13 Vancouver International Airport Authority	33.3	16.0
14 Greater Orlando Aviation Authority	29.2	257.4
15 Greater Toronto Airports Authority	27.8	5.9
16 Port of Seattle	27.7	10.8
17 Airports Authority of Thailand	27.3	86.7
18 Massachusetts Port Authority	27.1	54.1
19 Civil Aviation Authority Singapore	26.1	205.0
20 New Tokyo International Airport Authority	25.7	−9.4
21 Aeroporti di Roma	24.7	55.0
22 SEA Milan Airports	23.6	45.7
23 Munich Airport	21.3	40.8
24 Zürich Airport	20.9	64.1
25 Brussels International Airport Company	20.0	24.0
26 Kansai International Airport Company	19.9	−214.4
27 Manchester Airport	17.8	46.5
28 Copenhagen Airports	17.4	52.2
29 Aer Rianta Irish Airports	16.5	42.0
30 Düsseldorf Airport	15.9	14.7

Note: [1] Only includes traffic from main airports which the airport operator owns.
Source: Airline Business and annual reports.

to different accounting practices and taxation regimes, are eliminated. In aggregate terms the airports in Latin American and the Caribbean, and the Pacific both made a loss when net profits were considered but a profit when the EBITDA value was considered. Airports in the other regions appeared profitable when both measures were used.

The International Civil Aviation Organization also surveyed a smaller sample of 252 airports in 1998 which accounted for 91 per cent of all passengers carried by world scheduled airlines. The survey looked at profit after depreciation and interest and found that around three-quarters of the airports were profitable or at least broke even. It was noted, however, that only about two-thirds of the airport sample showed realistic costs associated with depreciation and interest. For the other airports, these costs were either not reported or were very low which must have had the effect of overestimating profit levels in some cases (ICAO, 2000).

Revenue and cost structures

Airport revenue is usually classified into two main categories: aeronautical (or aviation) and non-aeronautical (or commercial) revenues (Table 3.2).

Aeronautical revenues are those sources of income that arise directly from the operation of aircraft and the processing of passengers and freight. Non-aeronautical revenues are those generated by activities that are not directly related to the operation of aircraft, notably income from commercial activities within the terminal and rents for terminal space and airport land. The International Civil Aviation Organization has a long list of activities which can be classified as non-aeronautical including cattle farming, concrete-post manufacturing, baseball training camps, mannequins and models show and pipeline inspection shows (ICAO, 1991)! Then there are a few categories of income that can be classified as either type of revenue. For example, handling revenues are usually treated as aeronautical revenues unless handling is undertaken by handling agents or airlines when the associated revenue (rent or fee based on turnover) is included under rents or concession revenue items. Income received

Table 3.2 Airport operating revenue sources

Aeronautical	*Non-aeronautical*
Landing fees	Concessions
Passenger fees	Rents
Aircraft parking fees	Direct sales (shops, catering and other services provided by the airport operator)
Handling fees (if handling is provided by the airport operator)	Car park (if provided by the airport operator)
Other aeronautical fees (air traffic control, lighting, airbridges etc.)	Recharges (for gas, water, electricity etc.)
	Other non-aeronautical revenue (consultancy, visitor and business services, property development etc.)

by the airport from aircraft fuel companies or from airlines as a fuel through-put fee could be regarded as directly related to aircraft operations and hence an aeronautical revenue. Alternatively, this income could be considered as commercial income and hence a non-aeronautical revenue. Overall, landing and passenger fees are by far the most important aeronautical revenue sources. Most of the non-aeronautical revenue comes from concessions and rents. Revenues, such as interest received and income earned from subsidiary companies, are usually included under a different 'non-operating' revenue category.

From the 1999 ACI survey it is apparent that aeronautical revenues represented just under half of all revenues (Figure 3.1). The Pacific region had the highest percentage of non-aeronautical revenues which reflected, claimed the ACI, the importance of non-aeronautical sources at large airports such as Sydney, Seoul and Singapore and the dominance of international passengers at these airports. The African and Latin American/Caribbean regions appeared to have the lowest share of non-aeronautical revenues, mostly due to the lower

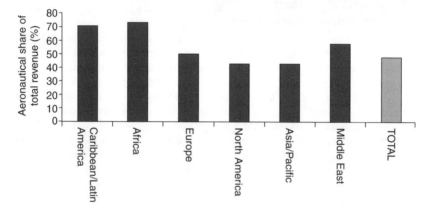

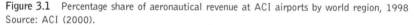

Figure 3.1 Percentage share of aeronautical revenue at ACI airports by world region, 1998
Source: ACI (2000).

income per capita, the generally smaller sized airports which had less non-aeronautical opportunities, and because the non-aeronautical policies tended to be less developed than in many other parts of the world. The ICAO economic survey also found the highest share of non-aeronautical revenue in North America (56 per cent) and the lowest in Africa and Central and South America (21–22 per cent), broadly confirming the ACI results. The overall average was lower at 36 per cent but is likely to be less accurate because of the relative smaller coverage of the survey in some areas.

A breakdown of revenues for a sample of European airports is shown in Table 3.3 for 1983–99. The table shows that aeronautical revenues account for around half the total revenues within Europe which is very similar to the results of the ACI survey. The dominant trend up until 1998 was a decline in the importance of aeronautical revenues with a subsequent increase in reliance on non-aeronautical sources. This not only reflects pressures from airlines and regulatory bodies to keep airport charge increases to a minimum but also the

Table 3.3   Average revenue and cost structures at European airports, 1983–98

	1983	1988	1993	1998	1999
Revenue shares (%):					
Aeronautical	58.9	55.5	54.1	52.0	55.9
Non-aeronautical	41.1	44.5	45.9	48.0	44.1
Total	100.0	100.0	100.0	100.0	100.0
Cost shares (%):					
Labour	45.6	43.8	39.2	36.6	34.5
Depreciation	18.2	20.6	21.6	23.4	21.9
Other	36.2	35.6	39.2	40.0	43.6
Total	100.0	100.0	100.0	100.0	100.0

Source: Annual reports.

increased focus being placed on commercial activities. At some airports the increase in the proportion of non-aeronautical revenue over the fifteen years from 1983 to 1998 has been considerable – for example, at Copenhagen airport the share increased from 41 per cent to 54 per cent and at Geneva airport it rose from 40 per cent to 51 per cent. One of the most notable increases in commercial revenues has been with BAA plc airports – Chapter 7 outlines how this was achieved. The situation changed in 1999 because of the impact of the abolition of EU duty- and tax-free goods in this year with the average non-aeronautical share declining slightly to 44.1 per cent.

Unlike with revenues, there is no industry standard for the reporting of airport operating costs. From published accounts, however, it is usually possible to identify the three separate cost items associated with labour, capital and other operating costs. Within Europe labour costs account for an average 36 per cent of total costs with depreciation representing a further 23 per cent. Over the years the labour costs have decreased in importance (Table 3.3). In part this is due to more outsourcing being undertaken by airport operators and in some cases a more productive labour force. There may also be higher depreciation charges due to additional investment at the airports to cope with the traffic growth and a more accurate representation of depreciation at some airports because of their transfer from public sector accounting procedures to more commercial practices.

These average values hide the variation between individual airports which in some cases in quite considerable. Table 3.4 shows these values for a number of European airports. The revenue figures reflect differences in strategies towards aeronautical and commercial activities and also differences in the functions carried out by the airport operator itself. For example, Düsseldorf, Frankfurt, Hamburg and Vienna in 1999 were heavily involved in handling. Gatwick and Heathrow, with their aeronautical charges regulated, were much more dependent on commercial activities.

The labour costs also vary quite considerably at airports. At Vienna and Frankfurt labour costs account for over half the total costs, again reflecting their heavy involvement in the labour-intensive handling activity. By contrast airports such as Basel-Mulhouse and Amsterdam which are not involved with some many activities, have much lower staff costs.

Table 3.4 Revenue and cost structures at a selection of European airports, 1999

Airport	Revenue shares (%):			Cost shares (%):			
	Aero	Non-aero	Total	Labour	Depreciation	Other	Total
Amsterdam	48	52	100	23	19	58	100
Basel-Mulhouse	41	59	100	21	44	35	100
Birmingham	69	31	100	32	18	50	100
Copenhagen	53	47	100	41	31	28	100
Düsseldorf	72	28	100	40	23	37	100
Frankfurt	56	44	100	50	17	33	100
Geneva	49	51	100	40	15	45	100
Glasgow	63	37	100	33	20	47	100
Hamburg	71	29	100	40	15	45	100
London Gatwick	40	60	100	27	17	56	100
London Heathrow	40	60	100	21	20	59	100
Manchester	50	50	100	31	26	43	100
Milan	74	26	100	62	12	26	100
Newcastle	70	30	100	47	23	30	100
Oslo	57	43	100	23	35	42	100
Rome	57	43	100	43	12	45	100
Vienna	72	28	100	52	17	31	100

Source: Annual reports.

Factors influencing costs and revenues

There are many factors that affect an airport's level and structure of costs and revenues. Some of these are more easily influenced by airport management than others. First, the volume and nature of the traffic, which the airport operator only has limited control over, can have a major impact on the airport's economic performance. As airports increase their traffic throughput the costs per unit of traffic, or unit costs, declines. Studies of British airports in the 1970s showed that unit costs, measured in costs per passenger handled or per work load unit (a WLU is equivalent to one passenger or 100 kg of freight) fell dramatically as total traffic increased to around 1 or 1.5 million passengers or WLUs. Then at a traffic level of around 3 million passengers or WLUs, the unit costs tended to flatten out and ceased to exhibit a strong relationship with airport size (Doganis and Thompson, 1973). Studies of Australian and Spanish airports have produced similar findings (Assaily, 1989; Doganis, Graham and Lobbenberg, 1995). The 1999 ICAO economic study found that costs per WLU or unit costs for airports of less than 300 000 WLUs averaged US$15, were US$9.4 for airports with WLUs between 300 000 and 2.5 million WLUs and were US$8.00 for airports between 2.5 million and 25 million (ICAO, 2000). More complex analyses also suggest that airports experience economies of scale – with the effects being most significant for smaller airports (Gillen and Lall, 1997; Pels, Nijkamp and Rietveld, 2000). It is likely that for small airports there will be certain fixed costs associated with the provision of infrastructure and services which will be incurred at the airport irrespective of the traffic levels. Many small airports experience poor utilization which will also push up unit costs.

Moreover larger airports are normally in a better position to provide a greater range of commercial facilities for passengers and other consumers and tend therefore to have a greater reliance on non-aeronautical revenues. The ICAO survey found that on average airports with more than 25 million passengers generated 58 per cent of their revenue from non-aeronautical sources compared with the sample average of 36 per cent.

Costs associated with international passengers tend to rise as this type of traffic requires more space in the terminal for customs and immigration, these passengers spend longer in the terminal. International passengers also have more luggage. For example, in Heathrow's Terminal 1 it has been estimated that international passengers on average have 1.3 bags compared with 0.5 for domestic passengers. BAA plc has estimated that for a hypothetical terminal of 8 million passenger capacity, the cost associated with an international passenger is likely to be 1.62 greater than the cost of domestic passengers. The cost multiple for EU passengers is less, namely 1.36, which gives a cost multiple between international and EU traffic of 1.20 (Toms, 2000). These passengers tend to spend more money at the airport on commercial facilities such as retail and catering which will push up unit revenues – particularly if they have access to duty and tax free shopping.

Charter passengers will not usually need certain facilities such as airline lounges which will influence the airport's cost and revenue levels. Charter passengers also have different spending patterns to scheduled terminal passenger as do transfer passengers at hub airports (a more detailed description of different spending patterns is given in Chapter 7). Moreover hub airports with a true 'wave' pattern of flights will have well-defined peaks and troughs of traffic which will be more costly to handle than a more evenly spread distribution of flights. Likewise, airports serving holiday destinations may have a problem with peakiness and uneven capacity utilization which may push up costs.

Airports operators are relatively free to choose their own physical and service standards which are considered desirable to provide an acceptable level of service to passengers although in practice many of the standards at airports are fairly similar. Nevertheless if an airport does decide to aim, say, for a more exclusive product, as with the business airport London City which put leather seats in the departure lounge, this will clearly have resource implications. At the other extreme, a number of low-cost carriers such as Ryanair and easyJet have expressed preferences for operating out of low-cost terminals with only basis facilities, with no provision of airbridges, in order to keep down the cost of airport charges. More space for passengers than is strictly necessary may be deliberately provided at some airports which are keen to develop their retail and catering activities in order to increase their non-aeronautical revenue.

There is no 'typical' airport when it comes to looking at the services and facilities an airport provides. Beyond the basic operational functions, different airports have little in common. Some airport operators will provide activities such as security, air traffic control, handling, car parking, duty-free shops, cleaning and heavy maintenance, while others will contract these out. In the extreme case, terminals may also be leased as is the situation in the USA and Australia. All this will impact on both cost and revenue levels. For example, SEA the Milan airport operator traditionally has been heavily involved in handling and generated over 50 per cent of gross revenues from this source. This is very different from airports such as London Heathrow or Amsterdam Schiphol which generate a relatively small amount of revenues from this activity in the form of rents and concession fees paid by the airlines and handling agents. In some cases the situation may be even more complicated as the government may choose to pay for the provision of certain services, as is typically the case with the provision of policing, security or fire and rescue.

Economic comparisons in any industry have to acknowledge the accounting policies adopted by individual operators. Within the airport industry accounting procedures vary quite considerably particularly since some airports adopt government or public authority accounting methods rather than commercial practices. With government-owned airports it is possible, for example, to find that the airport's land will not be considered to be an airport's asset and hence will not appear in any balance sheet. Views related to how assets should be depreciated differ. For example BAA plc depreciates runways for up to 100 years while Amsterdam airport uses thirty to forty and AdP uses just ten to twenty years. The ICAO 1999 economic survey found that one-third of airports did not show realistic costs associated with depreciation and interest. Moreover, airports will be subject to different taxation regimes, with many public sector airports, for instance those in the USA, being exempt from most business taxes. This will have an impact on any comparative analysis of net profit levels.

The ownership patterns can also influence other factors such as funding arrangements and the cost of capital. In addition, an airport's performance is likely to depend very much on where it is positioned in the investment life cycle, since investment at airports tends to be large and 'lumpy' rather than continuous and gradual. When major developments have taken place, capital costs are likely to be high and poor utilization may push up the operating costs. Later in the cycle the capital costs will reduce and utilization will hopefully improve.

There are many other factors dependent on an airport's location and geographic situation which, to a large extent, will be beyond the airport operator's specific control. For instance, weather-related expenses, such as snow removal and de-icing facilities, will only be incurred at certain airports. Location is also likely to influence the actual layout and design of the airport and the positioning of both airfield and terminal facilities. For example, an airport may require two or more runways not to meet traffic needs, but because of wind conditions or some other particular climatic or geographic characteristic. Environmental limits, imposed to reduce noise or other adverse impacts of air transport, may also mean that the airport cannot make the most efficient use of all resources. An airport may be forced to close at night even if there is sufficient demand to make night flying feasible. In a more general sense, locational factors may also effect the cost and quality of labour and the availability of capital for investment.

Measuring economic performance

Growing interest in performance assessment

Until the 1980s, the systematic monitoring and comparing of airport economic performance was not a widely practised activity within the airport industry. This can largely be attributed to insufficient commercial and business pressures for airports and the general lack of experience of benchmarking techniques within the public sector as a whole. The difficulties involved with producing meaningful comparisons, such as varying involvement in airport activities and different accounting policies, only further discouraged most airports from seriously attempting to analyse their comparative performance.

With airport commercialization and privatization has come a marked interest in performance comparisons and benchmarking. As airports become more commercially oriented, they have been keen to identify the strong performers in the industry and adopt what are seen as best practices. Senior managers can use performance measures to help them define goals and targets. Comparative performance analysis can also give valuable insight into issues such as whether privatized airports are more efficiently run than public sector airports, what is the best organizational framework for an airport and whether airports operated as part of national networks or systems perform better than individual airports. There is, thus, a growing recognition of the value of continuous performance appraisal within the airport industry.

Many other organizations external to the airport sector are also showing a keen interest in using performance measures to compare achievements between airports. Such organizations will have a different ultimate objective for comparing performance and, hence, are likely to view the findings from a different perspective. Investors and bankers, traditionally much more used to using financial ratios and other benchmarking techniques than airport operators, are anxious to identify possible business opportunities and to ensure that their chosen airport investments continue to perform well. Airlines, now operating in a much more cost-conscious and competitive environment, have an interest in identifying which airports are being inefficiently managed – particularly to add substance to any lobby against increases in user charges. Economic regulators of privatized or autonomously managed airports also have good reason to monitor airport performance to ensure that users are being fairly charged and that the airports are run efficiently (see Chapter 5).

The growing acceptance of airport performance monitoring is further illustrated by various international industry bodies showing an interest in such activities. For example, in 1991, ICAO listed ten indicators which it identified as being some of the key measures for assessing economic performance (ICAO, 1991). In the late 1990s the ACI-Europe Economics Committee started work on producing comparative airport performance indicators for its member airlines.

Analysing an airport's economic performance has therefore become an important task for many of those involved, directly or indirectly, with the airport industry. Economic performance appraisal is, of course, only one aspect of airport performance which needs to be assessed. There are a wide range of operational activities which need to monitored by looking at measures relating to airside delays, baggage delivery, terminal processing times, equipment availability and so on. In addition consumer satisfaction levels also need to be assessed, typically through passenger surveys. These non-economic areas are considered in detail in the next chapter but the interrelationships between these different aspects of performance must be recognized. Clearly any decision on service levels or operational procedures will greatly influence an airport's cost and manning levels and vice versa.

Performance concepts

Performance measures analyse the relationship between inputs and outputs at an airport. This relationship can be expressed in both financial and physical terms. As with other businesses, labour and capital are the major inputs of the airport system. The simplest physical measure of the labour input is the total number of employees. Any part-time and temporary staff should be converted to full-time equivalents. To capture the effect of the cost of labour as well as productivity per head, the labour input can also be measured in financial terms, namely employee wages and salaries.

Determining a reliable measure of the capital input is much more difficult. In physical terms, capital input is measured by the production capability or capacity of the system. At an airport this cannot be assessed by one measure. The capacity of the runways, terminal, gates and so on all have to be considered. Capacity can be measured on an hourly, daily or annual basis. Depreciation or asset values can be used to measure the financial capital input. These will, however, reflect the accounting policies of the specific airport and may not always be closely related to its economic production capability.

The financial measurement of output is relatively straightforward and can be measured by considering the total revenues generated. Physically, the output of an airport can be assessed in three ways: in terms of quantities of aircraft, passengers or freight. These measures do not cover all aspects of an airport, for example, its role as a retail facility, but they do capture the key outputs. The use of aircraft movements is not ideal as such measures will not differentiate between different sizes and different types of aircraft. Since most airports handle both passengers and freight, this suggests the use of an output measure which combines the two, such as the WLU. The WLU originated from the airline industry and uses a weight criteria for combining these two types of traffic (i.e. one WLU = one passenger or 100 kg of freight). Some argue, however, that the focus should be on passenger numbers since freight handling at airports is very much an airline activity and has little impact on an airport's economic performance.

The WLU, although probably the most widely accepted measure, is a rather arbitrary method of linking the two outputs since the same weight of passengers and freight does not involve using the same resources. Ideally the WLU formula should, therefore, reflect the relative importance or value of the different outputs and, perhaps, include an aircraft movement element. Costs or employee numbers associated with the different outputs could theoretically be used to determine the scaling factor but there is the major problem of joint costs or joint tasks undertaken by the staff. An alternative scaling parameter is the relative prices of the outputs but this assumes a close relationship between price and cost which is not usually the case because of market imperfections, regulation and government interference and, sometimes, cross-subsidies between different traffic. There is the additional problem that there are even different costs and revenues associated with different passenger types, the most notable examples being international and domestic passengers and terminal and transfer passengers.

There has been some research undertaken in this area to investigate whether a more appropriate output measure can be found which takes into account all three key outputs of an airport (Vallint, 1998). The Transport Research Laboratory (TRL, 2000) has suggested that the use of the airport throughput unit (APU) where

$$\text{APUs} = \frac{(\text{WLUs})^2}{\text{ATMs}}$$

Airport throughput units are used in some of TRL's performance assessment but have yet to be adopted elsewhere.

To summarize, performance measures or indicators are all about relating one or more of the outputs to one or more inputs. By using a number of these indicators, an airport can assess different aspects of its performance and identify where its strengths and weaknesses lie. These indicators can be grouped into certain categories such as cost-efficiency, labour and capital productivity, revenue generation and commercial performance, and profitability. In addition to these input:output ratios, a few other key measures such as the share of revenue from aeronautical sources or the percentage of costs which are allocated to staff can give further insights into comparative performance. There are around fifteen to twenty indicators which are commonly used (Ashford and Moore, 1999; Doganis, 1992; Humphreys and Francis, 2000). Table 3.5 presents the most popular indicators. Some of these have been used for the analysis of specific markets such as France (Assaily, 1989), Australia (Doganis, Graham and Lobbenberg, 1994) or the UK (CRI, 2000) or more generally to compare airport performance within Europe (Doganis and Graham, 1987; Doganis, Graham and Lobbenberg, 1995; Graham and Lobbenberg, 1995) or around the world (TRL, 2000).

While airport managers will be very keen to understand how efficiently the airport is using its infrastructure and how cost-effectively it is doing so, the financial sector will be more focused on ratios related to the business potential of the airport such as profit levels, liquidity ratios and capital expenditure levels. In the international financial markets, profit excluding depreciation is known as EBITDA and profit including depreciation is known as EBIT. Another indicator which can be used is the EBITDA or EBIT margin which is earnings expressed as a percentage of revenue. Operating profit:total assets is commonly referred to as return on capital employed (ROCE) or return on assets. Putting the traditional indicators in these financial terms enables comparisons to be easily made with other business sectors. Other standard financial ratios such as the interest cover (EBIT:interest) the dividend cover (post-tax profit/dividends), or gearing (debt as a share of shareholders funds) can be used to assess the

Table 3.5 Performance indicators commonly used to assess economic performance

1 COST EFFICIENCY
    Costs excluding depreciation
    per WLU
    Costs including depreciation
    per WLU
    Depreciation costs per WLU
    Labour costs per WLU
    Depreciation share of
    operating costs
    Labour share of operating
    costs
2 LABOUR PRODUCTIVITY
    WLU per employee
    Revenues per employee
3 CAPITAL PRODUCTIVITY
    WLU/ total assets
    Revenues/total assets
    Total assets per employee
	4 REVENUE GENERATION
	    Revenues per WLU
	    Aeronautical revenues per WLU
	    Non-aeronautical revenues per WLU
	    Aeronautical share of total revenues
	5 COMMERCIAL PERFORMANCE
	    Concession plus rental revenues per passenger
	    Concession revenues per passenger
	6 PROFITABILITY
	    Revenues: costs ratio
	    Operating profit excluding depreciation per
	    WLU
	    Operating profit including depreciation per
	    WLU
	    Operating profit including/excluding
	    depreciation/total assets
	    Net retained profit after interest and taxation
	    per WLU

Notes: 1 Only operating revenues and cost have been included (i.e. interest, extraordinary items, taxation and dividends are excluded) with the exception of last indicator (net retained profit after interest and taxation per WLU).
2 Some analysts use passenger numbers rather than WLUs and may include aircraft movements as an airport output measure as well.

financial well-being and capital structure of the airport company. Capital expenditure (Capex) per WLU, employee or revenues can also give an indication as to the amount of investment which is taking place.

For the few publicly quoted airport companies such as BAA plc and Vienna, additional indicators associated with the value of the company can be used. A number of these ratios relate the enterprise value (EV), which shows the market value of the company's core businesses, to sales, earnings or throughput (e.g. EV:total revenues; EV:EBITDA; EV:EBIT; EV:WLU). Reference has already been made to these 'value' ratios in Chapter 2 when privatization trends were considered. The price earnings ratio (PER), which shows the relationship between the price of the share and earnings attributable to that share, can also be used (ABN AMRO, 1998; Vogel, 1997; WDR, 1998).

The information needed for these basic performance indicators is normally available from sources in the public domain, such as published reports and accounts. More detailed and disaggregate performance measures can usually only be produced internally within an airport unless airports agree to voluntarily provide additional information. For this reason London, Paris and Amsterdam airports in Europe have an agreement to swap data on a regular basis. The availability of more disaggregate data enables more specialized comparative analyses to be undertaken for different areas of operation. For example, indicators commonly used by the retail industry such as sales per square metre of space and sales by location and type of outlet can be applied to airport commercial areas (CAS, 1998; ICAA, 1985).

Inter-airport performance

Producing meaningful inter-airport performance indicators is fraught with diffi-culties because of serious problems of comparability – particularly due to the varying range of activities undertaken by airport operators themselves. Comparing indicators from the raw data can give misleading impressions as airports involved with more activities would inevitably have higher cost and revenues levels.

This problem can be overcome by standardizing or normalizing the airport data so that each airport's performance is presented as if it undertook a uniform set of activities. For example, if an airport operator undertakes ground-handling activities itself, the costs, revenues and staff numbers associated with this can be deducted in order to make the data more comparable with airports with no involvement with this activity. A hypothetical concession income from handling agents can then be added to the airport's revenues. Ideally, the accounts of each airport could also be adjusted to conform to a common treat-ment of depreciation, asset values and so on as well, but normally this is too difficult a task. It is never possible to achieve total comparability between airports but at least making adjustments when large discrepancies exist enables more meaningful assessments to be made. The measures must be viewed as 'indicators' of performance to be used as a management tool to aid perfor-mance improvement, rather than as precise and accurate absolute values of economic performance.

Another issue to be faced in comparing airport performance is the difference in cost of living between countries. Official exchange rates may not be a close reflection of relative prices at different airports in different countries. This problem can be addressed by using purchasing power parity exchange rates, rather than market exchange rates. Purchasing power parity exchange rates are calculated by dividing the cost of a given basket of goods in one currency by the cost of the same basket of goods in another country. So, effectively, they convert currencies on the basis of equalizing buying power rather than on the basis of prevailing market conditions. They also overcome problems of currency fluctuations during the period under investigation.

European comparisons

To illustrate how individual airport performance may be measured on an inter-airport basis, a selection of the three indicators have been calculated for a sample of European airports. The fifteen airports represent a cross-section, from the largest European airport, London Heathrow, to small airports such as Newcastle. The airports come from seven different countries, five of which are within the EU. The sample includes privately owned airports such as Glasgow, partially privatized airports such as Copenhagen, publicly owned but indepen-dent corporations such as Amsterdam and airports run as concessions such as Nice. The sample also includes the unique bi-national airport of Basel-Mulhouse, which has two check-in concourses and arrivals halls, one of each in France and Switzerland. The data has been normalized and converted into purchasing power parities.

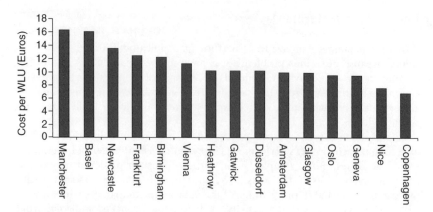

Figure 3.2 Cost per WLU for European airports, 1999
Source: Annual accounts.

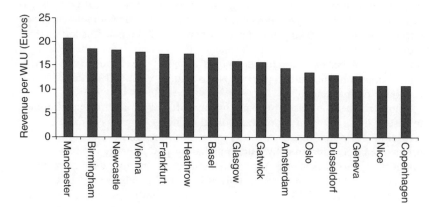

Figure 3.3 Revenue per WLU for European airports, 1999
Source: Annual accounts.

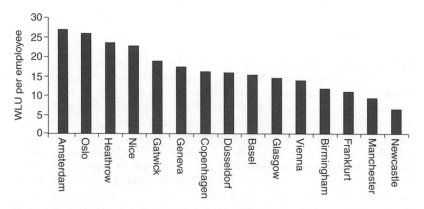

Figure 3.4 WLU per employee for European airports, 1999
Source: Annual accounts.

It may be seen from Figure 3.2, which shows the costs per WLU, that even when the data is normalized that the values for each airport are very different, with some of the lower cost airports having half the costs of higher-cost airports. The revenue figures are as varied and the ranking of the airports is similar – which is hardly surprising given that all the airports are profitable. There is also a wide spread of values of WLU per employee with some of the large airports such as Heathrow, Gatwick and Amsterdam achieving high labour productivity while at other large airports such as Frankfurt and Manchester the staff do not seem to be so productive.

The global picture

A similar methodology is used in the annual global study of performance which is undertaken by the TRL. The study looks at thirty-four different indicators. One of these indicators, total revenue per employee, is shown in Figure 3.5 for the global sample of airports. This indicator combines the effects of both staff productivity and the revenue generation ability of the airport. Most of the airports with high values have larger than average revenue-earning capabilities, with the exception of Vancouver and Calgary where there are flexible working practices which brings down staff numbers.

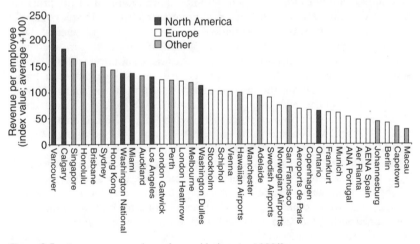

Figure 3.5 Revenue per employee for world airports, 1998/9
Source: TRL.

A single efficiency measure?

The performance measures in Table 3.5 are partial measures in that they give an indication of performance which relates specifically to the inputs and outputs that have been chosen. They can highlight strengths and weaknesses in certain areas but they cannot give an overall picture or identify the 'best in class'. This short-coming can be overcome by investigating the relationship between the combined inputs and combined outputs to produce a single efficiency measure. In contrast to other transport operations and public sector organizations there has been little exploration of the use of such methodologies until the 1990s, with the airport sector preferring to concentrate mostly on partial measures (Lemaitre, 1998).

There are various different ways in which overall efficiency can be assessed (CAA, 2000). A parametric or statistical approach can be adopted by using stochastic frontier analysis. This method involves the estimation of a 'frontier' and the airport is only efficient if it operates on the frontier. The model is based on the estimation of a production or cost function which recognizes several variables influencing performance. Examples of this approach include an assessment of the performance of BAA plc airports and a sample of European airports (Pels, Nijkamp and Rietveld, 2000, Tolofari, 1989).

Alternatively, a non-parametric index numbers approach, called Tornqvist total factor productivity (TFP), can be used. This requires the aggregation of all outputs into a weighted outputs index and all inputs into a weighted input index. The prices of the inputs and outputs are the weights which are applied to the quantities of outputs and inputs. Such a technique has been used to assess the performance of Australian airports (Hooper and Hensher, 1998; PSA, 1993).

A linear programming technique, called DEA, also produces a weighted output index relative to a weighted input index similar to the non-parametric TFP measure. The key advantage of DEA is that the weights for the inputs and outputs are not predetermined but instead are the result of the programming procedure. DEA is therefore a more attractive technique than the Tornqvist TFP because it has less demanding data requirements. DEA techniques have been used to undertake a comparison of the performance of twenty-five European airports and twelve Australian airports with the results showing that generally the Australian airports on average achieved higher efficiency scores than was the case for European airports (Graham and Holvad, 1997). Parker (1999) also used DEA to study BAA plc and concluded that there has been no noticeable change in efficiency since privatization. Gillen and Lall (1997) and Vasigh and Hamzaee (2000) used DEA to assess US airports and Martin and Roman (2000) used it with Spanish airports.

A multiattribute approach has also been used to assess airport performance. This combines a number of partial performance measures as a weighted sum of inputs. For each measure airports are measured according to how they perform relative to other airports – with a score of 1 for best performer and 0 for worst performer. The weighted sum of these scores gives an overall summary efficiency measure. This method has been used with a sample of around thirty global airports with six performance measures, namely: ROCE; concession revenues per passenger: aeronautical revenues per air transport movement; WLUs per unit of asset value; WLUs per employee; and operating costs per passenger (Jessop, 1999; TRL, 2000).

References and further reading

ABN AMRO (1998). *European Airports Review*. ABN AMRO.
Airport Council International (ACI) (2000). *ACI Airport Economics Survey 1998*. ACI.

Ashford, N. and Moore, C. (1999). *Airport Finance*. 2nd edn, Loughborough Airport Consultancy.

Assaily, C. (1989). *Airport Productivity*. Institute of Air Transport.

Centre for Airport Studies (CAS) (1998). *Airport Retail Survey 1998 Edition*. CAS.

Centre for Regulated Industries (CRI) (2000). *Airports Statistics 1998/9*. CRI.

Civil Aviation Authority (CAA) (2000). The use of benchmarking in airport reviews. Consultation paper, CAA.

Doganis, R. (1992). *The Airport Business*. Routledge.

Doganis, R. and Graham, A. (1987). *Airport Management: The Role of Performance Indicators*. Transport Studies Group Research Report 13, University of Westminster (formerly Polytechnic of Central London).

Doganis, R., Graham, A. and Lobbenberg, A. (1994). *A Comparative Study of Value for Money at Australian and European Airports*. Cranfield University.

Doganis, R., Graham, A. and Lobbenberg, A. (1995). *The Economic Performance of European Airports*. Department of Air Transport Research Report 3, Cranfield University.

Doganis, R. S. and Thompson, G. F. (1973). *The Economics of British Airports*. Transport Studies Group Research Report 1, University of Westminster (formerly Polytechnic of Central London).

Gillen, D. and Lall, A. (1997). Developing measures of airport productivity and performance: an application of data envelopment analysis. First Air Transport Research Group conference, Vancouver, July.

Graham, A. and Holvad, T. (1997). Efficiency variations for European and Australian airports. EURO XV/INFORMS joint international conference, Barcelona, July.

Graham, A. and Lobbenberg, A. (1995). Benchmarking European airports. *Airports International*, May, 12–14.

Hooper, P. and Hensher, D. (1998). *Measuring Total Factor Productivity of Airports – an Index Number Approach*. Institute of Transport Studies Working Paper ITS-WP-98-2, Monash University.

Humphreys, I. and Francis, G. (2000). *Traditional Airport Performance Indicators*. Transportation Research Board, no. 1703.

International Civil Airports Association (ICAA) (1985). *Commission recettes extra-aeronautiques*. ICAA.

International Civil Aviation Organization (ICAO) (1991). *Airport Economics Manual*. Doc. 9562, ICAO.

International Civil Aviation Organization (ICAO) (2000). Financial situation of airports and air navigation services. *ANSConf Working Paper No 3*, ICAO.

Jessop, A (1999). A multiattribute assessment of airport performance. Twenty-fifth Euro working group on financial modelling of the Institute fur Finanzierung und Finanzmarkte, Vienna, November.

Lemaitre, A (1998). The development of performance indicators at airports. Air Transport Research Group conference, Vancouver, July.

Martin, J. and Roman, C. (2000). An application of DEA to measure the efficiency of Spanish Airports prior to privatization. *Journal of Air Transport Management*, **7**, 149–57.

Parker, D. (1999). The performance of BAA before and after privatization: a DEA study. *Journal of Transport Economics and Policy*, **33**(2), 133–46.

Pels, E., Nijkamp, P. and Rietveld, P. (2000). Inefficiencies and scale economies of European airport operations. Fourth Air Transport Research Group conference, The Netherlands, July.

Prices Surveillance Authority (PSA) (1993). *Inquiry into the Aeronautical and Non-aeronautical Charges of the Federal Airports Corporation.* PSA.

Symonds Travers Morgan (STM) (1998). *Review of Airport Performance 1998.* STM.

Tolofari, S. R. (1989). *Airport Cost and Productivity Analysis: Summary of Research Results.* Department of Transport Technology, Loughborough University.

Toms, M. (2000). Critique of cost benchmarking. CAA workshop on benchmarking of airports: methodologies, problems and relevance to economic regulation, London, September.

Transport Research Laboratory (TRL) (2000). *Airport Performance Indicators 2000.* TRL.

Vallint, J. (1998). The suitability of the work load unit as a measure of airport output. Unpublished MSc transport thesis, University of Westminster.

Vasigh, B. and Hamzaee, R. (2000). Airport efficiency: an empirical analysis of the US commercial airports. Fourth Air Transport Research Group conference, The Netherlands, July.

Vogel, H. (1997). Privatization of European commercial airports: motivations, valuations and implications. Unpublished MBA thesis, Emery-Riddle University.

Warburg Dillon Read (WDR) (1998). *Airports Review 1998.* WDR.

4

Service quality and its measurement

Increasing emphasis on quality

The 1980s saw many service industries placing increased emphasis on managing quality. Traditional ideas of quality, which had evolved from manufacturing industries and had been based on the conformance to standards defined by operations management, began to be replaced by customer-focused notions. This required close consideration of what the customers wanted and how their needs could be met. Different dimensions of service were defined and customer satisfaction, considered to be the gap between perceived and expected service, was assessed. Quality management began to be viewed as an overall process which involved everybody from top management down to junior staff rather than just to do with concentrating on the employee-customer interaction. New approaches such as total quality management and continuous improvement programmes began to be applied by an increasing number of service industries (Lockwood and Wright, 1999).

The airport industry was not immune to this 'quality revolution' which was taking place – although it was rather late in adopting some of the principles. Structural changes such as commercialization, privatization and globalization, together with increased competition between airports, encouraged airports to place more emphasis on quality. Airports which had become regulated in their post-privatization stage, such as the London and Australian airports, also found that their service quality became the subject of increased scrutiny. Moreover, pressure was coming from the travelling public who were becoming more experienced and demanding consumers of the airport product.

With most service industries there is a particularly problem with measuring the quality of service because of the characteristic uneven spread of demand. With many airports for instance, a terminal will look and feel very different on a quiet Tuesday in winter compared to a busy summer Saturday in the school holidays. Likewise, passenger flows in the early morning or evening at an airport dominated by short-haul business traffic will be considerably greater than at other times of the day. This is bound to play a major role in influencing the passenger's perception of the quality of service provided.

Airports have the additional problem that the overall service is produced as a result of the combined activities of various different organization such as airlines, handling agents, customs and immigration officials, concessionaires and so on. These different bodies may have different ultimate objectives and conflicting views on what determines satisfactory or good service (Lemer, 1992). In effect, the airport operator only has partial control of all the processes which make up the final product. Areas of responsibility, therefore, have to be very clearly identified and the airport operator must define a common goal for all as regards service quality.

Airports tend to serve passengers with very different expectations – and so it is very difficult to please everybody! Traditionally very little segmentation has taken place at airports, with the most notable differentiation being separate check-in for economy and business-class passengers and remote stands rather than air bridges for passengers travelling on charter or low-cost airlines. The level of segmentation has now increased with more and more businesses travellers having access to fast-track systems which guide them swiftly through various processes such as immigration and customs, and provide other services such as valet parking. The expanding use of airline lounges has also helped to separate business and leisure travellers. It is not just the airlines which are providing such services now. In 1999, London Stansted launched an interesting airport upgrade product on its website which meant that for a fee of £20 passengers could have access to a special lounge, express security clearance, a reserved premium short-stay car parking space, currency exchange at reduced rates and a range of other additional offers. In 2000, London Heathrow opened its first pay-as-you-go lounge which gives passengers, for a £25 entrance, shower facilities, shoe shine, a clothes valet and hot and cold drinks. Another example is Manchester airport which opened a new premier lounge in its Terminal 2 in 2000. This lounge, which has an entrance fee of £15, consists of three seating areas. There is the 'hot desk' business area where office facilities including internet access is available. Then there is the 'comfort zone' where shops and catering facilities are available, The third area is the 'oasis of calm' with comfortable seating and a calm water feature!

In spite of these developments, most of the time airports still tend to offer one overall product which has to appeal to a very heterogeneous collection of passengers. Some passengers may want to get through the airport as quickly as possible with a minimum of distractions while others enjoy the opportunity of being able to shop and take refreshments.

Measuring the quality of service

Quality of service can be assessed with both objective and subjective measures. Objective indicators measure the service delivered and can cover areas such as flight delays, availability of lifts, escalators and trolleys, and operational research surveys of factors such as queue length, space provision, waiting time and baggage reclaim time. To be accurate these surveys need to be undertaken regularly and at varying time periods when different volumes and types of passengers are being processed through the airport. 'Mystery shoppers' who sample the airport product by anonymously pretending to be passengers can also be used.

The advantages of these measures is that they are precise and easy to understand (Maiden, 2000). They can also link into the passenger service standards which many airports adopt. An example of the service standards used by Manchester airport is given in Table 4.1. The standards are set and revised in the light of customer levels of satisfaction by surveying passengers to find out, say, when they become dissatisfied with the waiting time that they experience. Direct observations or camera shots can also be used to assess real-life situations when queue lengths start to have a negative impact on passenger behaviour. As with all the service measures, the airport is faced with the dilemma that not all types of passenger groups will have the same expectations and so a compromise standard in most cases has to be reached.

These objective measures can only cover a limited range of issues and service dimensions. For instance, while they can measure the reliability of equipment, they cannot tell whether consumers feel safe, assured and satisfied with their use of the equipment. Similarly, a passenger's perception of the time that they have spent waiting in a queue may be very different from the actual waiting time. Subjective measures, looking at passenger satisfaction ratings, are also needed. These measures will enable the quality of service to be assessed through the eyes of users rather than airport management.

There are two key types of subjective measures, comment/complaints cards and customer surveys. Focus groups may also be used to investigate important or topical issues in greater detail. Comment cards are cheap and immediate. If the comments are favourable they may provide a positive public relations opportunity. The airport operator, however, has very little control over this type of feedback. The comments will not come from a representative sample of travellers at airports and will usually only record extreme views since customers will not be motivated to comment unless they feel very strongly about their experience at the airport. While such a system may be able to identify a weakness which can be rectified swiftly, it is not systematic enough to be used for quality improvement programmes or target-setting.

Consumer surveys are more suitable. Typically such surveys will ask passengers about their usage of facilities and services, and their opinion of them in terms of comfort, congestion, cleanliness, value for money and so on. Also, if

Table 4.1 Service standards used by Manchester airport

Space

Queuing space
- 0.6 m^2 per passenger without baggage or accompanying visitor
- 0.6 m^2 per passenger with baggage or awaiting reclaim
- 1.2 m^2 per passenger seated and 0.9 m^2 standing passengers

Holding lounge
- 20% space allowance for circulation excluding major through corridors

Check-in desks

Scheduled services
- Sufficient check-in desks will be provided to allow handling agents to offer a multiclass service. Also a sufficient number to achieve queuing times of less than 3 minutes for 95% or, peak periods less than 5 minutes for 80% of passengers

Charter services
- Sufficient check-in desks will be provided to allow a minimum of 1 check-in desk per 130 passengers at peak periods

Seating

Concourse
- Seating will be provided for 25% of people present including general catering areas

Departure lounge
- Seating will be provided for 75% of people present including general catering areas

Gate lounges
- Seating will be provided for 70% of people present. Gate areas where departures are predominately short-haul international or domestic scheduled flights may be reduced to a figure of 65%

Security

Outbound control
- Given present security regulations 95% of passengers will queue for less than 3 minutes or at peak periods, 80% will queue for less than 5 minutes

Immigration

Arrivals
- The acceptable queuing times have been detailed by the immigration services. Maximum queuing times under normal operating circumstances are as follows:
  - UK passports – 15 minutes
  - EU passport – 20 minutes
  - other passports – 30 minutes

Departures
- Passengers should queue for less than 3 minutes after collection of their hand baggage from security check

Bussing	A maximum of 5% of passengers in any one year to be handled on remote stand
Connection/ Transfer times	Minimum connection times: international to international – 45 minutes international to domestic – 45 minutes domestic to international – 45 minutes domestic to domestic – 30 minutes (maximum)
Car parking Courtesy coach Pay stations Barriers Level of service	No customer is to wait on average more than 5 minutes for a courtesy coach A maximum queuing of 3 minutes for customers at any pay station An automated failure of less than 5%, i.e. less than 5% of car park users should arrive at the barriers with invalid out tickets To provide a level of service at least comparable with off airport parking companies
Equipment Baggage processing	Outbound: baggage acceptance process can always proceed by take-away belts immediately accepting baggage into the system Inbound: international flights – 90% of first bags to be delivered within 20 minutes of declared arrival time. Last bags within 35 minutes of arrival time on 90% of occasions. Last bag within 15 minutes of arrival time on 90% of occasions domestic flights – first bag within 12 minutes of arrival time on 90% of occasions. Last bag within 15 minutes of arrival time on 90% of occasions
Baggage trolleys	Target availability for total system to be 98% Trolleys to be available for all passengers who require one
Vehicles and plants	Target availability for all lifts, passenger conveyors, escalators and airbridges to be 98% including planned maintenance Target availability for all operations vehicles to be 92% including planned maintenance

Source: Monopolies and Mergers Commission (1997).

passenger profile information is collected, the survey findings can be used to investigate relationships between usage and satisfaction of services with demographics, attitudes and experiences of travellers. Clearly consideration has to be given to the sample size, interview time and most appropriate place to survey. Departing passenger may be keen to participate while waiting in their departure lounge having completed all the major essential processes, but tired arriving passengers may be less co-operative – being anxious to find their luggage and return home. The main drawback of surveys is, of course, their high cost. The results are also not so immediate as comment cards and may require careful interpretation (Maiden, 2000).

In 1998, ACI investigated quality of service measurement at airports through a survey of its members (ACI, 2000). One hundred and twenty airports responded with the sample ranging from large airports such as Cairo, Johannesburg, Copenhagen, Paris, Frankfurt, Rome, Amsterdam, Dallas, Houston, Chicago, Sydney, Hong Kong and Tokyo to some very small regional airports. All geographical regions were fairly well represented except for South America. Forty-three per cent of respondents said that they used objective criteria, while 62 per cent used subjective criteria. Both criteria were adopted by 32 per cent of all the airports. Some of the most popular objective measures were related to the availability of trolleys, lifts, escalators, moving walkways, conveyors and taxi services. The assessment of waiting time and queue length at check-in, security and immigration was a fairly common practice. Baggage delivery was also measured by a large number of airports, as was cleanliness. Analysis of complaints and comments was viewed as important as well. The subjective measures which were identified considered overall satisfaction with all the general processes at the airport together with more detailed measurements looking at specific service dimensions (Table 4.2).

With any performance analysis, the results should be made available to all interested parties so that corrective action can be taken and targets can be set. Some airports publish summaries of their results, mostly as a public relations exercise. Table 4.3 reproduces the survey results from BAA plc's annual report of 1999/2000 for the London airports. The quality of survey monitor (QSM) is based on a sample of over 150 000 passengers for the UK airports and uses a rating scale which gives a value of 5 for an excellent score and 1 when the aspect of service is considered extremely poor. BAA plc also uses its QSM at the international airports where it has an involvement, such as Naples and Melbourne. Other airport operators such as the Brussels International Airport Company also publish summary results of their quality monitors by identifying the percentage of satisfied passengers associated with the following service dimension: look, cleanliness, choice, quickness, personnel and overall service (Brussels International Airport Company, 2000).

It is worth reiterating that service quality is just one area of performance at an airport which should be assessed alongside economic or financial efficiency. Systems of performance measures at airports can be defined from different management perspectives such as the financial perspective, the operational perspective (the objective quality measures) and the marketing perspective (the subjective quality measures) (Lemaitre, 1998). The environmental perspective and the measurement of environmental good practice are

Table 4.2   Criteria most frequently used to measure quality of service at ACI airports

Airport process	Objective criteria	Subjective criteria
General	Response to/analysis of complaints/mail comments Availability of lifts/escalators/ moving walkways etc. Availability of trolleys Cleanliness	Overall customer satisfaction in terms of attractiveness/convenience/quality Quality of signage/ease of finding one's way Quality of public announcements Terminal atmosphere/temperature Availability/quality of trolleys Cleanliness (especially toilets) Seating areas Telecommunication facilities Security/airport safety
Flight information displays, information desk/telephone service		Overall satisfaction
Check-in Security check Immigration	Waiting time/queue Waiting time/queue Waiting time/queue	Overall satisfaction
Catering		Overall satisfaction Quality of goods Value for money Choice
Shops, commercial services (banks, post offices etc.)		Overall satisfaction Range of goods Value for money Staff courtesy
Baggage delivery	Delivery time	Overall satisfaction Waiting/delivery time
Ground access	Taxi availability/ waiting time	Overall satisfaction: ground access/public transport

Source: ACI (2000).

Table 4.3   Summary of quality of service monitor scores 1999/2000 at BAA London airports

	Heathrow 99/00	Variance	Gatwick 99/00	Variance	Stansted 99/00	Variance
Cleanliness	3.8	–	3.9	–0.1	4.1	–
Mechanical assistance	3.8	–0.1	3.9	–	3.9	–
Procedures	4.0	–	4.0	–	4.1	–0.1
Comfort	3.9	–	3.9	–0.1	4.2	–0.1
Congestion	3.6	–0.1	3.5	–0.2	4.0	–
BAA staff	4.0	–	4.1	–0.1	4.2	–

Note: Rating scale 5 = Excellent, 4 = Good, 3 = Average, 2 = Poor, 1 = Extremely Poor
Source: BAA (2000).

also becoming increasingly important. An airport's performance in any one of these four areas will inevitably be linked to its performance in other areas – so none of the performance monitoring systems should be considered in isolation.

While most of the focus in the past with quality monitoring has been within internal performance, airports are now appreciating that it is equally important to make international comparisons and to benchmark themselves against other airports – just as with economic performance analysis. Such an exercise is particularly problematic because of the lack of consistency or common format of each airport's consumer survey. However, since 1993 IATA has undertaken quality of service passenger surveys for a sample of airports around the world. This global airport monitor survey began with just over thirty airports and a sample size of 40 000 passengers but now covers fifty-seven airports and over 60 000 passengers. The 1999 survey covered nineteen European airports, twenty-two North American airports, three in the Middle East and thirteen in the Asia-Pacific rim (IATA, 2000a).

Some of the questions are related to what is called 'Airport Service' which are the services provided by the airport operator, airport concessionaires and tenants and includes such measures as ease of finding one's way through the airport and quality of the shopping and washroom facilities. Then there are 'Airline Service' questions which are services associated with airline activities which can be provided by airlines, handling agents or the airport operator itself. These cover areas such as the efficiency and experience of check-in or the efficiency and punctuality of boarding. Travel profile information such as purpose, class and frequency of travel and transfer details is also collected, as is demographic data in order to give a greater insight into the satisfaction levels of the different market segments.

In 1999 Copenhagen achieved the overall highest ranking in the survey. It also obtained this position when just leisure passengers were consulted (Table 4.4). Business passengers ranked it in second place. Helsinki, Singapore and

Table 4.4 Overall passenger satisfaction levels: best performing airports from IATA's 1999 global airport monitor

All passengers:	Business passengers:	Leisure passengers:
1 Copenhagen	1 Singapore	1 Copenhagen
2 Singapore	2 Copenhagen	2 Helsinki/Singapore
3 Helsinki	3 Vancouver	3 Vancouver
4 Vancouver	4 Helsinki	4 Manchester
5 Manchester	5 Kuala Lumpur	5 Cincinnati
6 Kuala Lumpur		
7 Cincinnati		
8 Perth		
9 Amsterdam		
10 Hong Kong		

Source: IATA (2000a).

Vancouver achieved consistently high rankings while other airports such as Birmingham, Brussels and New York's JFK were noted for their significant improvements in rankings. It is interesting that quite often the results tend to favour moderately sized airports serving smaller national or regional populations, such as Manchester, Cincianti and Perth. Passengers using these airports may have a much greater sense of pride in their airport, seeing it as a local asset – a view which is often lost at the larger airports which may be considered congested and impersonal. The more detailed IATA survey information can indicate to the airport how it is performing as regards each service element or dimension. For example, the 1999 survey showed that Copenhagen, Zürich, Hong Kong, Amsterdam and Oslo airports were considered 'best in class' as regards ground transport to and from the airport. As with all surveys of this type unforeseen bias and inaccuracies may occur but the reasonably large sample and the regularity with which the survey is undertaken has meant that it has been generally accepted within the industry. Its role in airport marketing has become important, with airports which perform well using the findings to publicize and sell their airport to their customers.

Most comparative studies of airport quality look at quality from a passenger's point of view (Lemaitre, 1998). Research into the airlines' point of view is less common. One rare example was a study undertaken by Adler and Berechman (2000) which looked at airline factors such as delays, runway capacity, cost of local labour force and the reliability of air traffic control for a sample of twenty-six airports in Western Europe, North America and the Far East. The information obtained from the airlines was used in a data envelopment analysis to rank airports relative to their quality level.

The emphasis so far has been very much on the individual passenger. The airport has a rather unique relationship with these customers as it does not actually directly sell its core product to them. Most airports concentrate on terminal facilities, although it may be, with greater encouragement of public transport use at airports, that surface access and the quality of transport links will be given much greater consideration in the future.

Individual airport operators obviously need to consider all their customers, including passengers, visitors, airlines, handling agents, freight forwarders, concessionaires and so on. At BAA plc airports for instance, feedback from their tenants is assessed through formal surveys, informal meetings, focus groups and hospitality events. They have two types of survey. A tenant survey involves interviewing the property managers of each organization to assess the managers' views on whether they think their needs are met, the efficiency of the relevant BAA plc processes, the quality and value for money of the accommodation and the overall performance of BAA plc as an landlord. In addition there is also an occupier survey which deals with the actual user of the property. Areas covered include quality and cleanliness of common areas, the effectiveness of the heating, the image of the building, the effectiveness of the building security and BAA plc's speed of response. Performance targets are set. For example, BAA plc aims to resolve 95 per cent of all faults within four working hours and to issue 95 per cent of draft standard tenancy documents within five days of terms being agreed (Le Marquand, 1996).

Service level agreements

A key airport customer is clearly the airlines – in fact many airlines will argue that they are the only true customers at the airport! However, for airline customers the exact quality of service for facilities which are covered by airport charges is rarely specified. This problem can be overcome by having service level agreements (SLAs). In general terms, these are arrangements between the service provider and its customers. The agreement requires the service to be quantified and the acceptance of minimum levels – taking into account the interests of both parties (Van Looy, Van Dierdonck and Gemmel, 1998). There has been increased use of SLAs in the service industries in recent years, and there is a growing interest in the air transport industry to use such agreements in order to formalize service provision between airport operators and airlines and other key users.

Service level agreements can involve a one-way commitment when the airport aims to achieve defined service quality levels or a two-way reciprocal commitment when both parties in the agreement aim to achieve service quality levels. These agreements can be contractural and incentivized, based on penalty payments for poor performance, or just a 'best endeavours' commitment based on performance targets. Areas of operation which the airlines would like to be covered include baggage systems, queuing standards, aircraft stand availability, aircraft aerobridge serviceability, people mover systems serviceability, and transfer standards. Such SLAs can be incorporated into more broader use agreements or strategic partnership agreements (SPAs) between airports and airlines (see Chapter 5) (Cruickshank, 2000; IATA, 2000b).

One of the few airport operators to introduce SLAs is BAA plc. This has been partly due to pressure from the regulatory body which feels that the absence of quality standards in the regulatory regime could mean that the price cap imposed on the airports could produce inadequate, or reductions in, levels of quality (Monopolies and Mergers Commission, 1996). In the late 1990s BAA plc began developing SLAs with BA and by 1999 four SLAs were in place at London Heathrow, Gatwick and Stansted. The agreements are one-way best endeavours types based on agreed minimum service levels and targets. They are not legally binding and no penalty payments have to be made for poor performance. The areas covered are stand availability, jetty availability, security queuing and the availability of 'people movers' (Table 4.5). In addition a specific facility agreement related to the handling of transfer baggage was established. This sets out the roles and responsibilities of each party with the transfer baggage facilities and includes performance targets.

A review of these SLAs by the UK CAA has found that generally these standards are thought to have led to some improvement in the service quality, although it was felt that there was also a need for improvement in the specification, measurement and range of facilities covered by the agreements. Penalty payments, which are favoured by many airlines, and whether these should be reciprocal still remain the most controversial issues (CAA, 2000a; 2000b).

One of the problems with airline customers, as with passengers, is that they all have different demands of service quality. Some airlines may be prepared

Table 4.5   BAA London airport service level targets, 1999

	Heathrow	Gatwick	Stansted
Stand availability (%)	99	98	98
Jetty availability (%)	98	98	98
Security queues length less than 10 minutes (%)	95	95	95
People movers[1]:			
Availability (%)	98–99	97–99	97–99
Mean time to repair[2]			
– transits	1 hour	1 hour	1 hour
– other	2 hours	2 hours	5 hours

Notes: [1] Includes passenger conveyors, excalators, transits. Targets vary for different equipment.
[2] By early 2000, BAA had abandoned this target at Heathrow and Gatwick.
Source: CAA (2000a).

to pay more for premium service whereas others may be willing to accept lower service levels in return for lower airport charges. A good example of this is the rebate given at some airports for remote stands which involve transferring the passengers by bus to the aircraft. Many of the new low-cost carriers have shown that they are prepared to accept a trade-off between service standards and cost by choosing to fly from airports with a less developed product. Considerable friction has arisen between both easyJet and its airport base, Luton, and Ryanair and its airport base, Dublin, when the airlines complained of paying for airport facilities which they do not want. Perhaps these problems could be overcome by identifying a standard quality product and then also by having additional individual agreements with different airlines which want lower or higher service levels. This could lessen the need for a strict regulatory regime (CAA, 2000c).

Level of delays

A crucial measure of airport performance for airlines and passengers, that airport operators often prefer not to focus on, is the level of delays. This may be because there are many factors that lead to flights being delayed which are outside the airport operator's remit (e.g. en route air traffic control, bad weather or technical problems with the aircraft). It is therefore inevitable that aircraft will deviate from the published schedule, which adds an unpredictable element to the time at which any given flight will wish to use the runway. Maximum runway throughput can only be achieved with queuing of aircraft (on the ground for departing flights or through speed control and 'stacks' in the air for arriving flights) so that there is always an aircraft ready to use the runway. Airports which are operating close to their runway capacity are therefore likely to impose additional delays on flights and exacerbate delays originating from other causes. An airport with spare runway capacity has more scope to accommodate delayed aircraft without disrupting other flights and may be able to avoid queuing aircraft in most cases.

Shortcomings in terminal capacity can also delay aircraft. If there are insufficient stands available, arriving aircraft may be held on the taxiways or apron before they are able to unload. At the day-to-day level, this may be an airline operational decision to await the availability of a preferred gate or avoid bussing passengers from a remote stand. In the longer term however, airports have the opportunity to expand or upgrade facilities to address these problems. Congestion within the terminals may lead to passengers who have checked in failing to reach the aircraft in time thus delaying departure; flights may also be held awaiting crew or transfer passengers, creating a knock-on of delays from one flight to another. In the USA it is common practice for the last flight of the day from a hub to be held much longer than earlier ones as it does not present reactionary problems for subsequent flights and enables as many passengers as possible to get home that night.

The airlines can take account of expected queuing times related to shortages of airport runway capacity in planning their schedule. This enables them to maintain a similar level of punctuality performance at congested airports, but at the expense of longer scheduled flight times and the resultant increase in costs from poorer utilization of aircraft and crew. If one considers the Frankfurt–London Gatwick route it can be seen that a morning flight from Frankfurt to Gatwick, scheduled for 1 hour 25 minutes in 1982 had increased to 1 hour 50 minutes by the year 2000 (Table 4.6). As a slightly faster aircraft type is now being operated, this must be due primarily to airport-related delays on a sector where the actual flying time is only about 1 hour. If one compares the Copenhagen–Amsterdam route of the same distance but with less congested airports this is still scheduled for 1 hour 25 minutes. Ryanair's low-cost alternative on the Frankfurt–London route is a Hahn–Stansted service, using secondary airports at each end and scheduled for 1 hour 20 minutes. This means that Ryanair can accomplish four round trips per day with one aircraft but the same aircraft could manage only three round trips if operating on the Frankfurt–Gatwick route. There is thus a penalty of about a quarter in aircraft and crew costs from operating to the more congested major airports.

Airlines thus include a contingency allowance for delays in their schedule. This means that published comparisons of schedule performance tend to understate the total time wasted compared with the theoretical minimum journey time and airlines can improve their punctuality performance by extending their scheduled

Table 4.6 Increasing scheduled journey times at congested airports

From	To	Miles[1]	Year	Depart	Arrive	Aircraft type	Sector time
Frankfurt (FRA)	London (LGW)	396	1982	0735	0800	BAe1-11	1:25
Frankfurt (FRA)	London (LGW)	396	2000	0725	0815	B737	1:50
Frankfurt (HHN)	London (STN)	396	2000	0940	1000	B737	1:20
Copenhagen (CPH)	Amsterdam (AMS)	393	2000	0900	1025	B737	1:25

Note: [1] IATA ticketed point mileage.
Source: *OAG Flight Guide/ABC World Airways Guide.*

Table 4.7   Delays at major European airports on intra-European scheduled services, 1999

Airport	% departures delayed more than 15 minutes	% arrivals delayed more than 15 minutes
Milan Malpensa	54.0	57.1
Madrid	48.4	48.6
Rome Fiumicino	37.4	40.9
Munich	36.7	33.1
Paris CDG	36.4	41.3
Brussels	35.4	34.1
Frankfurt	33.5	39.7
Zürich	32.5	35.7
Paris ORY	30.8	38.1
Amsterdam	30.3	22.9
Manchester	27.2	29.5
London Heathrow	25.7	32.8
Düsseldorf	23.6	28.0
London Gatwick	20.9	27.3
Stockholm	18.5	21.1
Copenhagen	18.3	19.7

Source: AEA (2000).

journey times. Comparisons between airports and airlines, therefore, have to be treated with caution. Of the intra-European scheduled services of Association of European Airlines (AEA) member airlines 30.3 per cent operated more than 15 minutes late in 1999. Table 4.7 shows that the worst affected airports were Milan Malpensa and Madrid with around half the flights significantly delayed. The London airports, Düsseldorf and Amsterdam were better with only a quarter of flights delayed more than 15 minutes. The Scandinavian airports had the best punctuality. At airports such as Munich and Zürich which are operating well below their theoretical runway capacity, the scheduling of peaks of activity for hubbing purposes creates congestion comparable to the most intensively used airports. The Association of European Airlines attributed the principal cause of delayed departures in 1999 to airports and air traffic control (AEA, 2000).

Post-privatization experience in Australia

When the Australian airports were privatized in 1997 and 1998 (see Chapter 2) a regulatory framework comprising a package of measures was introduced. This covered aeronautical charges and financial accounting reporting. It also made specific quality reporting requirements. This is in marked contrast with the earlier privatization of BAA plc where there were charging and reporting conditions but no specific formal requirements as regards service quality. In spite of this, service quality comes under close scrutiny when the UK airports are investigated every five years by the Competition Commission (previously the Monopolies and Mergers Commission).

The quality-monitoring programme in Australia was introduced to assist in the review of prices at the airports, to improve transparency of airport performance and to discourage operators from abusing their market power by providing unsatisfactory standards. The monitoring concentrates on facilities or services provided by, or strongly influenced by, the airport operator. This is in order to prevent the airport operators underinvesting and lowering the quality of services provided. This could well be an issue since the airports are not only having to

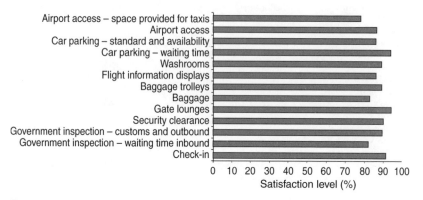

Figure 4.1 Passenger survey results at Brisbane airport, 1999/00
Source: ACCC (2000).

Table 4.8 Survey results of seven major airlines[1] at Brisbane airport, 1999/00

Facility	Aspect	Very Poor	Poor	Satisfactory	Good	Excellent
Runways	Availability			2	8	4
	Standard			2	10	2
Aprons	Availability		1	5	6	2
	Standard			5	6	3
Taxiways	Availability			3	7	2
	Standard			3	6	3
Gates	Availability			7	6	
	Standard			6	7	
Aerobridges	Availability		2	4	7	
	Standard			5	8	
Ground service	Availability		2	4	6	
	Standard		2	3	7	
Freight equipment	Availability		1	4	5	1
	Standard		1	4	5	1
Check-in facilities	Availability		3	5	5	2
	Standard		1	5	9	
Baggage processing	Availability		1	3	9	2
	Standard		2	4	8	1
Airline concerns				6	6	3

Note: [1] Air New Zealand, Ansett Australia, BA, Cathay Pacific Airways, Japan Airlines, Qantas Airways and Singapore Airlines.
Source: ACCC (2000).

produce commercial returns to satisfy private investors, but also are being faced with declining aeronautical charges because of post-privatization economic regulation (ACCC, 1998a). The Airports Act 1996 provided for the regulator, the Australian Competition and Consumer Commission (ACCC), to monitor the quality of services against criteria defined by the ACCC. It stipulated that records had to be kept in relation to quality of service and that the ACCC should publish the results of the quality of service monitoring exercise (ACCC, 1998b).

The regulation reports of the airports show the quality of service information which is provided through passenger perception surveys and they also publish 'static indicators' as required by the Airport Act 1996. In addition, the ACCC also undertakes surveys among airlines, Australian Customs Surveys and Airservices Australia, the air traffic control agency. By way of illustration the summary results of this quality assessment for Brisbane airport in 1999/00 are presented in Figures 4.1 and Tables 4.8 and 4.9. It is apparent that passengers were most satisfied with the gate lounges, check-in and waiting time at the car park, and least pleased with the space provided for taxis, baggage handling and inbound government inspection. The airlines were generally more satisfied with the airfield facilities (runways, aprons, taxiways) than the terminal facilities.

Table 4.9 Static quality indicators at Brisbane airport, 1999/00

Indicator	Value
Number of international aircraft parking bays	11
Number of aerobridges	8
Percentage of passengers (embarking) using an aerobridge	98.6%
Percentage of passengers (disembarking) using an aerobridge	98.6%
Number of check-in desks	54
Number of baggage inspection desks	19
Number of inbound immigration desks	26
Number of outbound immigration desks	20
Number of security clearance systems	3
Number of seats in gate lounges	1246
Capacity of outbound baggage handling equipment (bags per hour)	6000
Capacity of inbound baggage reclaim system (bags per hour)	9000
Throughput of the car park per year	1 779 470
Aircraft movement in busiest 30 half hours (annual average)	24
Aircraft movement in busiest 60 half hours (annual average)	23

Source: ACCC (2000).

Quality management at airports

At an increasing number of airports, measuring quality of service is just part of the overall quality management system which has become all about the continuous process of identifying customers needs, assessing their level of satisfaction and taking corrective action when necessary. All employees and all processes are considered to contribute to the long-term success of this system. Effective quality management is now considered to be key element in many services businesses and is viewed as giving companies a competitive edge and a way to increase customer confidence. Potential benefits include increased employee motivation, enhanced communication and teamwork within the organization and increased productivity and efficiency. Theoretically the 'cost of quality' does not have to be expensive as good quality management through quality appraisal and prevention schemes aims to minimize the costly situation when the service is unacceptable and has to be rectified (Lookwood and Wright, 1999).

In some cases airports have chosen to certify their quality system and gain external recognition by using the International Standards Organization's (ISO's) ISO 9000 family of standards. ISO 9001 is the most comprehensive standard and it covers the following elements: management responsibility; quality system; contract review; design control; document and data control; purchasing; customer supplied product; product identification and traceability; process control; inspection and testing; inspection, measuring and test equipment; inspection and test status; control of nonconforming product; corrective and preventive action; handling, storage, packaging and delivery; quality record; internal quality audits; training; servicing and statistical techniques. ISO 9002 does not include the design requirements. ISO 9003 has the least requirements as it concentrates very much on the final inspection and test. The ISO standard does not tell the airports how they should set up their system but simply gives guidance on the elements which should be included. Certification involves inspection by an independent registration body (ACI, 2000).

There are diverse examples of services at European airports which have been certified. For example, Brussels airport is ISO 9002 certified for its centralized technical management, Frankfurt airport has ISO 9001 for its handling services while at Shannon airport, the subsidiary organization Shannon Aviation Fuels is ISO 9002 certified. The Milan Airport company SEA had its ramp operations and baggage handling certified with ISO 9001 in 1997, followed by the security and emergency areas in 1998. It is hoping also to have the commercial activities and supervisory activities and technical activities and maintenance certified as well. Aeroport de Paris gained ISO 9002 certification in 1998 for its aircraft noise monitoring system. Singapore airport is ISO 9002 accredited for its emergency services and ISO 9001 accredited for its training processes. Vienna airport was the first airport to receive ISO 9001 creditation for the total organization, in 1995.

The ACI survey of quality of service asked airports about whether they had any ISO certification for their services. Out of 120 airports, only seventeen had ISO certified services – ten of which were in Europe. ISO 9002 was the most popular. A further twenty-four airports were planning to be certified in the future. Four airports had equivalent quality systems such as the Malcolm Baldridge Award in North America but the majority, seventy-five, of airports had no services certified.

There is a considerable debate as to the merits of becoming ISO certified. As well as giving external recognition and guarantees, certification is often thought to help improve the quality management system of an organization by clearly identifying roles, responsibilities and processes within the business and encouraging a quality culture. However, the certification process is a costly one, requiring much paperwork and extra workload. For example, when Munich airport was preparing for certification of its terminal and passenger services department in 1998, it prepared a very detailed 104-page quality manual which identified all the responsibilities and processes associated with the 214 employees within the department to do with activities such as information services, telephone exchange, VIP special handling services and other services such left luggage, dry cleaning, sale of underground train tickets and so on (Penner, 1999). One of the fundamental principles of the ISO certification concept is that every process should be written down and regularly updated. This procedure is often criticized as being more suitable to the manufacturing industries, where it originated, rather than the services industries where many process are more difficult to formally identify and more flexibility is preferred.

Total quality management at Vienna airport

Vienna Airport is a partially privatized airport which handled over 11 million passengers in 1999 (see case study in Chapter 2). It is worthy of consideration in relation to quality issues since it has been a leading airport in the implementation of total quality management systems. In 1995 it was the first airport in the world to gain ISO 9001 certification for its entire airport operations. This required the culture of the airport company to be changed. The total quality management philosophy, such as the focus on customer and employee satisfaction and the continuous improvement of all airport processes, was communicated to all staff through a series of training courses, workshops, meetings and informal discussions.

In 1997 the airport reorganized its processes to be more focused on customer needs and efficiency. This entailed introducing a new organizational structure. One of the central service divisions or corporate units, which supported the business and service units of the organization, was made responsible for total quality management (TQM) (Figure 4.2). The TQM corporate unit was to be involved with supporting the management board, heads of departments, middle management and all staff in achieving their quality-related goals. The overall quality policy and evaluation of the quality management systems, as with all total-quality focused companies, was given highest priority and was made direct responsibility of the management board. In addition, TQM co-ordinators were appointed to each business, service and corporate units to facilitate communication with the TQM unit and to look after the quality management system in their area of expertise.

A number of different elements are incorporated into Vienna airport's TQM model and corporate philosophy. An effective targeting system is considered crucial for all employees. The airport aims to keep all employees informed about the targets, such as how and why they were formulated and current progress, through various communication channels including the airport's intranet. In fact, staff knowledge of all TQM developments is considered to be very important and the airport uses a variety of different methods for communicating information – ranging from the intranet and TQM newsletter to TQM workshops and annual forums.

Within TQM philosophy, a high degree of staff motivation and satisfaction is considered to be essential. At Vienna airport a staff satisfaction survey in 1998

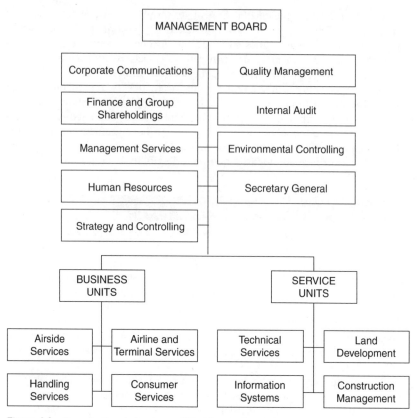

Figure 4.2 Organizational structure within Vienna airport, 1999
Source: Annual accounts.

found that 29 per cent of staff felt that they had enough information to be able to do their job well and 35 per cent were satisfied with the work routines in their department. Twenty-eight per cent felt that ideas regarding an improvement of the working situation were suitably appreciated by their managers. The survey was used as a starting point for more extensive surveys and for target setting (Kotrba, 1999). A target of 50 per cent of employees being highly satisfied or satisfied with communications, work processes and appreciation of their ideas was set for 1999. This target was exceeded with a score of 55 per cent (Vienna Airport, 2000).

Another important feature of Vienna airport's approach is the processes which it uses to find out about its customers and their needs and requirements. It started regularly interviewing its passengers in 1995 with two main surveys. First, there is the 'Passenger Map' which collects passenger profile information related to characteristics such as age, sex, residence, mode of transport to the airport, transfer details, ticket used, time spent at the airport, services used and purchasing patterns of departing passengers. The airport also undertakes a quality monitor in which passengers have to rate their opinion of airport facilities and services.

In addition, every other year the airport undertakes a 'conflict detector' which helps investigate, from a passenger viewpoint, the relative importance of facilities and services and to identify any conflicts which exist. Information from these surveys is also supplemented by ad hoc surveys of meeters, greeters and employees at the airport and regular feedback from other businesses at the airport. The results of this market research is used to analyse passenger and other customer requirements, define target groups, identify problems areas, support product development and to set quality targets (Pongratz, 1999).

Another way in which the airport has tried to improve its emphasis on customer orientation has been in encouraging its customers to get involved in the planning of future developments at the airport – so called 'customer imagineering' or the airport's 'one step ahead' approach. A prime example of this policy has been with the development and expansion of the terminal, the 'Terminal 2005' project. The airport has worked very closely with Austrian Airlines to define requirements for the expansion of the terminal and to ensure that the new facilities will enable Austrian Airlines to use the airport as a hub by offering quick and efficient transfers.

This co-operation was based on joint overall responsibility between the airport and airline with a mixed steering committee, mixed working groups and equal status project managers. Phase 1 involved two working groups 'Traffic Development' and 'Visions' preparing the groundwork for the future project work by considering forecast traffic levels and the activities and functions of the terminal and how these would affect the design. During phase 2, six other working groups, 'Airside Operations', 'Terminal and Aircraft Handling', 'New Information Technologies', 'Non Aviation', 'Working with Authorities' and 'Ecology and Infrastructure', then worked out the detailed requirements on the basis of the results from phase 1, which eventually led to the selection of the design of the terminal extension. The next planning and construction stages are also being co-ordinated jointly by Vienna airport and Austrian Airlines.

References and further reading

Airports Council International (ACI) (2000). *Quality of Service at Airports*. ACI.

Alder, N. and Berechman, J. (2000). Measuring Airport Quality from the Airlines' Viewpoint. Fourth Air Transport Research Group Conference, The Netherlands, July.

Association of European Airlines (AEA) (2000). European airline delays in 1999. Press release, 14 February.

Australian Competition and Consumer Commission (ACCC) (1998a). *Economic Regulation of Airports – an Overview*. ACCC.

Australian Competition and Consumer Commission (ACCC) (1998b). *Quality of Service Monitoring for Airport – Statement of the ACCC's Approach to Analysis, Interpretation and Publication of Quality Information*. ACCC.

Australian Competition and Consumer Commission (ACCC) (1999). *Brisbane Airport Regulatory Report 1998/9*. ACCC.

Australian Competition and Consumer Commission (ACCC) (2000). *Brisbane Airport Regulatory Report 1999/00*. ACCC.

British Airports Authority (BAA) (2000). *Annual Report 1999/2000*. BAA.

Brussels International Airport Company (2000). *Annual Report 1999*. Brussels International Airport Company.

Civil Aviation Authority (CAA) (2000a). *The CAA Approach to Economic Regulation and Work Programme for the Airport Reviews*. Position paper, CAA.

Civil Aviation Authority (CAA) (2000b). *Quality of Service Issues*. Consultation paper, CAA.

Civil Aviation Authority (CAA) (2000c). *BAA London Airports: A Regulatory Report*. CAA.

Cruickshank, A. (2000). Airport-airline agreements: what is the way forward? University of Westminster/Cranfield University Airport Economics and Finance Symposium, March.

European Commission (2000). *Protection of Air Passengers in the European Union*. Communication from the Commission to the European Parliament, COM (2000) 365 final.

International Air Transport Association (IATA) (2000a). *Global Airport Monitor*. IATA.

International Air Transport Association (IATA) (2000b). Service level agreements. *ANSConf Working Paper No 85*, ICAO.

Kotrba, F. (1999). Delivering quality in a globalized market. Ninth ACI Europe Annual Congress, Pisa, June.

Le Marquand, P. (1996). Pleasing the airport property customer. ACI Europe good communication and better airport marketing conference, Bologna, April.

Lemaitre, A. (1998). The development of performance indicators for airports: a management perspective. Eighth World Conference on Transport Research, Antwerp, July.

Lemer, A. C. (1992). Measuring performance of airport passenger terminals. *Transportation Research*, **26**A(1), 37–45.

Lockwood, C. and Wright, L. (1999). *Principles of Service Marketing and Management*. Prentice-Hall.

Maiden, S. (2000). Measuring service quality at airports. University of Westminster/Cranfield University Airport Economics and Finance Symposium, London, March.

Monopolies and Mergers Commission (1996). *A Report on the Economic Regulation of the London Airport Companies*. MMC.

Monopolies and Mergers Commission (1997*) A Report on the Economic Regulation of Manchester Airport plc*. MMC.

Penner, T. (1999). Terminal and passenger services certified according to ISO 9001. *ACI Europe Communique*, July, 5–6.

Pongratz, B. (1999). Market research and total quality management at Vienna International Airport. *ACI Europe Communique*, July, 9–10.

Van Looy, B., Van Dierdonck, R. and Gemmel, P. (eds) (1998). *Services Management: An Integrated Approach*. Financial Times Management. Vienna Airport (2000). *Annual Report 1999*. Vienna Airport.

5

The airport–airline relationship

The relationship between the airport operator and airlines is clearly fundamental to the success of any airport business. The sweeping changes which have occurred within the airline industry mean that airlines, more than ever before, are trying to control their costs in order to improve their financial position in an ever increasing competitive and deregulated environment. This is having an impact on the aeronautical policies of airports and their regulation. At the same time, demand is outstripping capacity at a growing number of airports and so the traditional mechanism for allocating slots has had to be revisited. All these issues are considered in this chapter.

The structure of aeronautical charges

Aeronautical charging traditionally has been relatively simple, with most revenue coming from a weight-based landing charge and a passenger fee dependent on passenger numbers. Many airports still generate their aeronautical revenue in this way. At other airports charging practices have become more complex and more market based. This reflects the increasingly commercial and competitive airport environment and the contemporary challenges faced by airports such as the growing pressure on facilities, environmental concerns and rising security costs.

Landing charges

Most airports have a weight related landing charge based on maximum take-off weight (MTOW) or maximum authorized weight (MAW). The simplest method is to charge a fixed amount unit rate (e.g. US$X per tonne) regardless of the size of the aircraft. A fixed unit rate will favour smaller aircraft types since tonnage tends to increase faster than aircraft capacity or payload. It will also benefit airlines which have high load factors or seating capacities. This simple method is used at many airports throughout the world including the USA and Australian airports, most of the German airports, Aer Rianta, Brussels and Copenhagen. Some airports have a unit landing charge which declines as the weight of the aircraft increases such as Manchester airport. At other airports, for example Amsterdam, Kuala Lumpur and the Italian, Spanish and Indian airports, the unit rate increases for larger aircraft. At a few airports, for example in Greece, the variable rate successively increases and decreases as the weight of the aircraft rises.

This charging mechanism uses 'ability to pay' principles, since airlines using larger aircraft are in a better position to pay higher charges. Some costs such as runway wear and tear do increase with weight and also larger aircraft require vortex separations, which can reduce the number of aircraft movements during a certain period. Overall, however, there is not a strong relationship between aircraft weight and airfield cost. A flat rate landing charge for all aircraft types may be more appropriate, particularly at congested airports. This is because the cost of occupying the congested runway is movement related and independent of aircraft size. Each aircraft movement will consume the same resource.

Very few airports have adopted a movement-related charge which clearly will tend to be very unpopular with airlines flying small aircraft types. Notable exceptions are Heathrow and Gatwick airports which have a fixed runway charge at peak times. Other airports have not gone this far, but have made an attempt to charge the smallest aircraft more to encourage general aviation traffic particularly to move away from congested major airports. For example, Frankfurt airport has a minimum landing charge set at 35 tonnes, Düsseldorf at 32 tonnes. Vienna airport has a large fixed movement element in its landing charge as well as a variable fee. In the USA most airports tend to stick to a very simple fixed unit rate. One such airport which was experiencing acute runway congestion in the late 1980s was Boston Massport. As a result of this, the airport attempted to introduce a movement-related element into its landing charge, but was forced to abandon such a policy when its airline and general aviation customers questioned the legality of this in the law courts.

BAA plc's fixed landing charge for all aircraft only applies to peak early morning and evening flights in the summer. Some other airports also have differential landing charges by season or time of day to reflect peaking of demand. For example, at Athens airport airlines pay a 25 per cent surcharge on landings from June to September between the times of 1100 and 1700. Toronto, Mexico City and Brussels airports have higher charges in the early morning. Some of the Spanish airports, namely Menorca and Ibiza, increase their landing fees slightly in the summer months.

Sometimes charges for ATC or terminal navigational facilities will be incorporated into the landing charge. At other airports, the airport operator may levy a separate charge. Typically this charge will be, like the landing charge, related to the weight of the aircraft. Clearly there is no logical cost rationale for this since each aircraft movement, regardless of the size of the airport, imposes the same costs on the ATC infrastructure. Alternatively, the airline will pay the air traffic control agencies direct and the airport operator will not involved in the financing of ATC services at all.

At some airports, for example, many of those in France and Italy, domestic, European or short-haul services pay a reduced landing fee. This is not a cost-related charge since the cost to land an aircraft is independent of its origin. Instead, it tends to exist to support local and regional services, which are comparatively expensive to operate. Sometimes such services will have a social role in linking together regional communities and so in effect the discount will be an unofficial subsidy. A few airports, for example Brussels and Macau airports and those in Spain and Portugal, offer a volume discount on the landing fee. This will naturally favour the established home carrier at the airport and European airports particularly have been subject to considerable criticism from having such a policy – particularly from the European Commission who in 2000 was threatening court action (Jane's Airport Review, 2000). The International Air Transport Association, the airline organization, is strongly opposed to such practices (IATA, 2000a).

A growing number of airports have noise-related surcharges or discounts associated with their landing charges as a result of increasing concerns about the environment. Some of these are based on airport or country specific aircraft acoustic group classifications as is the case with airports in France, Switzerland and Belgium. Elsewhere more standard ICAO 'chapter' classifications are used. (These classifications are based on the level of noise which aircraft make and the areas on the ground which are affected by the aircraft noise. There are currently three classifications: chapter 1 aircraft which are banned from airports, chapter 2 aircraft which are due to be banned in 2002 and chapter 3 aircraft which are the quietest aircraft). This is the practice at the German and London airports and those serving the cities of Amsterdam, Stockholm and Oslo. Airports may adopt different subclassifications within the chapter 3 group. Most airports in Germany have chapter 3 'bonus' or 'non-bonus' aircraft, whereas at London there are 'minus', 'base' and 'high' categories. Sometimes there is a separate noise tax as well as is the case at the French, Italian and Korean airports and at Sydney. There may be a cost rationale for such charging when the noise related revenue is used for noise protection and insulation projects but this is not often the situation.

At a number of airports such as Brussels, Manila, Oslo, Seychelles and those in Germany, the landing charges are higher at night, and at some airports such as Amsterdam and Manchester, chapter 2 aircraft are banned at night. In addition to noise disturbance effects there are increasing concerns about the impact that aircraft emissions are having on the environment (see Chapter 10 for a fuller discussion). As yet this has not been reflected in airport charges, with the notable exception of Zürich and Geneva airports in Switzerland and the Stockholm airports of Arlanda and Bromma which introduced emissions charges in the late 1990s.

Passenger charges

Passenger charges are the other main source of aeronautical revenue. These charges are most commonly levied per departing passenger. At most airports there tends to be a lower charge for domestic passengers to reflect the lower costs associated with these types of passengers. The French airports have three types of charges, namely domestic, EU and international. Aer Rianta airports have transatlantic, international and domestic charges, while Johannesburg airport has domestic, regional and international charges. The charges at Athens airport vary with distance, while in Spain and India neighbouring countries are charged less. As with the landing charge in some cases, there may be political or social reasons for keeping down the cost of domestic travel as well. Historically, such policies are often maintained to subsidize the national carrier which has a large domestic operation. It can be argued, however, that domestic passengers have less potential for generating commercial revenues and hence do not justify the lower passenger charge. Pakistan airports have different fees for passengers who are travelling first, business or economy class. With an increasing emphasis on airport safety in recent years, particularly the requirement for airlines to screen 100 per cent of hold baggage, security charges have become more popular. The passenger charge traditionally was considered to cover security costs but now a significant number of airports have separate security charges, very often levied on a per passenger basis.

A number of airports charge a smaller fee for transfer passengers (e.g. Amsterdam, Helsinki, Vienna and Copenhagen), or waive the fee completely in certain circumstances (e.g. Dublin, Rome, Milan, Stockholm, Brussels and Athens) to encourage this type of traffic. A lower transfer charge can be justifiable on cost grounds as such passengers will have no surface access requirements, will not have associated meeters and greeters, and very often will not need check-in, security and immigration facilities either. On the other hand, transfer passengers still require facilities such as baggage handling and may require special facilities in order that a rapid transfer is achieved. Some other airports also have differential charges to reflect peaking, such as East Midlands, Manchester and Luton airports in the UK which charge more in the summer. Passengers at London City airport pay more in the morning and evening peak times.

Other charges

There are also a number of other charges which tend to be fairly small compared with the landing and passenger fees. First, there is the parking charge which is usually based on the weight of the aircraft or, sometimes, on aircraft wingspan as in the case of Singapore, Malaysia, Oman, Malta and some US airports such as Boston, Houston and Miami. There is normally an hourly or daily charge with, perhaps, a rebate for using remote stands. Most airports have a free parking charge, typically ranging from one to four hours to allow the airline to turnaround at the airport without incurring any charges. A few airports, such as BAA plc's London airports, Frankfurt and Hong Kong, have no free parking charge to encourage the airlines to minimize turnaround time. BAA plc's airports charge per quarter hour and during peak times each minute counts as three. For those airports which have a twenty-four hour charge, such as Amsterdam, Düsseldorf, Manchester, Vienna and the Canadian airports, there is clearly no incentive for airlines to make the most effective use of the apron space.

There may be other charges for certain facilities or services which airports choose to price separately rather than including in the landing or passenger charge. For example, at the French and Italian airports and at Athens there is a lighting charge. At other airports, there may be an airbridge fee typically charged per movement or based on the length of time that the bridge is occupied. Sometimes, as an alternative to the passenger charge, there are cargo charges based on the weight of loaded or unloaded cargo as is the case at the Spanish and Swiss airports. There may be a lower fee for all-cargo aircraft, as is the case at Amsterdam and Brussels airports, or a higher charge as at Belfast International or the airports in Cyprus. There may be additional charges related to services such as fire-fighting, storage facility, hangar use and other airport-specific activities (Hague Consultancy, 2001).

Ground handling and fuel charges

Airlines incur three types of charges when they use an airport. First, they pay landing and passengers and, sometimes, other airport fees, which have already been discussed. Then there are ground-handling fees which the airport operator may levy if it chooses to provide some of these services itself rather than leaving it to handling agents or airlines. Finally, there are the fuel charges which are levied by the fuel companies which are normally independent of the airport operator. There a few notable exceptions, such as certain Middle Eastern airports like Abu Dhabi where the fuelling is provided by a government agency. Hence all services at the airport can be offered to the airline in one overall package.

It is rare to find published data relating to handling and fuel charges. These are usually negotiable and the agreed prices will depend on various factors such as the size of the airline, the scale of its operation at the airport in question and whether other airports used by the airline are served by the same handling and fuel companies. Further complexities occur since there are a variety of ways of charging for activities such as ramp handling, passenger handling, apron buses, aircraft cleaning, ground power, pushback and so on. In some cases there may be just one or two charges that cover everything, whereas elsewhere there may be a multitude of individual fees.

Government taxes

There is one final charge which airlines or their passengers sometimes experience at an airport – government taxes (see Table 5.1). This income does not directly go to the airport operator but does impact on the overall cost of the 'turnaround' from an airline's point of view (Pagliari, 1998).

Sometimes these taxes may have a travel-related objective as is the case with a number of taxes in the USA or in Australia where some of the tax directly funds the national tourist board. In Norway there is a tax to help finance

Table 5.1 Main aeronautical charges at airports

Charge	Common basis for charging	Income to airport operator?
Landing	Weight of aircraft	Yes
Terminal navigation	Included in landing charge or based on weight of aircraft	Sometimes
Airbridge	Included in landing charge or based on aircraft movement	Yes
Passenger	Departing passenger	Yes
Security	Included in passenger charge or based on passenger numbers	Yes
Parking	Weight of aircraft per hour or 24 hours after free period	Yes
Ground handling	Different charges for different activities	Sometimes
Fuel	Volume of fuel	No
Government taxes	Departing passenger	No

national transport links. Elsewhere such taxation is just used as means of supplementing general government taxation income from other sources. Mexico City has a tourist tax on international arriving passengers and a number of other countries such as Malta, Jamaica and Pakistan impose a tax on departing passengers. The Republic of Yemen has a 'Development Tax', a 'Tourism Tax' and a 'National Aid Tax'. In the UK, a departure tax which goes directly to the treasury, was introduced in 1994. This has been greeted with considerable opposition, especially from the new breed of low-cost carriers who complain that it is too large in proportion to the fares that are being offered. For example, in 2000 fares as low as £30 were on offer by low-cost carriers such as Ryanair and easyJet to European destinations with a third of this (£10) being the airport tax. If such a tax has to be levied, the low-cost carriers feel it would be fairer to base it on a percentage of the ticket price (Gill, 1998). As a compromise in 2001, a differential tax system with different amounts for economy and business-class passengers was introduced.

The level of aeronautical charges

It is very difficult to compare the level of charges at different airports because of the varied nature of the charging structures. To overcome this problem, comparisons have to be made by examining the representative airport charges for a Boeing 737 on an international route (Figure 5.1). A sample of twenty-four airports from around the world has been chosen. The costs are divided between aircraft-related costs which include landing charges as well as ATC and airbridge charges, if these exist; passenger-related costs which include passenger charges and any security charges; and government taxes. The data was not sufficient to allow ground-handling and fuel costs to be added. Only published charges were used, so the figures do not take account of any discounts that may be available.

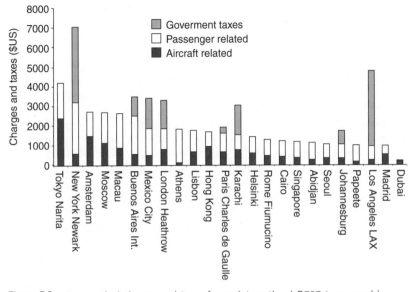

Figure 5.1 Aeronautical charges and taxes for an international B737 turnaround in 2000 at world airports
Source: Cranfield University.

There is a wide spread of charges (excluding taxes) ranging from less than US$300 dollars at Dubai airport to over US$4000 at Toyko Narita airport. Dubai has not increased its charges for many years. Charges at Narita airport have always been relatively high since it opened in 1984. Charges at the new Hong Kong Chek Lap Kok airport were also expected to be high and double the cost of the old Kai Tak airport – but were reduced because of airline pressure and the 1990s Asian crisis. Singapore has relatively low charges in spite of having a good reputation for service as was illustrated in the IATA Global Monitor (see Chapter 4). The situation changes somewhat when government taxes are included. Newark then becomes the most expensive airport and Los Angeles takes second position. Low airport charges may also be compensated for by relatively high handling charges as is thought to be the case, for example, at Madrid airport (Air Transport Group, 1998).

The impact of aeronautical charges on airline operations

In recent years airport charges have become subject increasingly to scrutiny from the airlines – particularly from the new breed of low-cost airlines in Europe. A more competitive airline environment and falling yields has forced airlines to focus on major cost-saving initiatives such as outsourcing, reductions in staff numbers and pegging the level of wages. These are all internal costs over which the airlines have a considerable degree of control. However, airlines have also been looking at their external costs such as airport charges, and demanding that airports adopt such cost-cutting and efficiency saving measures themselves, rather than raising their charges (Doganis, 2001).

In spite of this growing concern over the level of charges, airport costs generally represent a relatively small part of an airline's total operating costs. They are least important when long-haul operations are being considered, since the charges are levied relatively infrequently. Airport charges are the most significant for the charter and low-cost carriers as these airlines will have minimized or completely avoided some of the other costs which traditional scheduled airlines face. Most low-cost airlines operate short sectors which means that they pay airport charges more frequently. It is hardly surprising that it is this type of airline which has been most active in attempting to bring down their airport costs by negotiating incentive deals at airports or operating out of secondary or regional airports which have lower charges.

Accurate international figures illustrating this are difficult to obtain because many airlines do not now report the passenger fee as an airport charge and very often the airport charges may be combined with some other cost item. Figure 5.2 does, however, show the situation for UK airlines. Only landing and passenger charges are shown and so these figures do not represent the total turnaround costs for the airlines. British Airways, with a mix of long and short haul flights, has the lowest share of costs at around 8 per cent. This share is more than double for British Midland, which has a range of domestic and European services. These charges account for around 13–15 per cent of all costs for carriers with short-haul and mostly domestic services, such as British Regional and Brymon. A similar situation exists for easyJet although the charges would be much higher if its airport charges, for example at Luton airport, had not been heavily discounted. For the charter airlines of Britannia and Airtours, the airport charges represent around 20 per cent of total costs.

However, in a general sense, it is difficult to see how airport charges can have a major impact on airline behaviour. For most airlines the impact on demand,

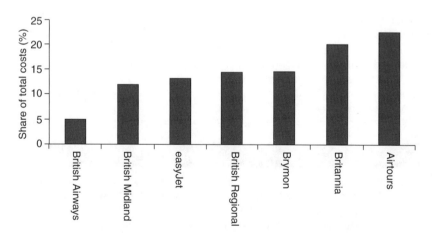

Figure 5.2 Landing and passenger charges as a share of total costs for UK airlines, 1998
Source: CAA airline statistics.

and on other costs which might be incurred if operations were changed to avoid certain airports or airport charges, would outweigh the impact on costs due to the airport charges. A recent study of UK traffic has suggested that a 50 per cent increase in all airport charges would only result in a 7.5 per cent reduction in total demand – although clearly the effects will differ according to both airport and traffic characteristics (DETR, 2000).

Peak charges have been introduced by some airports to make the airlines, which are generating the peak demand, pay for the peak capacity infrastructure costs. They have also been used with the intent of shifting some of the peak operations into the off-peak. This is unlikely to occur unless the differential between peak and off-peak pricing is very much higher than current practice. Airline scheduling is a complex task which has to take into account factors such as passenger demand patterns, airport curfews and environmental restrictions, crew availability, peak profiles at other airports and so on. If the airline were to shift operations to outside the peak period, this could well mean that the peak is merely shifted to another time. In effect, these schedule constraints coupled with the fact that charges make a relatively small contribution to airline total costs, mean that demand is fairly inelastic to changes in airport fees. Most peak pricing has very little impact on airline operations other than making it more expensive for airlines to operate in the peak. Moreover the impact on passenger behaviour also tends to be marginal since generally the different airport charges tend to be averaged out.

BAA plc is the only airport operator to have used a peak pricing charging system based on a detailed assessment of marginal costs. In theory marginal cost pricing leads to the most efficient allocation of resources as only the users, who value a facility at least as much as the cost of providing it, will pay the price for using it. In practice such pricing policies are complex and very difficult to implement. In the 1970s BAA plc introduced a peak surcharge on runway movements on certain summer days, and a peak passenger and parking charge based on marginal cost principles at Heathrow and Gatwick airports. It proved to be ineffectual in shifting any demand largely because of the scheduling problems already described, but also because the charging system was so complex that it was very difficult for the airlines to react. While BAA plc has retained the landing and parking peak charge, it has abandoned the more complex peak passenger charges. The airport operator faced widespread opposition from the airlines, particularly the US carriers, to such charges which were considered discriminatory. Also the airports are now effectively full in most hours and so the concept of the peak hour has become far less relevant. BAA plc claims that the new policy takes into account both economic pressures and the preferences of its airlines (Toms, 1994). In general, IATA remains opposed to peak pricing as it feels that it could lead to discriminatory practices and could be ineffective in addressing capacity problems (IATA, 2000c).

It is equally as difficult to influence an airline's choice of aircraft as it is to shift their schedules by using pricing mechanisms. At many airports the typical fee surcharge for a chapter 2 aircraft is about 20–25 per cent of the normal landing fee, which will be probably represent around 1 per cent of an airline's costs in most circumstances. This will be too insignificant alone to alter a carrier's choice of equipment (Dennis, 1996). To have any meaningful impact the surcharge probably has to be at least double the equivalent chapter 3 charge, as is the case in Germany. Between 1995 and 2000 Amsterdam airport increased its surcharges for chapter 2 aircraft between 50 to 100 per cent every six months. In 2000 for a 120-tonne aircraft the chapter 2 landing surcharge was 6075 Dutch guilders per landing compared with a basic runway charge (landing and take-off) of 2290 Dutch guilders. As a result chapter 2 aircraft at the airport have reduced from 15 per cent in 1999 to 0.6 per cent in the same year although, clearly, some of this fleet replacement might well have happened without such a charging policy – particularly with the banning of chapter 2 aircraft within Europe from 2002 (see Chapter 10) (Schiphol Group, 2000).

An airport charging policy probably has its greatest impact on airline operations when new routes are being considered – especially when being operated by low-cost airlines or on short regional sectors. This is due to the existence of airport incentive schemes or discounts. These are most likely to be offered at smaller airports which want to encourage growth and provide inducements to airlines which might otherwise not choose to use the airport. Such discounts have, in many cases, been a critical factor when low-cost carriers are selecting suitable airports for their operations.

One of the most popular methods is to waive or reduce the landing fee in the first few years of operation so that the airline only pays for the passengers it carries. If demand at the start of a service is initially low, the airline will pay very little. This means that the airport will share more of the risk when the airline is developing the route. At Norwegian airports discounts on both landing and passenger charges are available for new international services. In the first year of operation, there may be nothing to pay with the discount tapering in the second year to 70 per cent of the first year's discount and to 40 per cent in the third year. More sophisticated approaches include that of Belfast City airport which introduced a dual charging process in 1993. Airlines themselves could choose to come under a conventional charging structure or be charged an inflated passenger fee but with no landing charge. Of course, incentive schemes are not always popular with all airlines – particularly the full-fees paying ones who may be unhappy about effectively subsidizing the new carriers.

Between 1994 and 1999, Aer Rianta, the Irish operator had one of the most complex published discount schemes in existence (Table 5.2). The airport operator gave discounts on new routes and growth on existing routes, which reduced over time. In the initial years, airlines could be paying as little as 10 per cent of the standard landing and passenger charge. Various airlines, especially Ryanair, benefited significantly from this scheme – particularly because of the short-haul nature of their services and the price sensitivity of their leisure passengers. Aer Rianta terminated their discount scheme at the end of 1999, largely in preparation for the demise of EU duty- and tax-free sales. This was greeted with considerable opposition from Ryanair. Similarly easyJet in 2000 appealed unsuccessfully to the UK CAA to intervene when Luton airport announced that it would be charging easyJet its published, rather than discounted rate. Eventually easyJet's charges per passenger were increased from the original discount fee of £1.60 to a much higher compromise discount fee of £5.50 in 2001.

A particular area of concern for airlines as regards charging policies is cross-subsidization within an airport group under common ownership. This

Table 5.2   New growth and new route discounts available at Aer Rianta airports, 1994–9

New growth – landing and passenger fees	Discount rate (%)					
	1994	1995	1996	1997	1998	1999
94/3 growth	80[1]	70	60	50	40	30
95/4 growth		80	70	60	50	40
96/5 growth			90	90	70	70
97/6 growth				90	90	70
98/7 growth					90	90
99/8 growth						90
New route – passenger, landing and parking fees	80	80	90	90	90	90

Note: [1] passenger fees only.
Source: Aer Rianta.

typically occurs when a large international airport provides financial support for a smaller airport, usually serving primarily domestic services. Operators of airport groups argue that the individual airports need to operate as a system to make the most efficient use of resources and to produce cost savings. The airlines tend to be strongly opposed to such cross-subsidizing and argue that if the smaller airports really need financial help for social or economic reasons, that they should be supported by government funds instead (IATA, 2000e).

Another important issue is the pre-financing of future airport infrastructure through airport charges. A fundamental principle of the cost recovery policy in ICAO guidelines on airport charges is that charges should not be levied for any facilities until they become operational. The recommendations do, however, allow for airports to make a reasonable return on assets to contribute towards capital improvements. Pre-financing has traditionally not been an acceptable principle for a number of reasons. First, there is no guarantee that the airlines paying the charges will actually be the airlines which will benefit from the new infrastructure. Also there may be no certainty that the airport charges will be efficiently spent to provide new facilities. Moreover, the airlines tend to be fearful that they will pay twice for the infrastructure, both before it is built and once it is operational (IATA, 2000d).

In spite of these airline concerns, some airports have introduced fees for pre-financing purposes. The most notable example is the USA where PFCs go towards future development projects. A similar situation exists at some Canadian airports. In Greece higher passenger fees have been levied, in spite of airline opposition, to pay for the financing of the new Athens airport. Elsewhere, for example in the UK, the regulator takes into account the fact that some pre-financing will take place when setting the appropriate level of charges. Airports argue that self-financing in certain circumstances can provide a useful, cheaper source for funding investment in addition to loans and equity which can also be used as security for raising extra finance (ACI, 2000a; 2000b).

Airports claim that pre-financing also avoids large increases in airport charges when the infrastructure comes on stream as was experienced at Narita and Kansai airports in Japan or was initially proposed at the new Chek Lap Kok airport in Hong Kong – but was not fully implemented because of fierce opposition from the airlines.

The International Civil Aviation Organization has acknowledged that, with the growing commercialization within the industry and diminishing dependence on government sources for financing, pre-funding could perhaps be considered for the future. This would only occur if there was adequate economic regulation, effective accounting practices and prior consultation with users to ensure that such financing was considered fair and appropriate (ICAO, 2000a). The ICAO Conference on the Economics and Airports and Air Navigation Services (ANSConf 2000) therefore recommended that countries could consider pre-funding through airport charges but only in specific safeguarded circumstances.

The airport regulatory environment

Airports are subject to a number of different regulations at both international and national level. Many of these are technical regulations related to the operational, safety and security aspects of managing an airport. Airports are also increasingly becoming subject to environmental regulations which may, for example, restrict aircraft movements due to noise considerations or limit airport infrastructure development. These environmental issues are discussed in detail in Chapter 10. Then there is economic regulation with the main focus being on charge or tariff control. Other economic aspects of operation such as handling activities and slot allocation are also regulated in some areas of the world. Overall the economic regulatory interest in airports seems to be increasing at a time when, ironically, the airlines business is being progressively deregulated.

On a worldwide basis the 1944 Chicago Convention, which established an international regulatory air transport system, provides a basis for airport charging. Article 15 gives international authority for the levying of charges by ICAO member states and specifies that there shall be no discrimination between users, particularly from different countries. The International Civil Aviation Organization also produces more detailed guidelines with have an overriding principle that charges should be cost related. These also recommend that the charging system should be transparent and non-discriminatory and that consultation should take place between airport operators and their customers if changes are proposed (ICAO, 1992). Such principles, which are due to be revised as a consequence of ANSconf 2000, are only guidelines and are open to different interpretations. In spite of this, these guidelines have generally led to fairly similar overall pricing regimes being adopted by most airports, being broadly related to average cost pricing combined with some market or ability-to-pay pricing.

Airport charges can also be subject to the international obligations of bilateral agreements. For example, the UK/US bilateral air service, Bermuda 2, states that airport charges must be related to costs and should allow only reasonable profits. In addition, the European Commission has been proposing to introduce an airport charges regulatory framework for the whole EU. The first proposal appeared in 1985, and since then there have been several different attempts to seek approval for such legislation. The latest proposal has three basic principles (European Commission, 2000a):

1 *Non-discrimination by flight origin* – unless justified by cost differences.
2 *Cost related* – to ensure that overall the charges cover the total internal costs and external costs incurred because of the presence of the airlines. Pre-financing would only be allowed when there is an official decision regarding any future development of the infrastructure.
3 *Transparency* – achieved through consultation of airports and users, regarding both the way the charges are calculated and their actual level.

The airports have, in principle, been opposed to the Commission's plans. They claim that there is no need for such regulation since airports are adequately regulated by their own national governments and that competition and lower fares are exerting downward pressure on airport charges. Only when an airport has considerable market power, and consumer or trade law does not provide sufficient protection, do the airports generally consider that regulation might be necessary. There has been discussion about a self-regulation code of conduct to be developed jointly by the airports and airlines (Gethin, 1998). By contrast the airlines are in favour of the proposals, although they also want provision for a more effective actual mechanism to regulate charges and incentives to encourage airports to increase productivity and reduce costs (Clayton, 1997). A considerable amount of effort has been exerted by all interested parties in discussing the proposals – especially related to how to define cost-relatedness, what costs should be used as a basis for charge setting and the whole issue of self-financing. Eventually the draft directive on airport charges was adopted by the European Commission in 1997 and this should have enabled it to proceed through the European Parliament and the Council of Ministers (ACI-Europe, 1998). By 2000 little progress appeared to have been made, a particularly difficult area being the charging for airport networks (e.g. in Spain, Sweden, Finland, Portugal and Greece) and the whole issue of cross-subsidization.

In addition to international regulation, there can also be some kind of control at a national level. The degree of control varies considerably at different airports. Most airports still under public sector ownership usually need to seek government approval before changing their charging level or structure. In some cases this may be just a formality. At the other extreme it may the government's responsibility to set charges – perhaps after receiving recommendations from the airports. In Italy, airport fees are considered as taxes and there are actual laws associated with them. Elsewhere the level of charges may be automatically linked to the consumer price index, as is the case at Brussels airport. In 1999, the ICAO reviewed the situation at seventy-six member countries throughout the world. Fifty-seven per cent of countries stated that charges were determined by the airport operator with government approval, and a further 16 per cent of airport operators determined their charges independently. For the remaining countries, the government was directly responsible for setting the level of fees to be charged (ICAO, 2000b).

Regulation of privatized airports

The basic principles

When airports with considerable market power are privatized or even just commercialized, there are often serious concerns that they will abuse their monopolistic situation. This has resulted in new regulatory frameworks being established at a number of airports. This has involved using regulatory authorities which are already in existence or creating new bodies specifically for this purpose. While the regulatory systems at different airports vary, their common purpose is to allow the regulated airports a reasonable rate of return on capital while providing the correct incentives for an efficient operation and an appropriate investment policy. In choosing the most suitable regulatory system, consideration has to be given as to the best incentives to encourage appropriate investment, the treatment of commercial revenues and the maintenance of standards of service. A suitable review process also has to be established.

In general there are four key ways in which organization with monopolistic characteristics can be regulated:

1 Rate of return (ROR) regulation.
2 Price cap regulation.
3 Default price cap.
4 Reserve regulation.

The ROR mechanism, or so called cost based or profit control regulation, is the traditional mechanism which has been used extensively, for example in the USA and Australia, to regulate natural monopolies. The aim is to prevent regulated companies from setting prices that bear no relation to costs. A certain rate of return is established and price increases can only be justified when an increase in costs is incurred. While such a system can ensure that the prices are related to costs, it provides no incentives to reduce costs. The operator will be guaranteed a certain rate of return irrespective of efficiency. Costs inefficiencies can be built into the cost structure which can be passed on to the consumers through increased prices. Such a system can also encourage overinvestment. To ensure that this does not occur, the regulator has to scrutinize carefully the financial operations and development plans of the regulated companies.

To overcome these shortcomings, alternative regulatory systems have been sought. In the 1980s, price cap regulation began to be used – for example in the UK where a number of the state utilities such as gas and electricity, were being privatized (Helm and Jenkinson, 1998) This type of regulation was considered to be more favourable as it can provide the regulated company with incentives to reduce costs while simultaneously controlling price increases. It works by establishing a formula which provides a maximum price which can be set. Typically the formula will be adjusted for inflation and an efficiency factor:

Price cap = CPI – X or RPI – X

where CPI is the consumer price index, RPI is the retail price index and X is the efficiency gain target. Costs which are beyond the control of the company can be excluded from the regulation:

Price cap = CPI − X + Y

where Y is the external costs.

Since there is no cap on the profit levels, unlike the ROR method, any efficiency gains which the regulated company can make in excess of the required X will directly benefit the company. Such a method tends to be simpler to administer as companies can change their level or structure of prices as long as they still conform to the price cap without any justification from the regulator – which would be the situation with the ROR system. Opponents to such a system, however, argue that price cap regulation is not actually an effective alternative to cost-based regulation since the regulator will take into account the rate of return of the company, as well as other factors such as operational efficiency, planned investment and the competitive situation, when setting the price cap. Thus the regulated company may still have an incentive to overstate the capital expenditure needed, which will only be discouraged by careful scrutiny of the regulator. In spite of this shortcoming, price cap regulation has been the most popular approach adopted for privatized airports.

A 'default' price cap system works by having a price cap which is available to all users. However, individual users are permitted to set up alternative contracts with the airport operator outside the price cap condition if both parties are agreeable. Independent arrangements could therefore be established relating to levels of service quality, forms of price setting and any specific infrastructure developments. Any users wishing for a different level of service could, in theory, negotiate this with the airport operator. These contracts could have different duration for different users. This process could also allow for direct contracting for terminal facilities or up-front payment for specific facilities. Such an approach has yet to be used but would clearly lessen the direct regulatory involvement (CAA, 2000a; 2001a).

A further type of regulation is the 'light-handed' approach or reserve regulation. Here the regulator will only become involved in the price-setting process if the airport's market power is actually abused or if the company and its customers cannot reach agreement. In this case it is the threat of regulation, rather than actual regulation, which is used to provide an effective safeguard against anti-competitive behaviour (Toms, 2001). Sometimes, with so-called 'shadow' reserve regulation, there may be a predetermined regulatory model which will become effective at this stage.

When airports are regulated using price caps, decisions have to be made as to which airport facilities and services are to be considered under the pricing regime. There are two alternative approaches, namely the single till approach when all airport activities are included, and the dual till approach when just the aeronautical aspect of the operation are taken into account. With the single till concept growth in non-aeronautical revenue can be used to offset increases in aeronautical charges. Therefore, for the airport regulator the setting of the price cap will be a complex process which will involve a thorough investigation of both the aeronautical and non-aeronautical areas of operation. Within the airport industry such single till practices, when commercial activities are used to reduce aeronautical charges, are widespread. The single till principles are accepted by the ICAO in its charging recommendations (ICAO, 1992). The rationale for the single till is that without the aeronautical activities, there would be no market for the commercial operations and hence it is appropriate to offset the level of airport charges with profits earned from non-aeronautical facilities. This is the justification which the airlines use in favouring such a system which is clearly likely to bring the lowest level of actual charges for them (IATA, 2000g).

However, some major concerns about this approach have been voiced (Starkie, 2001). As traffic increases, the single till principles will tend to pull down airport charges. This may encourage growth and have the effect of increasing congestion and delays at the airport. The busiest most congested airports are likely to be in the best position to significantly offset commercial revenues against airport charges. Yet it is these airports which need to manage their limited capacity the most. Bringing down the airport charges for such scarce resources makes no economic sense. In addition, the airport industry argues that using commercial revenues to offset aeronautical fees prevents these revenues from being used to help finance capital investment, or to aid the development of better commercial facilities. There is less incentive to develop commercial operations to their full potential (ACI, 2000c).

By contrast, the dual till concept treats the aeronautical and non-aeronautical areas as separate financial entities, and focuses on the monopoly aeronautical airport services. In this case the X factor is established by just considering the aeronautical revenues and costs rather than the total airport operation. This is a difficult task because of having to allocate many fixed and joint costs between the aeronautical and non-aeronautical areas. At the London airports it has been calculated that the transfer from a single till to a dual till approach could mean that airport charges would have to be increased by 35 per cent (Monopolies and Mergers Commission, 1996). The method does, however, provide airports with incentives to develop the commercial side of their business which effectively are uncontrolled, unlike with the single till approach when any development in the commercial areas may well be accompanied by a reduction in aeronautical charges. Clearly there is a major logical argument in not including commercial activities within the regulatory framework since they cannot be considered as monopoly facilities.

While there is widespread evidence of single till practices, there are a few signs of a shift towards a dual till approach. For example, the South African government has stated its intention of moving away from the single till and it has been proposed that Sydney airport should transfer from a single to dual till system. Hamburg is also to be regulated by dual till principles. Elsewhere, in Switzerland for example, the government has proposed that only a certain share of commercial revenues should offset airport charges. In the UK, a considerable debate of the merits of the two systems has taken place prior to the airport regulatory review in 2001 (CAA, 2000b).

In addition to establishing whether a single or dual till approach is to be adopted, the regulator must also decide how the 'price' element of the formula is to be set. The main choice is whether to use a revenue yield or tariff basket methodology. The revenue yield formula means that the predicted revenue per unit (usually passengers, in the case of airports) in the forthcoming year will be allowed to increase by the CPI – X or RPI – X percentage. With the tariff basket definition the weighted average price of a specified 'basket' of tariffs or charges will be allowed to be raised by CPI – X. Both methods have their drawbacks, and their relative strengths have been fiercely debated by regulators and the industry. The tariff basket approach tends to be simpler since it operates directly on charges and is independent of any forecasts. Companies might, however, be encouraged to put the largest increases on the faster-growing traffic since the weights used in the tariff basket are from a previous period. With the revenue yield methodology, an artificial incentive may be created to increase passengers to inflate the denominator in the definition. This could lead to the setting of some charges below the marginal costs of the corresponding services. In general the tariff basket approach is considered to give airports greater incentives to move to a more efficient pricing structure (CAA, 2000c; Monopolies and Mergers Commission, 1997).

It is common practice to set the price cap in relation to the average costs, which will include consideration of any proposed investment programme, additional costs related to improvements in the quality of service and a reasonable rate of return. There has been some debate, however, as to whether industry benchmarking could have a much more active role in this process (CAA, 2000d; CAA, 2001b). Industry best practice could, in theory, replace an assessment of accounting costs as the basis for setting the price cap. This has already been used by the utility regulators for both England and the Netherlands (Burns, 2000; Kunz and Ng, 2000). This would mean that the regulatory control would be independent of any company action inappropriately influencing the key variables used in the regulatory formula, such as inflating the asset base. Alternatively benchmarking could be used much more as a cross-check to internal methods of setting the price, estimating investment costs or assessing the scope for efficiency and service quality improvements.

The adoption of such 'regulatory benchmarking' is fraught with difficulties because of the extensive problems of comparability associated with such an exercise, the subjective nature by which some of the associated problems are overcome and the lack of general consensus as to the optimal method of benchmarking (see Chapter 3). There is also the fundamental issue that such an approach assumes high costs are in fact the result of inefficiency, whereas in reality they may be due to a number of other factors. Only a very detailed assessment of the benchmarking data may be able to identify these factors (Shuttleworth 1999; 2000).

Another area of major concern within any regulatory framework is often the quality of service. When the regulation does not formally establish service standards or require an appropriate quality monitoring system, there may be little incentive for the airport operator to optimize quality. In reducing the service standards at the airport, the operator could be able to soften the blow of the price control. This could be overcome, in theory, by ensuring that there are measures of congestion and delays to assess the adequacy of the airport facilities and by assessing passenger and airline feedback to determine the operational efficiency of the airport. In practice as discussed in Chapter 4, defining service dimensions and attempting to adopt a standardized quality level is extremely difficult – particularly given the different expectations of different types of airlines and passengers. The default price cap mechanism can, in theory, overcome some of these problems.

In Australia, the regulatory framework does include some formal service quality monitoring and reporting. At BAA airports service quality comes under close scrutiny during the review process, although there are no explicit regulations. The review of service quality at London airports has played a major role in encouraging airports to consider entering into service-level agreements with their customers. The airlines are, understandably, in favour of some formal regulatory process to guarantee that service levels are maintained. This, and all of the other regulatory requirements, argue the airlines, should only be agreed after close consultation with the airlines and there should always be an independent review process. Table 5.3 summarizes the airlines views about the airport regulation.

Table 5.3 IATA's criteria for airport economic regulation

1   The starting base charges to be set at an acceptable level
2   The airport to be motivated to improve its productivity
3   Airlines to share the benefits of traffic growth and improved productivity
4   Commercial revenues to be taken into account
5   All charges to be regulated
6   The regulation to be transparent and simple to understand and administer
7   An effective and meaningful consultation process must be established
8   There must be an independent regulatory review process

Source: IATA (2000f).

Regulation examples

In the UK both BAA plc London and Manchester airports have been subject to single till price cap regulation since 1987/8. The price cap is reviewed every five years after an extensive assessment of the airport's operations, financial performance and future plans has been undertaken. The revenue yield approach has been adopted at these airports. Initially the price cap was the same at all airports, being RPI – 1 (Table 5.4). During the second five-year

Table 5.4 The X value used for the UK airport price caps

Airport	X value (%)				
	1987–91	1992–3	1994	1995–6	1997–2002[1]
Heathrow and Gatwick	1	8	4	1	3
Stansted	1	8	4	1	–1
	1988–92	1993–4	1995	1996–7	1998–2002
Manchester	1	3	3	3	5

Note: [1] The normal five-year charging period has been extended to six years because of the timing of decisions related to the possible development of Terminal 5 at Heathrow.
Source: Centre for the Study of Regulated Industries (1999).

review period in the early 1990s the price cap was far more restrictive, particularly for the London airports. For 1997–2002, the London airport formula did
not take account of the loss of EU duty- and tax-free sales in 1999. Instead, a
compensatory 15 per cent increase in charges over two years following abolition of sales was allowed. At Manchester, the abolition was considered when
setting the value of X. These airports can allow most increases in security costs
to be passed straight through to the airline. Initially 75 per cent of costs were
permitted to be passed through with this percentage rising to 95 per cent after
the first five-yearly review. A major impact of this single till regulation at the
London airports has been that the commercial aspects of the business have
been considerably expanded which has simultaneously led to a substantial
reduction in real charges to airline users. At Manchester airport, airport
changes still remain comparatively high which is one of the key reasons for the
more restrictive price cap for the 1998–2002 period.

The regulatory framework for the privatized Australian airports is fairly
similar to that adopted by the UK airports, in that there is a CPI – X formula
which also has a security element – but in this case 100 per cent of the charges
are allowed to be passed through to the airlines (Table 5.5) The Australian
airports use the basket tariff rather than the revenue yield approach. As in the
UK, the price cap has been set for an initial five years with the belief that
maybe another price cap will not be needed after this – although this will be
reviewed before any change in the system is introduced. The Australian regulatory framework has more formal conditions relating to relating to airport access
and quality of service monitoring which do not apply to the UK airports. Other
airports which have adopted a similar price cap regulatory mechanism include
those of Argentina and South Africa. In the first two years after private participation in the South African airports, aeronautical charges were allowed to
increase at the same rate as inflation before an X value to increase efficiency
was introduced.

At Vienna airport a slightly different approach has been adopted taking into
account both inflation rates and traffic growth patterns. The regulation is applied

**Table 5.5 The X value used for the Australian airport
price cap for five years after privatization in 1997/8**

Airport	X value (%)
Adelaide	4.0
Alice Springs	3.0
Brisbane	4.5
Canberra	1.0
Coolangatta	4.5
Darwin	3.0
Hobart	3.0
Launceston	2.5
Melbourne	4.0
Perth	5.5
Townsville	1.0

Source: ACCC (1998).

directly to the charges. There is a sliding scale which protects revenues when there is slow growth, while requiring productivity gains to be made when traffic growth is high. When there is a loss in traffic or no growth, the charges can be increased in line with the CPI. When the annual traffic growth is up to 7 per cent the sliding scale is used with the permitted charge increases being less than the CPI. If the growth is between 7 and 11 per cent, no increase is allowed. Above growth of 11 per cent, the charges must decrease (WDR, 1998).

Elsewhere, the Scottish airports in the UK and the major New Zealand airports are examples of reserve regulation practice. At Auckland and Christchurch airports, the privatization legislation allows for the airports to review their charges every three years and they are not subject to any formal price regulation. The legislation also calls for the regulator to conduct periodic reviews to assess whether price controls are necessary – this relies on general competition law and the threat of further heavy-handed regulation. The Bolivian airports are a rare illustration of airports which are subject to shadow pricing. There is a view that given the fact that airports are operating in an increasingly competitive environment that they should no longer be considered as monopoly providers and consequently in the future more governments will move towards a more reserved or light-handed approach (ABN AMRO, 2000). The Mexican airports are unusual in that they are regulated by the dual till principle. There are no examples of airports using default price cap mechanism although there has been considerable interest shown for such an approach in the UK. A number of the other privatized airports have a more relaxed regulatory regime. In Copenhagen, for instance, there is a set of guidelines which stipulates that the company is allowed to alter its charges in line with costs subject to the company ensuring that it continues to improve the efficiency of its operation.

Slot allocation

The steady rise in air traffic in recent years has put increasing pressure on airport capacity, particularly runway capacity, throughout the world. While timely capacity addition might theoretically provide a solution to this problem, in many cases environmental, physical or financial constraints have meant that in practice this has not been a feasible or desirable option. Instead, attention has been focused on more short term solutions to provide some relief for the shortage of capacity both by consideration of capacity or supply-side approaches and by the assessment of demand management options. In a climate of growing environmental opposition to new developments, such solutions may be politically more acceptable. Supply-side options aim to make more efficient use of existing capacity by improving ATC services and ground-side facilities, and thus provide for incremental increases in traffic. Demand management techniques consider the most appropriate mechanisms for allocating airport slots. Airport slots are usually defined as an arrival or departure time at an airport – typically within a 15- or 30-minute period. They are different from ATC slots which are take-off and landing times assigned to the airline by ATC authorities. There is a view, however, that the definition of a slot should be more broadly defined to take account of all the resources necessary to operate at the airport. Thus the slot would not only be defined by a time period for arriving or departing, but also by the stand, gate and terminal capacity that is needed and the share of environment capacity which is used (Pricewater-houseCoopers, 2000).

Alternative slot allocation procedures have to be considered at airports because the pricing mechanism fails to balance demand with the available supply. As already discussed, the current level of charges at airports and peak/off-peak differentials when in existence have a relatively limited impact on airline demand. Peak charges would have to be considerably higher to ration demand or to be the equivalent to the market-clearing price needed to match supply and demand or 'clear the market'. This is obviously not helped by the widespread acceptance of the single till concept which can pull down the level of charges to below that of the cost of supply (Starkie, 1998).

Currently in all parts of the world except the USA the mechanism for allocating slots is industry self-regulation by using IATA Schedule Co-ordination Conferences. These voluntary conferences of both IATA and non-IATA airlines are held twice a year for the summer and winter season with the aim of reaching consensus on how schedules can be co-ordinated at designated capacity-constrained airports. These airports, which number over 260, are designated at two levels:

1 *Schedule facilitated*: demand is approaching capacity but slot allocation can be resolved through voluntary co-operation.
2 *Fully co-ordinated*: demand exceeds capacity and formal procedures are used to allocate slots. The most important of these procedures is 'grandfather rights'. This means that any airline which has operated a slot in the previous similar season has the right to operate it again. This is as long as the airline operates 80 per cent of the flights – the so-called slot retention requirement or 'use it or lose it' rule. The airline does not, however, have to use its slots for the same services each year and can switch them, for example, between domestic and international routes. Preference is also given to airlines which plan to use a slot more intensively to make the most effective use of the capacity. For example, priority would be given to an airline which plans a daily service rather than one which is less than daily or a service which operates throughout the season rather than only in the peak.

The most recent IATA scheduling guidelines use level 1, 2 and 3 classifications for fully co-ordinated, schedules facilitated and non-coordinated airports. Each of the fully co-ordinated or level 1 airports has an airport co-ordinator, traditionally the national airline of the country, which manages the slot allocation process. Between 1990 and 1999, the number of fully co-ordinated airports increased by 18 per cent, while for schedule facilitation or level 2 airports there was a higher growth of 63 per cent. In 1999 there were 120 fully co-ordinated airports with more than ten others being fully co-ordinated in the summer months only. Around 80 airports were schedule facilitated. Over sixty of the fully co-ordinated were in Europe, with a further thirty in Asia Pacific and ten in Africa. Many US airports are also capacity constrained but do not come under the IATA Scheduling Committee mechanism (ICAO, 2000c).

Within the EU, slot allocation comes under the regulation number 95/93 which was introduced in 1993. While the IATA co-ordination system is voluntary, the

EU rules are a legal requirement. The IATA system developed primarily as a process to co-ordinate schedules and to avoid unnecessary congestion, whereas the EU regulation has other key objectives such as making the most efficient use of capacity and encouraging competition. However, many of the IATA features have been incorporated into the European law. For example, there are three levels of capacity constraints or co-ordination, namely non-coordinated, co-ordinated (comparable to the IATA schedule facilitation airports and fully co-ordinated airports) and each of the airports uses an airport co-ordinator. In 2000, there were thirteen co-ordinated and fifty-seven fully ordinated airports in the EU (PricewaterhouseCoopers, 2000). Table 5.6 shows the co-ordination status of major airports in the EU.

Table 5.6   Slot co-ordination status of major airports in the EU

Country	Fully co-ordinated airports	Non-coordinated airports
Austria		Vienna
Belgium		Brussels – Zaventum[2]
Denmark	Copenhagen – Kastrup	
Finland	Helsinki	
France	Paris – Charles de Gaulle, Orly	
Germany	Berlin – Templehof, Tegel; Schonefeld; Düsseldorf; Frankfurt – Main;	Munich
Greece	Athens; Thessalonika	
Ireland		Dublin[2]
Italy	Milan – Bergamo, Malpensa, Linate[1]; Rome – Fiumcino, Ciampino	
Netherlands	Amsterdam	
Portugal		Faro; Lisbon
Spain		Barcelona; Las Palmas; Madrid; Malaga; Palma de Mallorca
Sweden	Stockholm – Arlanda	Stockholm – Bromma
UK	London – Heathrow, Gatwick, Stansted; Manchester	London – Luton

Notes: [1] In 2000 Milan Linate was co-ordinated having switched from fully co-ordinated when the new Milan Malpensa airport was opened. This airport is the only major airport to be co-ordinated although there are a number of other medium-sized airports which fall into this category.
[2] Brussels and Dublin are expected to change to fully co-ordinated in 2000.
Source: PricewaterhouseCoopers (2000).

An important difference with the European regulation is that the co-ordinator must be independent of all airlines at the airport, thus enabling the process to be more transparent and impartial. In a number of countries, such as Denmark, France, Italy, the Netherlands, Sweden and the UK, an independent company has been established. In order for an airport to become co-ordinated, the legislation theoretically requires that a thorough capacity analysis and consultation process must take place. In practice this has rarely occurred primarily because many of the airports were already fully co-ordinated under the IATA system or perhaps because of some legal constraint such as a limit on aircraft movements at Düsseldorf airport.

The grandfather rights system is used with an 80 per cent slot retention requirement. Airlines are allowed to exchange slots with other airlines but not to trade slots. In reality it is generally recognized that a 'grey market' in slots already exists. Within this context an interesting decision was made in 1999 by the UK High Court when it ruled that the financial payment from BA to Air UK to 'compensate' for the exchange of some highly demanded slots with some less attractive slots did not invalidate the exchange (*Financial Times*, 1999).

The European legislation (Table 5.7), as with the IATA mechanism, aims to encourage new entrants, which are clearly disadvantaged by the grandfather rights system, by giving them preference of up to 50 per cent of any new or unused slots. New entrants are defined as airlines with less than 4 per cent of daily slots at an airport or less than 3 per cent of slots in an airport system, such as the London airports. They are also airlines which have requested slots for a non-stop intra-EU service where two incumbent airlines already operate. Under certain conditions, slots may be reserved for domestic regional services or routes with public service requirements – so called 'ring-fencing'.

Table 5.7   Key features of the 1993 EU slot allocation regulation

Slots are allocated on basis of historical precedence or grandfather rights
Airlines must use slots of 80% of time – 'use it or loss it' rule
There is a slot pool for new or returned slots
50% of slots in the pool are allocated to new entrants
Certain slots can be ring fenced if they are vital for social or economic reasons
Airports are non-coordinated, co-ordinated or fully co-ordinated
Co-ordination status is defined after capacity review and consultation
An independent co-ordinator supervises the allocation of slots

Source: European Commission (1993).

Alternative slot allocation mechanisms

The current scheduling committee system is widely accepted and has succeeded in providing a stable environment for allocating slots. However, there is considerable concern – as pressure on runway capacity continues – that it may not be the most effective mechanism, to manage the scarcity of slots or encourage competition. Critics claim that this procedure gives no guarantee that the scarce airport capacity is used by the airlines who value it most highly, it provides no guide to future investment requirements and is administratively burdensome. Most new entrants are still prevented from competing at airports, especially within Europe, partly because few new slots become available and partly because the definition of new entrant is very limited. There are also a number of issues related to the current structural changes taking place in the airline industry. For example, can a franchise partner gain slots by claiming to be a new entrant with the result of effectively increasing the number of overall slots for the larger incumbent carriers for which it is operating? Should some slots held by airlines in alliances be given up and reallocated to new entrants for competitive reasons?

There have been lengthy debates discussing whether a better system could be introduced (Reynolds-Feighan and Button, 1999). Various regulatory suggestions have been put forward such as giving preference to long-haul international flights, which normally have less flexibility in scheduling than short-haul flights because of night closures and other constraints. This could potentially have an environmental benefit by switching short-haul traffic from air to surface transport. Priority could be given to airlines which cause the least noise nuisance. Scheduled airlines could be favoured over charter airlines and passenger aircraft could have preference over cargo airlines. Alternatively, frequency caps could be placed on certain services once a daily maximum limit has been reached. Another suggestion is to give priority to larger aircraft which make the most efficient use of slots. The traffic distribution rules imposed at London Heathrow airport in the 1980s were an example of such administrative regulation in practice. These rules restricted assess to charter, general aviation and cargo flights – although the charter rule was subsequently relaxed in 1991 (Doganis, 1992).

While such mechanisms can be useful in pursuing some economic, social or environmental objective, they are still likely to be used in combination with grandfather rights. As a result any such system will again share the shortcomings of the traditional system, namely in not ensuring that the scarce runway slots are used by those who value them the most. Therefore, market-based options have also been considered. Within this context, the issue of who actually owns the slot is clearly very crucial. On the one hand, the grandfather rights system, historically giving airlines the rights to use slots for long periods of time, encourages claims of ownership by the airlines. There is no legal sense in this. On the other hand, airports maintain that they have created and own the infrastructure which enables slots to exist, and so the airlines are, in effect, just granted usage rights. Other suggestions are that slots, rather than being considered as a right in perpetuity, should be regarded as long-term concession rights at airports, which have to be handed back after a certain period of time. In reality airlines do view slots as a financial asset which are taken into account whenever airline purchases or mergers take place. There are a number of examples of purchases, for example when BA bought Cityflyer Express based at London Gatwick, and the most important financial asset of the airline being purchased was considered to be its slots. It is difficult to quantify the value of a slot but the 'slot exchange with compensation' between BA and KLM UK provides some guide. It was revealed that BA had paid around US$25 million for eight daily slots – thus representing around US$3 million per slot (O'Toole, 1998).

The simplest of all market-based options is the use of the airport charging mechanism to match demand and supply. However, as previously discussed, the market-clearing price would have to be set at a considerably higher rate that is the current practice with airport charges. An alternative suggestion is to use the auction mechanism as a means of allocating slots. These auctions could be held every six months like the scheduling committees, but this would clearly lead to considerable upheaval and disruption for both airlines and passengers. At the other extreme there could be just one auction, selling the slots rights in perpetuity and then any further changes would have to be implemented through slots actually being traded. Somewhere in between these two options, slots allocated under long-term lease agreements could be an attractive compromise. Individual slots or a combination of slots could be auctioned at one particular time (Jones, Viehoff and Marks, 1993).

Then there could just be a system of slot trading when airlines are able to buy and sell slots – so-called secondary trading. Officially airlines have so far been prevented from such processes, except with the case of four US airports (see 'Slot allocation' in 'The US experience' section). The merits of such a system is that airlines that value the slots the most can buy the slots. Such a mechanism, however, would be bound to favour the large incumbent carriers as they would be the airlines most able to afford to buy the slots. Any such process would also have to be seen as non-discriminatory to comply with international obligations. There is also the issue as to whether it is appropriate for existing slot holders to make windfall profits from slots for which they never actually bought (Doganis, 1992).

Alternatively lotteries for slots could be held. This might potentially overcome this anti-competitive problem but in practice could cause havoc with airlines' schedules and be very disruptive. Slots obtained at one end of the route might not match up with those at the other end and in general there would be a great deal of uncertainty.

Following the introduction of the European slot allocation regulation in 1993, the European Commission has been considering whether a better system of regulation could be introduced, particularly since there has been very little evidence that this regulatory process has encouraged competition or lessened the influence of the major flag carriers at the airports. This is hardly surprising given that the European regime has largely maintained the grandfather rights system. At the same time, delays and congestion at many European airports has increased. After a long period of review and consultation, the European Commission put forward some proposals in 2000. A major suggestion was that all new slots would be allocated on a ten-year concession basis. Slot trading was also proposed through an auction process and once slots were transferred by auction they would be subject to the concession system. No single airline would be able to buy more than 0.5 per cent of any slots in any one season. The 80 per slot retention rule would remain and the definition of new entrant broadened to encourage greater competition among the 50 per cent of new slots. If not enough slots were allocated to new entrants (at least 0.5 per cent), it was suggested that the incumbent airlines would have to give up some slots – on a non-discriminatory and proportionate basis. Another new feature would be consideration of environmental constraints with the possibility of higher priority being given to larger aircraft size or lower priority to services where surface alternatives existed (European Commission, 2000b).

One of the problems with the consideration of slot allocation processes is that often there are too many conflicting objectives. Frequently quoted aims are often to make the best use of existing resources while at the same time encouraging or enhancing competition. But are these two aims, as well as other aspirations, really compatible? For example, it may be feasible to focus on competition but that may cause sudden disruption in schedules. Likewise it may be possible to protect certain routes through ring-fencing but this may not produce the most effective use of the scarce runway slots. Slot trading may ensure that slots are allocated to those who value the slots the most, but it will always tend to favour the large incumbent airlines. Therefore it seems most probable that, in the near future at least, any new system is likely to use a combination of the different approaches, as has been proposed for the EU, rather than adopting just a single mechanism.

Ground handling issues

Ground handling activities at airports are very important to airlines. They impact both on an airline's cost and the quality of service which they provide for their passengers. Ground handling services cover passenger handling, baggage handling, freight and mail handling, ramp handling, fuel and oil handling and aircraft services and maintenance. Such activities are often divided between terminal or traffic handling, which is passenger check-in, baggage and freight handling, and airside or ramp handling, which covers activities such aircraft loading and unloading, cleaning and servicing. Sometimes these services are provided by the airport operators, although at most airports they are provided by airlines or handling agents. Historically often the national airline or airport operator may have had a monopoly or near monopoly in ground handling. Some airport operators such as Milan, Rome, Vienna and Frankfurt airport, which have been heavily involved in such activities, earn very significant revenues from such activities – sometimes over half the total income of the airport. In other cases the airport operator will just earn rental fees and perhaps a small concession fee from the airlines or agents which are providing the handling services. Countries in Europe where the national airline has had a handling monopoly include Spain with Iberia and Greece with Olympic.

A study of European airports in 1992 showed 44 per cent of aircraft movements were handled by airport operators, 27 per cent were self-handled by the national carrier, 8 per cent were handled by the national carrier for other airlines, 7 per cent were handled by independent ground handlers and the remaining 14 per cent were self-handled by other airlines. By contrast, in terms of passenger numbers, only 16 per cent were handled by the airport operator, again 7 per cent by independent ground handlers and the rest by airlines (Deutsche Bank, 1999). For operational reasons, it is far easier to have a number of airlines providing traffic handling rather than ramp handling – given capacity constraints of the equipment and space in the ramp handling areas.

Providers of monopoly services claim that providing competition, particularly for ramp handling would merely duplicate resources, lower efficiency and may also cause considerable apron congestion, particularly at airports which are already at full or near capacity. Critics of the situation, particularly the airlines, claim that ground handling monopolies are pushing up prices and, in some cases, reducing service standards (Bass, 1994). In 1993 the European Commission acknowledged that it had received a number of complaints related to ground handling activities at various airports including Milan and Frankfurt and at the Spanish and Greek airports (Soames, 1997). A study in 1997 of airline turnaround costs at a number of European airports commissioned for the AEA found that the nine most expensive airports all had ramp handling monopolies whereas the next fourteen, in descending order of price, operated in a competitive situation (AEA, 1998).

Within Europe many have argued that air transport cannot be fully liberalized unless the ground handling activities are offered on a full competitive basis. This has resulted in the EU's adoption of the Ground handling directive 96/67. The long-term purpose of this directive is to end all ground handling monopolies and duopolies within the EU by opening up the market to third party handlers, recognizing the right of airlines to self-handle and guaranteeing at least some choice for airlines in the provision of ground handling services (European Commission, 1996). The details of the directive, which provides for phased liberalization of ground handling services, are shown in Table 5.8.

Table 5.8 Key features of the 1996 EU Ground handling directive

From 1 January 1998	Airlines have the right to self-handling for airport terminal services
	For airports with more than 1 million passengers or 25 000 tonnes of freight, airlines have the right to self-handle for baggage, ramp, fuel and freight services
From 1 January 1999	For airports with more than 3 million passengers or 75 000 tonnes of freight, third party handling is allowed
From 1 January 2001	For airports with more than 2 million passengers or 50 000 tonnes of freight, third party handling is allowed
	At least one handler must be independent from the airport operator or dominant airlines with more than 25 % of the traffic

Source: European Commission (1996).

The directive does allow for service providers to be limited in the ramp area. Moreover in some exceptional circumstances airports may be granted temporary exemptions on the basis of space or capacity constraints in order to ease the transition from a monopolistic to competitive situation. Many supporters of ground handling liberalization are concerned that such conditions are only prolonging the existence of monopolies at airports. A number of monopoly handlers in countries such as Germany have applied for such exemptions. Frankfurt airport was one such company but only gained exemption from competition in ramp handling in certain areas. Other airports, such as Düsseldorf have been more successful.

It is too early to assess the impact of the directive – particularly since the introduction of the new ramp handler has in many cases, such as at Frankfurt and Vienna airports, been delayed until 2000. Undoubtedly for the airports which have previously provided monopoly services, there will be a loss of market share to the independent handlers. Airport operators still have the right to perform ground handling but these activities must be separated from their main role as airport operator. To compensate for a lesser involvement at their home airports, a number of airports such as Frankfurt and Rome have been actively expanding their handling activities at other airports. The airline share of the handling market might be expected to remain more constant because, although there might be some shift from monopoly airline handlers to the independent sector, there might also be a shift back to airline handling as a result of an increased number of airline alliance agreements (Mackenzie-Williams, 2000).

The impact of airline alliances of the ground handling industry is a very important issue. In the future ground handlers at airports may achieve economies of scale by negotiating common contracts with all alliance members rather than by consulting with the individual airlines. Some large international handling agents are emerging through a number of corporate mergers and takeovers, encouraged by ground handling liberalization and following the trends of internationalization and globalization in both the airline and airport industry. Swissport which in 2000 provided handling services at 115 airports in twenty countries is owned by SAir group, whereas another global player, GlobeGround, which had contracts at eighty-five airports in twenty-three countries, is owned by Lufthansa. Thus there exists a real threat to independent handlers that these agents will be favoured by members of either the Qualiflyer or Star alliances. As yet, however, there appears to be little concentration of the handling business in this way and independent international handling agents such as Menzies (which bought Ogden Aviation in 2000) serving fifty-seven airports in twenty countries and Servisair, providing handling at ninety-nine airports in eleven countries, have also experienced substantial growth (Coleman, 2000). In 1999 the five largest handling agents in terms of revenue were Globegrand ($707 m), Swissport ($625 m), Frankfurt airport ($445 m), Menzies ($404 m) and Servisair ($340 m) (Pilling, 2001).

The US experience

Airport use agreements

The relationship between airports and airlines in the US is unique and so is worthy of special consideration. The airports and airlines enter into legally binding contracts known as airport use and lease agreements which detail the fees and rental rates which an airline has to pay, the method by which these are to be calculated and the conditions for the use of both airfield and terminal facilities. A key reason for the existence of these agreements has been because private bondholders have demanded the security of such formal relationship between the airports and airlines before investing in the airport.

There are two basic approaches to establishing the airport charges: residual and compensatory. With the residual approach the airlines pay the net costs of running the airport after taking account of commercial and other non-airline sources of revenue. The airlines provide a guarantee that the level of charges and rents will be such that the airport will always break even, and so they take considerable risk. By contrast with the compensatory approach the airlines pay agreed charges and rates based on recovery of costs allocated to the facilities and services that they occupy or use. The risk of running the airport is left to the airport operator. The residual approach, therefore, is more akin to the single till practice, while the compensatory approach is more similar to the dual till approach. Airports have applied these two different approaches in various ways to suit their particular needs and some have adopted a hybrid approach, combining elements of both the residual and compensatory methodologies. A study in 1998 showed that for the large US airports the residual and compensatory approaches were each used by 41 per cent of the airports with the remaining 18 per cent of airports using some kind of hybrid model. For medium-sized airports the relative shares were residual (38 per cent), compensatory (19 per cent) and hybrid (43 per cent) (Federal Aviation Administration/Department of Transportation, 1999).

The use agreements traditionally have been long-term contracts of between twenty and fifty years. In more recent years they have become shorter to reflect the more volatile, deregulated environment. The length of use agreement will normally coincide with any lease agreements which the airlines have with the airport operator. In the USA it is common for airlines to lease terminal space or gates, or even lease or build total terminals – as in the case of JFK airport in New York. The airlines which carry most of the airport's traffic may also play a significant role in airport investment decisions if they agree to the majority-in-interest (MII) clauses in the use agreement. These clauses, which are far more common among residual agreements, typically mean that these signatory airlines have to approve all significant planned developments or changes at the airport. The anti-competitive nature of such agreements can be a problem if other non-signatory airlines are prevented from gaining access to terminal space and gates. As a result there has been an increasing use of 'use it or lose it' clauses in which the control of assets are returned to the airport if the airline does not use the facilities as intended (Federal Aviation Administration/ Department of Transportation, 1999). Capacity improvements which may bring more opportunities for competition may also not be approved by the signatory airlines. As a result some airport operators have tried to reduce the powers of the signatory airlines by requiring MII disapproval rather than approval or have limited the airlines' influence to only major projects. Some airports have discarded MII clauses altogether.

Airport fees and passenger facility charges

The landing fees at US airports are normally very simple, being based on a fixed rate per 1000 lbs. Signatory airlines may pay less. The charges do not vary according to noise levels or peak periods, unlike the practice at some European airports. The level of landing fees tends to be relatively low partly because the airport operator provides a minimal number of services itself. However, there are also a number of government taxes which push up the total amount paid by the airlines and their passengers. There is the air transportation tax, which goes towards the federal aviation trust fund to provide the finance for the airport grants which are available under the AIP. There are also separate taxes relating to agriculture and health inspection, and customs and immigration services.

Unlike most other airports in the world, US airports do not have passenger charges – although some of the costs associated with terminal and gate space which are normally incorporated into the passenger fee may be covered by airline lease payments. United States' airports are not legally allowed to levy passenger charges primarily because of fears that such revenues will be diverted from the airport to be used for non-aviation purposes. However in 1990, the federal government approved the levying of PFCs. These funds go directly to the airports rather into central federal funds as with the air transportation tax. This means that airports have greater control over this type of funding. Passenger facility charges are also largely independent of airline influence, unlike revenue bonds which may require guarantees from the airlines. Although the PFCs are legally and constitutionally different from passengers charges levied elsewhere in the world, they have a similar impact on airlines. The initial PFC legislation, allowed for airports to levy a US$1, US$2 or US$3 fee which had to be spent on identified airport-related projects or could be used to back bonds for the projects. In 2000 it was agreed that the maximum PFC could be raised to US$4.50. Airlines have no veto rights when it comes to PFC-funded projects nor can they have exclusive rights. If PFCs are used by large and medium-sized airports then the airports have to forego up to half their AIP funding.

Passenger facility charges were first used in June 1992. By November 1993 PFCs had been approved at over 150 airports which would generate around US$9 billion. As of 1 January 1998, 264 commercial service airports – almost half of all such airports – imposed a PFC – with about three-quarters of the seventy-one larger airports imposing such a fee. Between 1992 and 1998, the total approved collections for all airports was US$21.9 billion (General Accounting Office, 1999). This had increased to US$24.7 billion by 2000. Large amounts of PFCs have been approved at Denver (US$2331 million), Las Vegas (US$1585 million), Detroit (US$641 million), Boston (US$599 million) and Chicago O'Hare (US$484 million). Some PFCs have been approved for a long time (longer than thirty years) whereas others will be used for as little as three years.

Slot allocation

At most airports in the USA there is no formal slot allocation mechanism, such as the IATA scheduling committees, since these would be in conflict with antitrust laws. This means that instead there is open access to the airports, barring any environmental constraints, and airlines design their schedules independently taking into account any expected delays. This can result in considerable congestion at certain times of the day when many flights are scheduled around the same time.

The exception to this practice is at four airports which are subject to the 'high density airport rule'. This rule was introduced in 1969 by the Federal Aviation Administration (FAA) as a temporary measure to reduce problems of delay and congestion at JFK and La Guardia airports in New York, O'Hare airport in Chicago and Washington National airport (now Washington Reagan). The traffic was divided into three categories, namely air carriers, air taxi (now commuters) and other (primarily general aviation), with a different limit on the number of flights during restricted hours for each category. No slot allocation mechanism was defined but the relevant airlines were given antitrust immunity to discuss co-ordination of schedules.

Initially the rule worked relatively well, but the increase in traffic due to airline deregulation in 1978 and other factors, such as a major air traffic control strike, resulted in a new allocation system being introduced (Langner, 1995). This was the 'buy-sell' rule which effectively meant that after an initial allocation process based on grandfather rights, airlines were then be permitted to buy and sell their slots. Airlines were also allowed to 'lease' slots on a short-term basis. This is the only formal secondary trading market for slots in any part of the world. This trading of slots was limited to domestic operations (international routes being more complex because of international regulation) with air carriers slot being unable to be traded for commuter slots and vice versa. Slots used for essential air services were excluded. There was a 'use or lose it' rule requirement of 65 per cent and a slot pool was established for newly available slots. These were to be reallocated using a lottery – with 25 per cent initially being offered to new entrants. International slots were allowed to be co-ordinated through the IATA scheduling committees (Starkie, 1992; 1994).

Over ten years' experience of this slot trading has led to increasing criticism of the system. There have been few outright sales of air carrier slots and very few new entrants. The established airlines have actually increased their dominance at the airports. This has to be viewed, however, within the context of the US airline industry which itself has become more concentrated (Starkie, 1998). As a result of these concerns, in 2000 it was agreed that there would be a phasing out of these slot rules

A new airport–airline relationship

This chapter has shown how the airline–airport relationship is changing, being driven by trends towards greater competition, privatization and globalization within the industry. Airport charges have come under increased scrutiny from both airlines and governments. Moreover, as more airports are being privatized, economic regulation is becoming more commonplace. In short, the airline–airport relationship is starting to become much more to do with the linking of two privately owned international companies, rather than two state-owned organizations operated within the limits of national laws and regulations.

The normal contract between an airline and an airport traditionally is the published airport conditions of use, which describes the services provided in exchange for the aeronautical fees. This is not a formalized relationship as it does not identify the rights and obligations of both parties. For example, there is no agreement as regards the standard of services to expect and no process is identified should disputes between the airlines and airports arise. A number of airlines have therefore been considering a more appropriate, more clearly defined, contractual relationship with the airports which they serve. In the UK, for example, this type of agreement exists between the privately run railway infrastructure and train operators. For the airport industry, the only country which has the rights and obligations clearly defined and incorporated into a legally binding contract is the USA. The US agreements concentrate on the fees and rentals to be paid, the method by which these are calculated and the conditions of use of the facilities. Formalized service standards are not usually incorporated into these agreements. However, outside the USA, the airline industry has been looking at use agreement from a wider prospective, which includes quality of service aspects.

ACI-Europe has identified six types of use agreements which can exist between airports and airlines. First, there is the basic agreement which covers what the airlines receive for the main airport charges or the basic plus agreement which also identifies what additional facilities and services are available at the airport and their cost. Second, there is the facility agreement which is an additional arrangement between one or more airlines relating to just part of an airport. Then there are two types of service level agreements, either a one-way commitment by the airport operator to achieve defined service quality standards or a two-way commitment by both the airport and airlines to reach the required quality levels. Finally, there is the strategic partnership agreement (SPA) which, as the name suggests, is more strategic and covers areas such as future financial investment and rights, and obligations for both airlines and airports (ACI-Europe, 1999; Cruickshank, 2000).

In 1997, IATA set up a working group to develop a generic use agreement or SPA which could be used worldwide and adapted according to local circumstances. The airlines claim that such agreements could clarify the airline–airport relationship by identifying clear rights and obligations, protect both airlines and airports from uncertainty and risk by providing financial guarantees, and provide more financial security, as in the case of the USA, for the increasing number of private airports which are dependent on commercial borrowing. They could also help to minimize the conflict between the two parties – thus, perhaps, lessening the need for government economic regulation (Clayton, 1997; De La Camara, 1998). British Airways has suggested that a use agreement should contain the following elements: duration and termination; services to be provided in return to charges; service standards; additional services, rentals, fees and charges; capital expenditure; insurance and liabilities; security and policing; terminal navigation services; and disputes and arbitration (Monopolies and Mergers Commission, 1997). Such far-reaching SPAs have yet to be adopted at any airport although service level agreements are now being tested at a few airports.

References and further reading

ABN AMRO (2000). *Pan-European Airports Review*. ABN AMRO.

ACI-Europe (1998). *Big Issues: Airport Charges*. ACI-Europe working paper.

ACI-Europe (1999). *Airport Use Agreements*. ACI-Europe working paper.

AIB, SH&E and Warburg Dillon Read (1999). *Review of Strategic Options for the Future of Aer Rianta*. Report to the Minister for Public Enterprise and the Minister for Finance.

Air Transport Group (1998). *User Costs at Airports in Europe, SE Asia and the USA*. Research report 6, Cranfield University.

Airports Council International (ACI) (2000a). Pre-financing of airport capital expenditures. ANSConf Working Paper 52, ICAO.

Airports Council International (ACI) (2000b). Recommendations for new ICAO guidelines on pre-financing of airport capital expenditures. *Ansconf Working Paper No 55*, ICAO.

Airports Council International (ACI) (2000c). The single till. ANSConf working paper 48, ICAO.

Association of European Airlines (AEA) (1998). *Benchmarking of Airport Charges*. AEA.

Australian Competition and Consumer Commission (ACCC) (1998). *Economic Regulation of Airports – an Overview*. ACCC.

Bass, T. (1994). Infrastructure constraints and the EC. *Journal of Air Transport Management*, **1**(3), 145–150.

Burns, P. (2000). The use of benchmarking in regulatory proceedings. CAA workshop on benchmarking of airports: methodologies, problems and relevance to economic regulation, London, September.

Centre for Study of Regulated Industries (1999). *Airport Statistics 1998/9*. CRI.

Civil Aviation Authority (CAA) (1998). *The Single European Aviation Market: The First Five Years*. CAP 685, CAA.

Civil Aviation Authority (CAA) (2000a). The CAA approach to economic regulation and work programme for the airport reviews. Position paper, CAA.

Civil Aviation Authority (CAA) (2000b). The single till and the dual till approach to the price regulation of airports. Consultation paper, CAA.

Civil Aviation Authority (CAA) (2000c). Issues for the airport reviews. Consultation paper, CAA.

Civil Aviation Authority (CAA) (2000d). The use of benchmarking in airport reviews. Consultation paper, CAA.

Civil Aviation Authority (CAA) (2001a) Direct consulting between airports and users. Consultation paper, CAA.

Civil Aviation Authority (CAA) (2001b) Pricing structures and economic regulation. Consultation paper, CAA.

Clayton, E. (1997). A new approach to airport user charges. *Journal of Air Transport Management*, **3**(2), 95–8.

Coleman, N. (2000). European ground handling: new competitive dynamics. *Aviation Strategy*, October, 8–9.

Cruickshank, A (2000). Airport–airline agreements: what is the way forward?' University of Westminster/Cranfield University Airport Economics and Finance Symposium, March.

De La Camara, J. (1998). Airport charges and airport finance – the airline's perspective. ACI Airport Financial Management Seminar, Fortaleza, March.

Dennis, N. (1996). Airport charges – the key developments. University of Westminster/Cranfield University Airport Economics and Finance Symposium, March.

Department of the Environment, Transport and the Regions (DETR) (2000). *Air Traffic Forecasts for the United Kingdom 2000*. DETR.

Deutsche Bank (1999). *European Airports: Privatization Ahead*. Deutsche Bank.

Doganis, R. (1992). *The Airport Business*. Routledge.

Doganis, R. (2001). *The Airline Business in the Twenty-first Century*. Routledge.

European Commission (1993). *Council Regulation 95/93 on Common Rules for the Allocation of Slots at Community Airports*, 18 January.

European Commission (1996). Council Directive 96/67/EC on access to the groundhandling market at Community airports. *Official Journal of the European Communities*, L 272/36, App. A.

European Commission (2000a). The European regulatory framework. *ANSConf Working Paper 76*, ICAO.

European Commission (2000b). Draft proposal for amending council regulation No 95/93 of 18 January 1993 on common rules for the allocation of slots at Community airports. EC.

Federal Aviation Administration/Department of Transportation (1999). Airport business practices and their impact on airline competition. FAA/DOT.

Financial Times (1999). Air slots can be traded, High Court rules. *Financial Times*, 26 March, p. 20.

General Accounting Office (1999). *Passenger Facility Charges: Program Implementation and the Potential Effects of Proposed Changes*. GAO.

George, A. (2000). Industry fears EC slot shake-up plans. *Airline Business*, November, 23.

Gethin, S (1998). Airport charges proposal general fierce debate. *Jane's Airport Review*, May, 6–7.

Gill, T. (1998). Weakened by taxation. *Airline Business*, March, 35–7.

Hague Consultancy (2001). *Benchmark Airport Charges 1999*. Hague Consultancy.

Helm, D. and Jenkinson, T. (eds) (1998). *Competition in Regulated Industries*. Oxford University Press.

International Air Transport Association (IATA) (2000a). Charges discounts. *Ansconf Working Paper No 82*, ICAO.

International Air Transport Association (IATA) (2000b). Peak/off-peak charging. *Ansconf Working Paper No 81*, ICAO.

International Air Transport Association (IATA) (2000c). Marginal pricing. *Ansconf Working Paper No 80*, ICAO.

International Air Transport Association (IATA) (2000d). Forward pricing. *Ansconf Working Paper No 31*, ICAO.

International Air Transport Association (IATA) (2000e). Airport networks and airport cross-ownership. *Ansconf Working Paper No 33*, ICAO.

International Air Transport Association (IATA) (2000f). Airport economic regulation. *Ansconf Working Paper No 27*, ICAO.

International Air Transport Association (IATA) (2000g). The single till. *Ansconf Working Paper No 30*, ICAO.

International Civil Aviation Organization (ICAO) (1992). Statement by the Council to contracting states on charges for airports and air navigation services. 9082/4, ICAO.

International Civil Aviation Organization (ICAO) (2000a). Pre-funding of projects through charges. *Ansconf Working Paper No 31*, ICAO.

International Civil Aviation Organization (ICAO) (2000b). Economic regulation. *Ansconf Working Paper No 9*, ICAO.

International Civil Aviation Organization (ICAO) (2000c). Capacity management and slot allocation. *ANSConf Working Paper No 11*, ICAO.

Jane's Airport Review (2000). Italy and Spain warned over fees. *Jane's Airport Review*, September, 6.

Jones, I., Viehoff, I. and Marks, P (1993). The economics of airport slots. *Fiscal Studies*, **14**(4), 37–57.

Kunz, K. and Ng, C. (2000). Benchmarking and economic regulation: introduction and overview. CAA workshop on benchmarking of airports:

methodologies, problems and relevance to economic regulation, London, September.

Langner, S. (1995). Contractual aspects of transacting in slots in the United States. *Journal of Air Transport Management*, **2**(3/4), 151–61.

Mackenzie-Williams, P. (2000). Ground handling – the story so far. *International Airport Review*, **4**(3), 68–71.

Mecham, M. (2000). SFO flights delays by targeting United. *Aviation Week and Space Technology*, 1 May, 32–3.

Monopolies and Mergers Commission (1996). A report on the economic regulation of the London airport companies. MMC.

Monopolies and Mergers Commission (1997), A report on the economic regulation of Manchester airport. MMC.

O'Toole, K. (1998). KLM accounts hint at the true worth of BA slots at Heathrow. *Flight International*, 8–14 July, 8.

Pagliari, R. (1998). Taxing for take-off. *Avmark Aviation Economist*, September/October, 10–12.

Pilling, M. (2001). Empire building. *Airline Business*, January, 52–54.

PricewaterhouseCoopers (2000). *Study of Certain Aspects of Council Regulation 95/93 on Common Rules for the Allocation of Slots at Community Airports*. PricewaterhouseCoopers.

Reynolds-Feighan, A. and Button, K. (1999). An assessment of the capacity and congestion levels at European airports. *Journal of Air Transport Management*, **5**, 113–34.

Schiphol Group (2000). *Annual Report 1999*. Schiphol Group.

Shuttleworth, G. (1999). Regulatory benchmarking: a way forward or a dead-end?' *Energy Regulation Brief*, National Economic Research Associates.

Shuttleworth, G. (2000). Price caps, benchmarking and efficient costs. CAA workshop on benchmarking of airports: methodologies, problems and relevance to economic regulation, London, September.

Soames, T (1997). Ground handling liberalization. *Journal of Air Transport Management*, **3**(2), 83–94.

Starkie, D. (1994). The US market in airport slots. *Journal of Transport Economics and Policy*, September, 325–9.

Starkie, D. (1992). *Slot Trading at United States Airports*. Putnam, Hayes and Bartlet Ltd.

Starkie, D. (1998). Allocating airport slots: a role for the market? *Journal of Air Transport Management*, **4**, 111–16.

Starkie, D. (2001). Reforming UK airport regulation. *Journal of Transport Economics and Policy*, **35**(1), 119–35.

Toms, M. (1994). Charging for airports: the new BAA approach. *Journal of Air Transport Management*, **1**(2) 77–82.

Toms, M. (2001). Thoughts on airport regulation. University of Westminster/Cranfield University Airport Economics and Finance Symposium, March.

Warburg Dillon Read (WDR) (1998). *Airports Review 1998*. WDR.

6

The provision of commercial facilities

The importance of non-aeronautical revenues

A key development in the evolution of the airport industry has been the increase in the dependence on non-aeronautical or commercial revenues. This chapter will discuss the generation of non-aeronautical revenues by looking at the market for commercial services and assessing how the facilities can be planned and managed. It will consider factors which influence commercial performance. The most significant development of the late 1990s, namely the abolition of intra-EU duty- and tax-free revenue, will also be discussed. The focus of this chapter will be on individual consumers who buy commercial goods/services at airports. There are, of course, other consumers such as the airlines and handling agents who also generate concession and rental revenues by paying for the use of office space, check-in-decks, lounges, in-flight kitchens and so on. These activities are covered in Chapter 5 which considers the airport–airline relationship.

There have been a number of factors which have contributed to the growth in dependence on non-aeronautical revenues. First, moves towards commercialization and privatization within the industry have given airports greater freedom to develop their commercial policies and diversify into new areas. A more business-oriented approach to running airports has also raised the priority given to commercial facilities. Such facilities were traditionally considered to be rather secondary to providing essential air transport infrastructure for airlines. Managers are now eager to adopt more creative and imaginative strategies and to exploit all possible aeronautical and non-aeronautical revenue generating opportunities.

Moreover, the airlines have been exerting increasing pressure on the airport industry to control the level of aeronautical fees which are being levied. A more competitive environment and falling yields have forced many airlines to focus on major cost-saving initiatives such as out-sourcing, reductions in staff numbers, and the pegging of the level of wages. Increasingly airlines are demanding that airports adopt such cost-cutting and efficiency saving measures themselves, rather than raising their charges to the airlines (Doganis, 2000). Thus airport charges have become subject to more and more scrutiny from the airlines – particularly from the new breed of low cost airlines in Europe. In addition the ability of some airports to increase aeronautical charges is now restricted by government regulation as has been the case with BAA plc and Australian airports post-privatization (see Chapter 5). The impact of these pressures on the level of aeronautical charges, either from the airlines themselves or regulatory bodies, has encouraged the airports to look to alternative ways of increasing their revenues and growing their businesses by giving greater attention to commercial facilities. In effect the airports have had to broaden their horizons in managing their businesses.

At the same time, increasing numbers of people are travelling through airports and making more frequent trips. Hence passengers are becoming more sophisticated and experienced airport shoppers, and are generally much better informed. As a result of this, airport shoppers are becoming more demanding not only in the quality of service which is provided, but also in the range and value for money of the commercial facilities on offer. This reflects general trends in the high street where consumers have become more discerning with quality, value and choice at the top of their priorities (Freathy and O'Connell, 1998). Admittedly it is difficult to determine entirely whether the raised expectations at airports have been caused by a genuine need or desire of the consumers for expanded facilities or whether an airport's drive to maximize its commercial income by becoming a shopping centre has merely changed the expectations of passengers. It is also true to say that this increased emphasis on commercial facilities has not been welcomed by all the travelling public with significant groups of passengers, particularly those from the business community, often desiring a quick route through the airport as uncluttered as possible from the distraction of numerous shops and catering outlets.

Increasing airport competition, especially between airport hubs, has also played a role in the development of non-aeronautical revenues. The main reason for why a passenger will choose a certain airport will, of course, be the nature of air services which that airport offers and the convenience of the airport's location. Consideration of the retail and other commercial facilities is bound to be secondary. Transfer passengers may, however, be more influenced by the commercial facilities if they cannot perceive any significant difference between the convenience and quality of the choice of connecting flights at different airports. Certain airports, such as Amsterdam Schiphol and Singapore Changi, have run high-profile marketing campaigns emphasizing the quality and good value of the commercial facilities on offer to transfer passengers. Other airports have gone one stage further. For example, Manchester gave discounts on duty-free purchases to transfer passengers as part of their 'Manchester Connects' strategy to increase the use of the airport as an inter-line hub. In the Middle East a number of the airports such as Abu Dhabi, Dubai and Bahrain try to use their duty- and tax-free shops as a way of captur-ing competing traffic, particularly by using incentives like raffles with high value prizes, such as luxury cars.

The market for commercial facilities

Who buys at airports?

The airport environment is a unique location for shopping and other commer-cial facilities. The main shoppers, the passengers, make up a large captive market. They often tend to be more affluent than the average and they may have time on their hands to have a quick meal or snack. They may spend spontaneously to acquire the last minute essential or discount purchase for a holiday, or souvenirs and gifts while returning. They may even spend just to dispose of the last of their foreign currency. Airport retailing is, however, fundamentally different from high street retailing since passengers are going to the airport to catch a flight rather than to shop. Consequently the passengers will be far less familiar with the airport shopping environment than with their neighbourhood shops and this, coupled with a fear of missing the flight, may impose a sense of anxiety on the passengers.

To fully harness the commercial development potential of the airport traffic, the range of facilities on offer and even the product selection should match very closely the preferences and needs of the specific passengers types at the airports. To achieve this aim, airports, together with their retailing and catering partners, have increasingly been devoting more resources to getting to know their customers. At the most basic level this involves an analysis of the air services offered and the origin and destination of travellers. Even this detail of infor-mation about the market, which is automatically collected at airports, is the envy of most high street retailers. In addition, duty- and tax-free retailers can get information about travellers from their boarding passes which are shown when purchases are made. In many cases this is supplemented by market research, of varying degrees of sophistication, which will investigate the demographic, geographic and behavioural features of the passengers. Such research will often aim to determine who shops at airports and what they buy, who does not shop at airports and why, and attitudes towards the range of facilities on offer and the value for money of the products. This type of research needs to be updated regularly as customer demands and perceptions are continuously changing.

BAA plc, like other large European airport operators, regularly undertakes market research regarding commercial facilities. Results have shown that on average 53 per cent of passengers considered airport shopping to be important or very important. It was considered more important to certain subsegments such as eighteen to twenty-four year olds (64 per cent) and less important for others such as UK business travellers (34 per cent). Overall 70 per cent of passengers considered catering to be important or very important. The UK leisure market gave it a higher rating (77 per cent) while the European business market gave it a much lower rating. BAA plc has also investigated the non-buying share of the passenger population at its airport and the factors which might entice them to buy. Price was the key reason given, with 12 per cent of the sample claiming that they would shop if the prices were reduced by a tenth. A further 47 per cent, many of whom were UK leisure passengers, would have shopped if the prices were reduced by a quarter. Prior knowledge of the prices on offer would have encouraged 22 per cent more passengers to make purchases. Sixteen per cent said they would shop if they had more time (an extra hour) at the airport. Twenty-two per cent of the passengers, a significant share of whom were UK business travellers, claimed that they had no interest in the shops and would not be persuaded to buy (Maiden, 1995).

These examples illustrate the different spending profiles and preferences of different types of passengers. Leisure passengers have traditionally been favourites for impulse buys and the use of catering facilities. The new breed of leisure passengers on low-cost carriers often tend to have a lower spend profile, since they are more cost-conscious customers. Long-haul leisure passengers tend to spend more than short-haul leisure travellers. Regular business travellers typically have a shorter dwell time and are less likely to browse in shops. Moreover, the widespread adoption of airline lounges for business and first-class customers has further discouraged these passenger from having spare time to visit the main terminal shops. As a result of this business travellers make purchases relatively infrequently – although their average spend on a purchase tends to be high. Business travellers also tend to make high use of certain facilities such as banks, car hire and airport hotels. Within the business market there is an increasing number of women travellers who have different needs and preferences from the more traditional male traveller.

Then there are transfer passengers. They are unlikely to make use of facilities such as banks and post offices, and obviously will not need car hire or car parking facilities. They may want to make some retail purchases, particularly if the duty- and tax-free prices are competitive, but this will only be possible if there is sufficient time between flights. It is hard for an airport to maximize the commercial opportunities from transfer passengers if it also wishes to maximize its efficiency as a hub by providing swift connections. At most major hubs there will also be passengers who spend a considerable length of time in the airside area. Various airports have developed some quite imaginative airside facilities and services which can be shared between these and local passengers. For example, Singapore Changi airport has a swimming pool, a sauna, a karaoke lounge and a putting green and, if the transfer passengers stay for longer than four hours, they can go on a bus tour of Singapore. Amsterdam airport has an art gallery and casino. Most airports have business facilities such as meeting rooms, secretarial support, internet access and so on. A number of airports also have fitness and health centres. Vienna airport, for instance, opened its Wellness Plaza in 1999 where passengers can experience different massage techniques and make use of the fitness bar, solarium and showers. Bangkok airport offers head and foot massage, Frankfurt airport provides dental, optical, and foot reflexology services and a clinic which has become a specialist centre for laser operations to repair damaged shoulder and knee joints!

BAA plc has identified four key traveller groups associated with UK nationals – each of which have different shopping characteristics. First, there is the mass market leisure flyers who travel just once a year and are in the mood for treating themselves. They are impulse buyers and they tend to buy duty-free if they can. Then there are the young upmarket leisure flyers who travel several times a year and are high spenders. They will be brand conscious and prepared to pay for quality products. Older upmarket leisure flyers again travel several times a year and have a high disposable income. They will treat themselves at airports although they will be price-conscious buyers. They will make duty-free purchases if they can, and perfumes will be popular. Finally, there are the time-starved frequent business flyers who will be attracted by 'one-off' promotions and electronic products. They will use the airport as a convenience place to shop (Maiden, 2000). Another way of looking at passenger shopping is by segmenting the customers by behaviour. For instance, distinctions can be made between entertainment shopping (gift/novelty purchasing), purposive shopping (confectionery, books, toiletries), time-pressed shopping (last minute/emergency purchases), convenience shopping (wide choice of known brand names), essential shopping (restaurants/cafeterias, foreign currency exchange, insurance) and lifestyle shopping (high-quality international brand purchases) (Institute for Retail Studies, 1997).

Factors such as nationality, age, occupation and socio-economic group will also influence spending and shopping behavioural patterns. Nationals from countries in Scandinavia, which have relatively high taxes on alcohol, are favourites for buying such products at airport shops. A survey at Heathrow in the mid-1990s showed that 54 per cent of Scandinavians bought duty-free goods compared with 27 per cent of Japanese, 25 per cent of UK residents and 7 per cent of US residents. By contrast with tax-free goods other than perfumes and cosmetics, 35 per cent of Japanese made purchases, compared with 20 per cent of Scandinavians and 10 per cent of both UK and US residents (Maiden, 1995). The Japanese have traditionally been very high spenders at airports especially on gifts to take home to friends and relatives – although this is not so common for the younger more independent Japanese travellers. Americans, however, although being very fond of shopping have traditionally not expected to do their shopping at airports. As regards age differences, younger travellers tend to make much heavier use of facilities such as electronic entertainment zones and internet cafés which are becoming commonplace at many airports.

Most of the airport commercial facilities historically were provided for passengers. Many airports, however, have now recognized the commercial opportunities which exist with other consumer groups which use the airport and have introduced facilities wholly or partially for their needs. The airports have thus exploited their commercial potential of being business or commercial centres which generate, employ and attract a large number of visits – rather than just providing facilities for passengers who choose to use the airport. For example, staff employed by the airport operators and by the airlines, handling agents, concessionaires and governments agencies may wish to use airport commercial facilities, particularly as they may not be able to combine a visit to their local shops and their working life at the airport. Workers from nearby office complexes, or from airport industrial estates, may find the airport facilities useful. Popular services include supermarkets, banking services, hairdressers, chemists and dry-cleaners. Some of these services may used by arriving passengers – another potential market sub-segment which is generally considered to have significant spending potential but has only more recently been recognized by most airports.

Airports may also be attractive to the local residential community as an alternative shopping centre – especially if the airport is relatively uncongested and easily accessible with good road and rail links. Sometimes local residents will be encouraged to the airport by free parking or a certain period of free parking if a purchase is made. The growing popularity of the use of initiatives to encourage public transport use, however, may be in conflict with such commercial strategies. Indeed for certain large airports with severe surface access problems, encouraging additional visits to the airport will be the last policy that they want to adopt. Opposition may also be voiced from nearby local shopping centres as has been the case at London Gatwick airport with shopping facilities at the neighbouring town of Crawley. Environmentalists, such as the Friends of the Earth in the UK, consider such developments to be flouting government policy, which is against out-of-town retailing.

Airports may be particularly popular as alternative shopping centres if there are legal restrictions on shopping hours imposed on the high street. For example, Frankfurt airport was one of the first airports to develop its landside shops into a shopping mall concept, benefiting from downtown shopping hour limits which were only relaxed in the mid-1990s. Amsterdam airport opened its landside shopping 'Plaza' of forty shops in 1995. This has a shopping area of 5400 square metres and is easily accessible by private and public transport. Many of the shops are well-known quality international branded outlets which are relatively difficult to find elsewhere in the Netherlands. Only around 30 per cent of the Plaza's customers are passengers (Gray, 1998a).

Meeters and greeters and other visitors to the airport will also need catering services, and, perhaps, additional facilities such as florists and gifts and souvenir shops. Car-parking revenue can be generated from them. Air travel still holds a strange fascination for certain people and for these enthusiasts specialist shops and merchandise can be sold. Viewing platforms, tours and exhibitions can also be provided on a commercial basis. They can have a dual purpose in acting as a public relations function or service to the community. For instance, Munich airport visitors park is one of Bavaria's most popular day-trip destinations, consisting of an interactive multimedia centre, an observation hill, a 'behind the scenes at the airport' display, guided bus tours and catering and retail facilities. Visitors may also be attracted to airports if leisure facilities are provided. A notable example is the new Kuala Lumpur airport. Within the boundary of this airport there is a Formula One motor-racing track, an adventure park, rock climbing, a shooting range, golf course, cinema and equestrian park!

For the business community, conferences and meeting facilities can be provided (Table 6.1). Most major airports offer these. The good transport links

Table 6.1   The different markets for commercial facilities at airports

Market segment	Facilities provided
Passengers (departing/arriving, terminal/transfer, business/leisure, different nationalities, ages etc.)	Wide range of retail, catering and other essential and leisure services dependent on passenger type
Workers at the airport and in the surrounding areas	Convenience shops, banks, chemists and other essential services
Local residents	Shops, catering and leisure services
Visitors – meeters and greeters	Catering, gift and souvenir shops
Visitors – air transport enthusiasts	Specialist aviation shops, tours, visitor terraces, exhibitions, catering
Local businesses	Office/meeting facilities, land for business development/light industry

which airports generally possess can make them ideal for international business events. These facilities can be shared by business passengers, local businesses and other customers. For example, Munich airport opened its new commercial centre in 1999 consisting of offices, conference facilities, medical clinic, catering and shops – aiming to appeal to a number of the different consumer groups at the airport. The new offshore Inchon International airport in Korea will have a business centre with two hotels with over 1000 rooms, a shopping mall of 12 000 square metres and six office buildings on 39 000 square metres (Kim, 2000). Numerous airports have also expanded beyond the boundaries of the traditional airport business by using neighbouring land for hotels, office complexes, light industries, freight warehousing, distribution centres and business parks. The small UK regional airport of Southend relies on its property business for its survival and, unusually, is involved in buying electricity in bulk and then reselling it. Cork airport in Ireland, is one airport of many which opened a business/technology park in 1998. One of the larger developments is Brisbane airport which, in partnership with other organizations, has created the Australia TradeCoast economic development area which uses 2 700 000 square metres of airport-owned land.

While airports can measure their potential passenger market quite accurately, it is much more difficult to obtain meaningful figures for the other consumers at an airport. A 1995 survey of forty-seven European airports showed that on average meeters and greeters made up 34 per cent of the customer volume (Schwarz, 1996). At individual airports the size of this market is quite varied, which must partly reflect traffic and cultural characteristics but also the methodology used to estimate the figures. For example, in 1999 it was assumed that in addition to the 8.5 million passengers, there were 8.5 million visitors and meeters and greeters and 3 million staff/employees at Ben Gurion airport in Tel Aviv (Kostelitz, 2000). At Frankfurt airport it was estimated that 46 million passengers were joined by 7 million meeters and greeters, 8 million other visitors and in addition there were 60 000 employees at the airport (Middecke, 2000). In the same year Malpensa Milan airport was predicted to handle 3.25 million meeters and greeters and 15 000 airport staff along with 13 million passengers (Amore, 1999).

At most airports, however, it is the sales in the airside area of the airport which still brings in the most revenue for the airport operator – although the abolition of Intra-EU duty- and tax-free sales may have a major impact on this in the future. A study of fifteen airports of varying size in Europe in 1998 showed that on average landside shops occupied 37 per cent of an airport's retail space but only 22 per cent of total sales. Airside sales per square metre were 6.8 times greater than in landside shops, and sales per passenger were thirty-two times greater. At these airports, 64 per cent of the landside purchasers were passengers, 16 per cent employees, 13 per cent meeters and greeters, with the remaining 7 per cent being local residents and others. (Meznarsic, 1999). Some landside facilities such as post offices, travel agents or booking agencies may not bring in huge amounts of revenues to the airport but may be perceived as adding value to the airport product from the point of view of the passenger and other consumers.

Geographical characteristics

Many of the most successful airports in terms of non-aeronautical income generation are situated within Europe. This is due to a number of general factors such as the large international traffic volumes within Europe and the relatively high income per capita. European airports have also led the way in terms of commercialization and privatization trends with the development of non-aeronautical revenues being one of the most notable outcomes of these more advanced evolutionary stages of the airport industry. The 1999 ACI airport economics survey (ACI, 2000) shows that European airports as a whole generated US$10 per passenger from non-aeronautical sources in 1997 compared with a global mean of US$7 (Figure 6.1). Concession income is the most important non-aeronautical revenue source. Shopping generates the most concession income and is likely to continue to do so in spite of the abolition

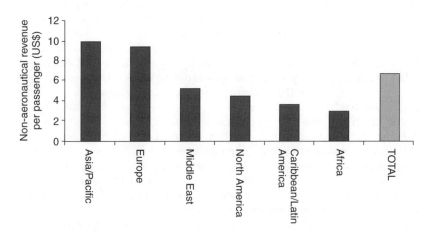

Figure 6.1 Non-aeronautical revenue per passenger at ACI airports by world region, 1998
Source: ACI (2000).

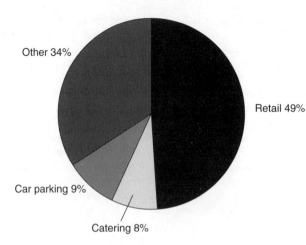

Figure 6.2 Concession revenue: Brussels airport, 1999
Source: Annual report.

of EU duty- and tax-free sales. For example, shop or retail sales accounted for 49 per cent of all concession revenue at Brussels airport in 1999 (Figure 6.2).

According to ACI non-aeronautical revenue per passenger for North American airports was much less than in Europe – averaging only US$5. These airports are dominated by domestic passengers who spend less. Also at hub airports, emphasis is placed on swift efficient connections rather than providing passengers with the time to browse and shop. The dependency on the car and the lack of adequate public transport access to many airports means that the two single most important non-aeronautical sources were car parking (US$1.87 per passenger) and car hire (US$0.99 per passenger). Shopping was much less important, with a revenue per passenger value of only US$0.66 compared with US$6.47 in Europe. Again the important role that the car plays can be seen when looking at the concession sources at the Washington airports (Figure 6.3). Car parking and car hire together accounted for three-quarters of the concession revenues compared with much less at Brussels airport. For the Washington airports, the ratio of catering to retail revenue was also much higher. This is typical of most US airports, which have relatively more of the total commercial area being allocated to catering concessionaires. This also reduces the overall concession income per square metre for US airports.

It is surprising that the USA, which is world famous for its shopping malls, only began to fully recognize the commercial potential of airports in the 1990s – well behind the European airports. Branded shops and catering outlets were rarely found at US airports until this time, in spite of their widespread use elsewhere in the country. The turning point came about in the early 1990s at around the time when BAA plc acquired a fifteen-year contract to manage the commercial facilities at Pittsburgh airports. The company replaced the typical newsagent outlet and general store with well-known brands and developed other concepts which it had used with its European airports, such as

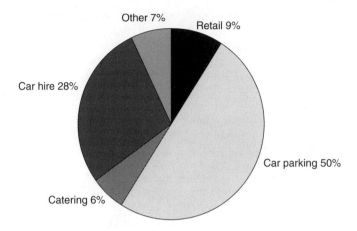

Figure 6.3 Concession revenue: Washington airports, 1999
Source: Annual report.

pre-ordering products. Similar practices have been introduced by BAA plc at Indianapolis, Newark and Harrisburg airports. Another forerunner in airport commercial development in the USA was Portland airport which was of the first airports to introduce a mall concept to the airport with its 'Made in Oregon' mall (Citrinot, 1999a).

Duty-free and tax-free sales are not very significant at most North American airports with the exception of certain airports such as San Francisco, Los Angeles and Honolulu which handle a large proportion of Asian traffic. The situation in Asia is very different where duty-free and tax-free income is much more important. Compared with in Europe, where traditionally most of the sales have been associated with core products such as liquor, tobacco and fragrance, in Asia the duty-free and tax-free revenue is generated from a much wider range of products. There are also arrival duty-free and tax-free shops at many of the major Asian airports. Singapore Changi airport has built up a worldwide reputation for good shopping – a reputation which new airports such as Kuala Lumpur's Sepang and Hong Kong's Chek Lap Kok also wish to acquire.

The passenger profile at these airports is changing with the upper-class high-spending Asian nationals being joined by an increasing volume of Asian travellers who are of a younger average age and are from the rapidly growing middle classes. Moreover, inbound passengers are now a much more diverse, more cost-conscious group of travellers (O'Conner, 1999). Spending patterns are consequently changing, with more emphasis being placed on 'value-for-money' goods. Nevertheless the ACI survey still found that the average non-aeronautical spend per passenger in this region was the highest globally – albeit that the sample was dominated by large airports such as Singapore and Seoul which handle international passengers who have higher spending patterns. The Asian sample also included the major airports from Australia who have been developing their commercial facilities because of privatization and also due to the downward pressure on airport charges due to regulation.

The Middle East is an interesting area where there is a considerable amount of competition between airports and where shopping is used as a major marketing tool to attract passengers. For instance airports such as Abu Dhabi, Bahrain and Dubai have developed extensive duty-free facilities. In Abu Dhabi and Dubai prices can be kept low since the shops are operated as a division of the Department of Civil Aviation and can be subsidized. In Bahrain, the management expertise of Aer Rianta International has been brought in to run the shops. All three airports have a history of launching major marketing initiatives to strength passenger awareness of the shopping services and to encourage passengers to use their airports.

In other areas of the world, such as in Africa and South America, there generally tends to be less reliance on non-aeronautical income. This is partly because many of the airports in these regions have relatively small numbers of passengers and also because the spending power of the local population is more limited. The airport management, often closely tied to its government owners, has neither the expertise nor the commercial pressures to fully exploit the non-aeronautical opportunities at these airports. The developing economic conditions in some countries, particularly in South America, are encouraging growth in traffic and broadening the customer base for commercial facilities. In addition in a number of these countries the airports have been privatized and have brought in experienced European and North American airport managers who are introducing many tried and tested commercial strategies which have been used elsewhere.

Approaches to the provision of commercial facilities

Most airports have come a long way since they just provided the generic newspaper, book and gift shop, the traditional duty-free shop with its internationally branded products and the bland catering services with no recognizable identity. In the 1980s many European airports began to recognize the attraction of speciality retail outlets and the advantages of using familiar brand names such as the Body Shop, Tie Rack and Sock Shop. The specialist retail chains which had grown so quickly in the high streets started to appear at airports. The branding provided reassurance for the traveller, who was aware of the quality and price level of the goods within the branded outlet. More variety was also introduced into the catering outlets by again bringing in famous brand names as McDonald's and Burger King. The catering area began to be split into a number of different, sometimes competing individual outlets. In most cases, the large sit-down restaurant, which took up considerable valuable floor space, became a relic of the past.

However, the widespread adoption of branding at airports has meant that there is now greater similarity between the shopping facilities at many airports and less diversity. Brand fatigue can become a problem – particularly for the frequent traveller who can find that airport shopping can become rather dull and boring. Hence most airports are trying to blend together famous brand outlets with local outlets which can give the airport some kind of identity and can distinguish it from other airports. The character and the culture of the city or the country which the airport serves can be represented by selling local merchandise or gourmet products such as cheese from Switzerland, chocolates from Belgium or Parma ham from Italy. A flavour of the local environment can also be provided by theming the commercial facilities. For instance, at Las Vegas airport a number of the outlets are themed after hotels in the city and at Orlando airport there are shops representing the major theme parks in the area. The skill is in finding the correct balance between international recognized global brand retailers and local shops and catering outlets which give the airport an individual identity.

Aeroport de Paris is just one example of an airport company which launched a new retail strategy in 1994. The airport operator decided that it would get rid of its traditional duty-free, tax-free and fragrance shops and replace them with a new retail concept based on the large Parisian avenues called Passenger City. In this area AdP put in world-famous brands such as Hermes, Cartier, and Christofle but also shops representing the tradition of Paris and France such as Musées de France and others selling gourmet French products. Madrid airport has its 'Palaces and Museum's' outlet which has merchandise inspired by Spain's culture and heritage. Hong Kong's Chep Lap Kok airport tries to reflect its unique 'East meets West' culture with a wide range of international retail shops combined with both Asian and western restaurants and fast-food outlets. Manchester airport has its 'Donkey Stone' pub which is stocked with the local beer Boddingtons and it has a Manchester United football club shop. Vancouver airport is themed to represent the physical characteristics and cultural heritage of British Columbia, while the new terminal at Santiago airport in Chile tries to depict Chile's diverse geography from desert to Antarctic conditions (Byrd, 2000).

Some airports have chosen to enforce and promote an airport brand rather than the individual brands of the high street retailers. Amsterdam Schiphol and Singapore Changi airports are good illustrations of such a policy. For example, at Amsterdam airport all the shops in the airside area are branded under the 'See Buy Fly' identity and the outlets are grouped by product type such as electronics, fragrances, confectionery and so on, rather than according to who sells them. All the staff wear the same uniform. All sold products are placed in bright yellow branded shopping bags which have become a very recognizable feature in Europe and beyond.

The development of airport terminals into shopping centres has not been universally popular. Certain passenger types, particular business travellers who are seeking a quick transit through the terminal, favour a more streamlined airport service. Airlines have been responding to these needs by developing automatic ticketing and self check-in which theoretically should speed up the travel process and reduce the time a passenger has to spend in an airport before departure (Conway, 2000). While flight departure 'tannoy' announcements have long since been abandoned at most airports because they have proved ineffective and annoying, a few airports, particularly since the demise of intra-EU duty- and tax-free shopping, have made 'shopping announcements' instead which have further increased resentment to airport shopping from certain passengers.

The airlines, while welcoming the fact that non-aeronautical income can reduce an airport's reliance on aeronautical charges, have periodically expressed concerns that the shopping function of the airport has interfered with the normal flows of passengers through the airports. Clear signage to gates, for example, is difficult to achieve if the airport is cluttered with retail and catering signage and branding. There have been claims that passengers have delayed flights because they have been lost in the duty-free shops – so some airports have now placed flight information systems in the commercial outlets as well. Some airlines have also complained that airports have been giving too much attention to developing commercial facilities while ignoring basic operational requirements. For instance, at Heathrow airport BA complained about the lack of airline information desks at the entrance to the Terminal 1 departure area because the space was being occupied with commercial facilities, while at Gatwick airport Airtours, a major charter airline, was aggrieved that their request for greater space in the gate lounge areas had been refused although extra space had been provided for duty-free outlets (Monopolies and Mergers Commission, 1996). A correct balance between commercial and operational space is needed so that the non-aeronautical revenue is optimized without compromising the operational effectiveness – but this is no easy matter.

As well as adopting high street preferences for speciality shopping and branded products, airports have also been applying other tried and tested retail practices. This has been partly as a result of airports employing professional retail managers from the high street rather than always making internal appointments. Some concessionaires are appointing service assistants to greet customers in an attempt to make the shopping experience a more personal one (Anderson, 1999). Airport operators such as BAA plc and Aer Rianta have encouraged loyalty purchases at airports by introducing loyalty cards such as BAA plc worldpoints and the Dublin airport executive club. At Amsterdam airport, the See Buy Fly retailers are partners in KLM's Flying Dutchman frequent-flyer programme. As with high street shopping, the schemes not only provide the airport operators with a mechanism to encourage repeat buying but also enable them to find out about their customers and communicate with them when new products and services are being introduced. However, the perceived value of such initiatives tends to fall as they are adopted by more and more operators.

Moreover, airports have also introduced value and money-back guarantees which have been commonplace on the high street for many years. These are seen as particularly important because of the perceived expensive 'rip-off' reputation of many airports. For example Singapore Changi airport has two such guarantees:

1 The price of liquor, tobacco, perfumes and cosmetics will be no higher than at other major airports in the Asia Pacific region. Prices for other goods will be no higher than established downtown shops. If higher prices are found at the airport, a refund of double the price difference will be given.
2 A full refund or exchange will be given for any goods whether they are faulty, inappropriate or unwanted purchases.

No discussion about retail activities would be complete without references to the impact of the internet and e-shopping. In some ways, the internet must clearly be seen as a threat because there is a whole new range of discounted goods which are now available and easy to access. It must be remembered, however, that many purchases at airports are made on impulse and form part of the 'leisure travel experience'. The internet can also bring many opportunities for airports if strategies are developed in conjunction with the terminal facilities. Many airport web sites now give details of the commercial facilities which are available and so passengers can be more prepared when they visit the airport. They may be better able to plan their shopping in the limited time period which they have available. Information provided on the web can complement or replace more traditional promotional methods, such as Amsterdam airport's practice of supplying travel agents and KLM offices with their 'See Buy Fly' catalogues, and can achieve far greater widespread coverage.

With some airports, for example Copenhagen, products can be pre-ordered for collection at the airport. At Vancouver airport, aboriginal arts and crafts can be bought on the airport web site. In the case of BAA plc and some other airports merchandise can be delivered to home addresses and so consumers can, in effect, now participate in 'airport shopping' without leaving the comfort of living room! Such a development will no longer mean that airport shopping has to be limited to what the passenger can carry. E-commerce may also offer other non-aeronautical revenue opportunities for airports in the form of web advertising and the selling of travel related products. BAA plc has already bought a share in the last minute specialists lastminute.com.

The commercial contract and tender process

There are various ways in which commercial facilities can be provided at airports. Most airports have chosen to contract out these services to specialist retail and catering companies. This lower-risk option is usually chosen because the airport operator does not have specialist skills required or a detailed understanding of the market environment. Some airports, particularly smaller ones, may opt to offer their airports as a total retail package to a master concessionaire who will then in turn seek specialist operators to run the individual outlets. There are a few companies, such as Aer Rianta and BAA plc who have chosen to provide some facilities themselves, such as duty-free and tax-free products. For Aer Rianta this is primarily because it has built up much expertise in this area being directly involved with such operations since the first shops were opened in the 1940s. BAA plc only adopted this approach in 1990s to enable it to have total control over the whole retailing process from suppliers to warehouses to customer purchases and to provide it with opportunities for international expansion. Car parking tends to be the only commercial activity which is provided by a substantial number of airport operators themselves since it generally requires less specialist skills and also greater capital investment by the airport operator.

The contractual details

When airport operators contract out their commercial facilities they usually enter into a concession contract with the companies providing the services. This typically involves the concessionaire paying a percentage of sales to the airport operator often in addition to agreeing a minimum annual guaranteed amount. The turnover fee may vary from as little as 5 per cent for some landside commercial activities to up to 50 per cent for facilities with higher profit margins – notably duty-free and tax-free sales. The fee may also increase at a faster rate than the level of turnover in the belief that concessionaires will be in a better position to pay higher fees once all basic fixed costs have been covered (Freathy and O'Connell, 1998). The airport operator will usually only provide the shell for the outlet and it will be up to the concessionaire to provide the capital investment for fitting out the facility. A typical length for the concession will be around five years, although this can vary quite considerably and there may be options for renewal. Such an arrangement will be relatively low risk for the airport operator which will tend to have little responsibility over the commercial facilities. The airport operator will be assured of a certain amount of revenues. However, since this revenue stream will be linked to the concessionaire's sales rather than profit volumes, there is no guarantee that the concessionaire will aim to maximize its sales as it may be more concerned with profit margins.

Alternatively the airport operator may choose to enter into a management contract with the retail or catering company. These have been used for car-parking facilities at airports for many years. It is currently not a popular approach for other commercial activities but the idea has generated some interest – particularly since the abolition of intra-EU duty- and tax-free sales in 1999. BAA plc used this type of contract with its duty-free retailers in the 1990s before it operated these facilities itself. Other examples include a number of regional UK airports, such as Birmingham airport, which now have profit share style management agreements for several concessionaires (Savage, 2000). This type of arrangement can be on a profit- or sales-sharing basis or a mixture of the two. It should enable the airport operator and the concessionaire to develop a much more longer-term relationship with each other than is typical with a traditional concession contract. They have to work together following common objectives to optimize revenue and profit levels and sharing the risk. This may not be an easy path to go down, however, and such an approach may be costly in management time both while the contract is being negotiated and once the agreement is in place (Gray, 2000).

A third option is to have a joint venture arrangement when the airport operator enters into a partnership with the specialist retailer or some other organization to provide the commercial facilities. Examples of this practice at home airports are relatively rare – Amsterdam airport used to have such an arrangement with its catering facilities. There are perhaps more opportunities for this type of arrangement when an airport operator is wishing to expand its involvement to other airports. Aer Rianta, for example, entered into a number of joint venture agreements in order to provide commercial facilities in the CIS and the Middle East.

Within Europe, North America and Asia an increasing number of concession contracts are automatically put out to tender when they come up for renewal. Such a practice is not so widespread in some other more developing areas but is usually the most effective way of ensuring the best contractual arrangements.

While selection criteria will vary from airport to airport, generally the evaluation of offers will consider both the financial terms (i.e. the concession fee paid) and the more qualitative terms (i.e. quality, vision, innovation etc.). Some airports will just choose the bid which will generate the highest revenue – indeed, in some countries such as Singapore and Israel they are required to do so by law. This has led to a tendency to overbid in offers, particularly in Europe, in recent years. While in the short run this will benefit the airport operator with high levels of concession revenue, such a situation will not be sustainable in the longer term. The concessionaire will loss money and have to renegotiate conditions with the airport operator or be forced to abandon its airport operations completely.

The problem of overbidding is one of the key reasons behind ACI Europe's attempt to develop a tender code (ACI-Europe, 1999). The objectives of this code are to facilitate tender processes by recommending standardized tender procedures and to establish generally recognized selection criteria based on a combination of qualitative and quantitative factors. A points system is being developed which considers three different areas, namely appraisal of the tenderer's qualities (size and range of activities, specific experience, financial reliability), appraisal of the business plan (market analysis and product strategy, shop design, turnover forecast, organization/personnel/investments) and assessment of the concession fee offered.

Non-aeronautical performance

Factors driving success

Choosing the right concessionaire and negotiating the most appropriate contractual agreement is crucial if an airport is going to fully exploit its commercial opportunities. Many other factors which will also play a role. The airport operator may be able to influence some of these factors – but by no means all of them. Clearly the nature of the airport traffic needs to be taken into account. For instance, an airport handling predominantly domestic business travellers is likely to be in a less favourable position for generating commercial income than an airport with many long-haul leisure passengers. Understanding the mix of passengers and planning the facilities to match as closely as possible their needs and preferences is paramount to maximizing the revenue generating opportunities and return on investment. Also small airports with limited passenger traffic are at a distinct disadvantage since they will not have the critical mass, thought to be around 5 million passengers, necessary to diversify and support specialist retail and catering outlets (Gethin, 1997).

Spending by all passengers will be influenced by the general economic climate. Factors to consider include growth in gross domestic product (GDP) and consumer expenditure, level of taxation, inflation rates and foreign currency fluctuations. Purchasing patterns will also be affected by delays at an airport. A delay of an hour or so for a departure slot may give passengers extra time to visit the shops or catering outlets. Such a delay may be popular with the commercial department but not with anyone else! On the other hand, lengthy operational delays within the terminal, such as long queues for passport control, security or immigration will have the reverse effect, and reduce or even eliminate the dwell time that passengers have for browsing in the shops and having something to eat or drink.

Then there is the competition for airport commercial facilities, which can come from a variety of different sources. First, there are other airports. Notable examples of airports which are in a particularly competitive situation are those in the Gulf such as Dubai, Abu Dhabi and Bahrain and some Asian airports serving destinations such as Singapore, Kuala Lumpur and Hong Kong. There is also competition from the in-flight sales of airlines, particularly the charter airlines. These airlines, for instance the UK carriers Airtours and Britannia, allow pre-booking of goods in order to catch some business before the passengers can see what the airport competitor has on offer. In addition, competition can come from downtown tax-free outlets for international travellers, which are allowed in a number of countries, particularly in Asia. In Europe and North America competition exists with discounted electrical and other high street businesses and from the growth of factory outlets. E-shopping, as previously discussed, is quite likely to develop into a major competitor as well.

Just as in the high street, outlet size and mix is very important as is the location, space and design of facilities. However, a large proportion of the airports which are in use today were designed without taking sufficient account of the commercial opportunities which airport terminals can offer. All too often, concession planners get involved at a much too late stage of the terminal design and development process (Gray, 1998b; Walsh, 2000). This has meant that commercial facilities very often are not ideally situated or have been added on later as an afterthought. Successful concession planning, at least when passenger purchases are being considered, is all about providing facilities close to passenger flows and not in areas which are 'dead ends' or are too far from passengers' view. A change in the flow line of passengers can have a dramatic impact on concessionaire's sales. One option, adopted by Brussels airport to ensure that passengers pass by all outlets, is to place popular outlets like duty- and tax-free shops in the 'weak corners' outside the main flow lines and the less popular outlets in the 'strong corners' (Haugaard, 1998). The outlets should, ideally, be on the same floor levels as the departure gates, as having to go through the inconvenience of changing levels may deter some passengers from visiting the commercial facilities (Doganis, 1992).

Thus many airports cannot maximize their commercial spend because their facilities may have been inappropriately designed, located in secondary sites or because subsequent extensions of the terminal have significantly shifted the main direction of passenger flows. Particular problems can arise from terminals which are of a linear design, such as Munich airport, because very often facilities have to be duplicated which can be costly until there is sufficient throughput of passengers to support all the facilities. This was the situation with the fourth terminal at London Heathrow Airport when it first opened. Problems have also occurred for airports in European countries which have signed up to the Schengen agreement and have abolished immigration controls with other Schengen countries. At some airports this has caused unnecessary duplication of facilities, resulting in reduced custom for each outlets.

The amount of time a passenger has at an airport will obviously influence their shopping behaviour. Different types of passengers spend different average dwell times in the lounge. BAA plc has estimated that in the domestic lounge in Terminal 3 at London Heathrow the average dwell time for economy passengers is 49 minutes compared with 27 minutes for business class and 13 minutes for first-class passengers (Toms, 2000). BAA plc has also calculated that the incremental airport spend for each additional ten minutes available time is £0.80 for domestic passengers and £1.60 for international passengers (Maiden, 2000). Passengers also need to feel relaxed when they shop and so they tend to have a preference in buying from outlets which are situated within the vicinity of the departure gates – once all essential processes such as check-in and security screening have been completed. They also will not want to walk long distances to be able to shop. Landside shopping is different as convenient locations not only for passengers, but also for staff, meeters and greeters and local residents, must be found. Catering outlets can compete with passengers' dwell time in shops and so they need to be positioned near to the retail facilities but must not interrupt the flow. Shops and catering outlets have to be large enough so as not to give a congested and overcrowded image, but not too large that consumers may be deterred by an appearance of inactivity and empty space.

Measuring non-aeronautical performance

Airports, with their concessionaire partners, have become increasingly active in monitoring their non-aeronautical performance. This is partly due to a drive for better performance monitoring of all aspects of the industry and also because retail experts, with experience of assessing retail performance at other locations, are being bought in to manage airport facilities. Consumer satisfaction levels and perceptions of value for money are assessed by many airports through customer surveys (as described in Chapter 4). In addition, airports use indicators such as sales per passenger, passenger penetration levels and sales per square metre to analyse the economic performance of their commercial facilities. The latter measure has the advantage in that it can be used to compare airport performance with other retail facilities at other sites such as shopping malls.

Making inter-airport comparisons is difficult because of the commercially sensitive nature of the information required and lack of reliable industrywide data. One of the most comprehensive benchmarking studies was undertaken in 1998 by the consultancy group, Centre for Airport Studies. Twenty-four major airports in Europe, Asia Pacific and North America were investigated. The study looked at performance indicators such as retail revenue per passenger and retail revenue per square metre both airside and landside, and analysed various factors which helped explain the comparative results which were obtained. These included geographic location, ownership model, the volume and nature of traffic, the number, size, location, mix, density of outlets and the area devoted to retail (Centre for Airport Studies, 1998; Favotto, 2000). One of the indicators used, retail revenue per square metre, is presented in Figure 6.4 with the average value indexed at 100. This shows the clear dominance of Europe among the best performing airports (Heathrow, Gatwick, Vienna, Copenhagen and Frankfurt) and the USA among the worst performing airports (Orange County and the New York airports of JFK, Newark and La Guardia).

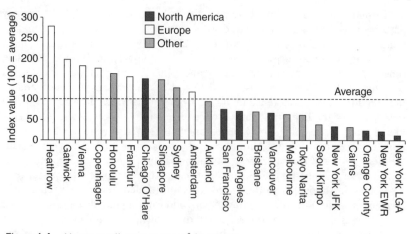

Figure 6.4 Airport retail revenue per m² in 1997/8
Source: Favotto (2000).

The ending of EU duty- and tax-free sales

Background

For much of the travelling public, airport retailing is all about duty- and tax-free shopping and nothing much else. This is in spite of the expansion in the range and type of other retail activities on offer. Moreover few passengers are actually totally aware of the differences between tax free shopping (when the sales/value added tax – VAT – on goods such as perfumes and cosmetics, clothes and electrical equipment is not charged) and duty-free shopping (when the higher 'duty' tax on alcohol and tobacco is excluded). Value added tax rates within Europe vary from above 20 per cent in Denmark, Sweden and Norway to around 15 per cent in Spain, Portugal and Luxembourg. In some countries, such as Austria and Germany, most VAT-free sales are not allowed. Duty taxes are again highest in the Scandinavian countries and lowest in Greece, Spain and Italy. Consumer perception of value for money at airport duty- and tax-free shops will thus very much depend on their country of origin.

The first duty- and tax-free airport outlet was opened in 1947 at Shannon airport in Ireland. In 1951 another shop was opened in Prestwick airport in Scotland. These shops were designed to be attractive to transatlantic passengers on refuelling stops (Freathy and O'Connell, 1998). The shops sold a small range of alcohol, tobacco and perfumes and a few other items. By the 1960s other airports had opened similar shops and had started to expand the range of merchandise on offer. This was primarily in response to the rapid increase in passenger traffic at that time and particularly the growth in package holidays and other forms of leisure travel. Amsterdam Schiphol airport, for example, was one of the first airports to offer tax-free electronics and photographic material. Then came a retail boom in duty- and tax-free shopping with many airports substantially increasing the area dedicated to such shops and offering a much more diverse and varied product selection, ranging from the traditional alcohol, tobacco and perfume products to camcorders, watches and jewelry, sports clothing and other fashion accessories.

The 1990s were a period of uncertainty for most EU airports. It was originally intended that all EU duty- and tax-free sales would be abolished on 1 January 1993 as the single market was 'born'. The rationale was that it was illogical and incompatible to have such a system when the EU should be behaving as a single market with open borders. In addition, these shopping privileges were considered to distort competition between modes of transport with no access to these sales, such as rail, and to be unfair trading in relation to downtown shopping. It was argued that EU consumers were subsidizing not only duty- and tax-free outlets but also air and ferry travellers.

In response the airports, charter airlines, ferry companies and associated manufacturing industries collectively argued that duty-free privileges did not distort or hamper the development of the single market and that abolition would result in millions of jobs being lost. It was claimed that the cost of travel would have to rise substantially to compensate for the loss of income, which would have a knock-on effect throughout entire national economies. Through active lobbying of government ministers, the proponents to the abolition managed to achieve a six-and-a-half-year extension of these sales until 30 June 1999.

During this reprieve period the arguments for and against abolition were hotly debated. Anti-abolition lobbyists (airports, ferry companies, manufacturers and so on) co-ordinated their work through the International Duty Free Confederation (IDFC) which was based in Brussels, and other bodies such as charter carriers and regional carriers associations, and the Federation of Transport Workers Unions. The European Travel Research Foundation (ETRF) commissioned various studies to support the lobbyists' arguments, looking at the impacts on the airport, charter and low-cost scheduled airline industry. The main specific findings of the potential impact on EU airports were (Air Transport Group, 1997; ETRF, 1997):

1. EU airports would lose at least 40–46 per cent of their total duty- and tax-free sales and at least 58–64 per cent of duty- and tax-free profits.
2. The replacement of lost sales volume and profit would not be achieved by extending the duty/tax paid products on offer. To recover this lost revenue, airport aeronautical charges would have to be increased by an average of 20 per cent for all services or by 40 per cent if the increases were just applied to EU flights.
3. The airports which would be worse affected would be those which had a high reliance on intra-EU flights (particularly regional airports with a large proportion of charter traffic), had a well developed retail policy or which had planned heavy investment programmes.

It was argued that this large sales loss would fundamentally alter the cost structure and profit potential of airport retailing. This was because the negotiation position with suppliers would be weakened, the gross margin achieved on duty/tax sales would fall and lessen investment opportunities, and customer choice would be reduced with suppliers less eager to provide marketing support and trial new products (Institute for Retail Studies, 1997).

In total it was estimated that for all EU airports, 55 per cent of all duty- and tax-free sales were at risk, representing US$1.9 billion in 1996 prices. Of this amount major income streams of US$485 million in the UK, US$211 million in Germany and US$188 million in France could potentially be lost. Deutsche Bank (1999) looked at the likely impact on a sample of fourteen major Europe airports of airport groupings, namely AdP, Aeroporti di Roma AENA (Spain), Aer Rianta (Ireland), Amsterdam, ANA (Portugal), BAA (UK) Copenhagen, Frankfurt, Hamburg, Manchester, Munich and Vienna. It was estimated that airports such as Aer Rianta, Copenhagen, AENA, ANA, Hamburg and Vienna would be worst affected since EU sales represented over 85 per cent of total duty- and tax-free sales. The potential loss of revenue was estimated to be as much as US$85 million at Aer Rianta airports and US$61 million at Copenhagen in 1997 prices. The larger airports, such as Paris, Frankfurt and Amsterdam had higher shares of non-EU traffic and so it was estimated that EU duty-free sales accounted for only around half of the total income. In absolute terms, however, the loss of potential revenue was estimated to be as much as US$69 million at Paris, US$54 million at Frankfurt and US$44 million at Amsterdam.

The IDFC launched a major awareness campaign at airport terminals, ferries and in other public places. Messages such as 'Act now to keep your Duty Free', '1999: Travelling would never be the same again' or ' Duty-Free: It doesn't have to go' were displayed on placards, plastic bags and in leaflets. By 1999 almost all governments had been persuaded in favour of another thirty-month extension to the abolition date in order for the industry to be adequately prepared. The Danish government, however, was not convinced by the arguments. Since unanimity among EU members was needed to approve the extension period, this meant that on 30 June 1999 intra-EU duty- and tax-free sales were abolished.

Airport strategies

In the first few months after the abolition of duty- and tax-free sales it quickly became apparent that the airport industry had focused too much of its attention on fighting the campaign to save the sales, with not enough effort being channelled into preparing for change if abolition were to occur. Admittedly a number of airports had broadened their retail mix and diversified into new activities in the 1990s, but the prospect of no EU duty- and tax-free sales was only one contributing factor, as well as changing consumer expectations and retail trends, which had led to this development. Also companies such as BAA plc and Aer Rianta had bought duty-free concerns outside Europe in an aim to grow their businesses in areas which would be unaffected by EU developments. Generally, however, a disbelief that abolition would really occur in 1999 meant that when 1 July arrived many airports were not nearly as ready as they could have been.

The immediate impact of loss of EU duty- and tax-free sales in many cases was much greater than was expected. This was largely the result of airports being victims of their own very successful awareness campaigns. The travelling public was sold the message that duty- and tax-free shopping would no longer

Table 6.2   Short-term impact of the loss of intra-EU duty- and tax-free sales on airport revenues

Airport	Impact on revenues
Amsterdam	Duty/tax free revenue down 12% in 1999 compared with 1998. Other concession income up 7%
Aer Rianta	Shops sales down 44% and related profits down 70 % July–December compared to January–June
BAA	Duty/tax-free revenue down by 26% in 1999/2000 compared with 1999/8. Tax-paid revenue up by 12%. Landing fees raised by 58 pence per passenger (around 12% increase)
Birmingham	Duty/tax-free revenue down by 46% in 1999/2000 compared with 1998/9
Brussels	Duty/tax-free revenue down by 22% in 19999 compared with 1998
Copenhagen	Duty/tax-free shopping centre revenue (includes duty/tax free) down by 23% in 1999 compared with 1998. Other concession revenue up by 14%. Landing charges up 15% in 1999 and 13% in 2000
Düsseldorf	Duty/tax-free revenue down by 20% in 1999 compared with 1998
Paris	Duty/tax-free revenue constant but spend per passenger down by 6% in 1999 compared with 1998. Total sales (including duty/tax-free) revenue up by 11%
Vienna	Shopping revenue (duty/tax-free and paid) down by 5% in 1999 compared with 1998

Note: For UK airports the impact is likely to be greater since the financial year runs from April to March, rather than January to December.
Source: Compiled by author from annual accounts.

be available after 30 June 1999, and hence stayed away from all airport shops – even those passengers who could still use them. At BAA airports for instance, retail income was down by 20 per cent in July 1999 compared with the equivalent amount in 1998. While for many airports, the situation improved after the initial reaction to abolition, the loss of revenue within the first year of operation after this development was in many cases considerable (Table 6.2).

To address the confusion among passengers, a number of airports launched major marketing campaigns, explaining what passengers travelling to EU destinations and beyond could and could not buy at airport shops. The key message that most were trying to get across was that there were still bargains to be found within the EU and that outside of this area the situation remained unchanged (Newhouse, 2000).

Many of the EU airports, in partnerships with their retail concessionaires, have absorbed the value added or sales tax themselves – effectively offering the merchandise still at 'tax-free' prices. Some airports are also selling a selection of liquor products at duty-free prices but at most airports cheaper tobacco is no longer available to EU-passengers. At many airports passengers for both EU and non-EU destinations share the same retail terminal area and so the airports have had to devise some method for identifying the merchandise which is on sale to these two types of passengers. At some airports, for example at BAA airports, goods which have been displayed in areas which are colour-coded blue are made available to EU passengers while products in green areas are available to non-EU passengers. Understandably, many passengers have been confused by such a system and this has prompted the airports to provide more explanatory literature to clarify the situation.

Elsewhere a number of European concessionaires, airports and ferry companies have joined together to form the Travel Value Association. All these organizations have adopted the common and recognizable 'Travel Value – Buy more for less' trade mark on their shops, merchandising and advertising in order to indicate to the travelling public that there are still good savings to be made when travelling. This organization also embarked on a large advertising campaign between Easter and autumn 2000. Some major airports such as Frankfurt, Vienna and Dublin are members of this association. At the same time the airports were anxious to put across the message that duty- and tax-free sales still exist, as normal, for non-EU passengers. At Manchester airport, for example, large notices were placed at check-in informing non-EU passengers of this fact. Airport web sites gave details about what passengers can buy. Non-EU European airports where duty- and tax-free sales can still be made have also been trying to capitalize on this situation.

Such strategies have undoubtedly enticed some passengers back to the shops and softened the blow of the loss of EU duty-free. However, EU airports have still been very much aware of the need to increase the volume of retail income if they are going to make up for the lower profit margins on EU sales. Some airports, such as Copenhagen, have introduced arrivals shops in the baggage reclaim area where discount purchases can be made while others, such as the Birmingham airport, have arranged for goods to be ordered on the outbound part of a journey and to be collected on return. Airports with significant amounts of domestic traffic have been making these passengers aware that for the first time they, too, can have access to discount shopping at airports.

Some airports are also planning to increase retail space both airside and landside, with the aim of increasing consumer spend. For example, Amsterdam airport is expanding its central lounge shopping area – the first phase of work was completed in August 1999. Once the second phase is completed the shopping area will have nearly tripled in size from 1250 square metres to 3700 square metres (Schiphol Group, 2000) Copenhagen is planning a major expansion of landside shopping facilities in the former arrivals area of Terminal 2 and has build a service centre on the nearby Oresund motorway (Copenhagen Airport, 2000).

Before abolition in June 1999 it was widely predicted by the ERDF and other bodies that aeronautical charges would have to be substantially increased to compensate for the reduction in non-aeronautical revenue. Only a few airports have adopted this strategy of increasing their dependency on aeronautical fees. Copenhagen raised its charges in January 1999 and 2000 by 15 per cent and 13 per cent respectively – although this airport had not raised their charges for a number of years prior to this. Aer Rianta wound up its discount scheme for new traffic and carriers. BAA plc's regulator allowed an increase in charges of 70 pence per passenger – equivalent to an increase of around 15 per cent. In the end BAA plc raised charges by 58 pence per passenger. By contrast the regulator did not allow Manchester to raise its charges even if it so desired. Other airports such as Amsterdam, Frankfurt and Paris decided not to increase their charges to compensate for the loss of non-aeronautical revenue.

Aer Rianta: becoming an international retailer

Aer Rianta is an interesting example as it was one of the first airport companies to expand beyond national boundaries and get involved with the management and operations of commercial facilities at other international airports. Aer
Rianta is the Irish state-owned airport company which has been responsible for
managing the country's three major airports, namely Dublin, Shannon and Cork
since 1937. It has a long history with the provision of commercial facilities, as
the world's first duty-free shop was opened at Shannon airport in 1947. It
continues to operate its own duty-free and travel-value shops at the three airports
and also provides fuelling and catering services at Shannon airport. It also runs
a college of hotel management in Shannon and in 1990 acquired a chain of
hotels, Great Southern Hotels.

In 1988, Aer Rianta International (ARI) was set up as a wholly owned
subsidiary of Aer Rianta. With a population of less than 4 million, Aer Rianta
recognized the limits of its own market and aimed to use ARI to promote
commercial activities in locations outside of Ireland. The first undertaking was
a joint venture company Aerofist with Aeroflot Russia, the Moscow airport
authority and ARI each having a one-third interest in the company. Aer Rianta
had originally developed links with the Soviet Union in the early 1970s with an
agreement whereby Aeroflot would trade airport charges for fuel at Shannon
airport. In 1988, Aerofist opened the first duty-free shop at Moscow airport. It
also began offering in-flight duty-free sales on international flights operated by
Aeroflot out of Moscow. In the next few years, joint venture companies with
ARI involvement were also set up to manage duty-free shops at St Petersburg
and Kiev airports as well as downtown shops in Moscow and two shops, which
are now closed, on the Russian–Finnish border.

In 1991, ARI expanded its involvement into the Middle East area with the
setting up of a joint venture company with local investors in Bahrain to be responsible for designing the duty-free shops, overseeing their fitting out and their day-
to-day management. Aer Rianta International further expanded operations in this
region by getting involved in the management of the duty-free shops at Karachi
airport in 1992 and at Kuwait airport in 1994. In 1997 other new duty-free shop
contracts were awarded in Beirut, Qatar (in-flight catering for Qatar airways),
Damascus and Egypt. In Europe, ARI's first retail operation outside of Ireland in
Europe was at the terminals of the Channel tunnel. The organization provided duty
free facilities from the tunnel opening in 1994 until the abolition of duty free sales
in 1999. In addition ARI opened two shop in Cyprus in the late 1990s – one at
Larnaca airport in 1997 and one in Paphos in 1998. In 1999, it took over operations of a number of duty-free shops at Greek airports, sea ports and at border
crossing in a joint venture with the Gebr Heinemann and Jacques Parsons.

Elsewhere, in China in 1996 ARI signed a consultancy contract with China
National Duty Free Corporation concerning the operation of duty-free shops in
Beijing Airport. This was ARI's first venture in the Far East. Aer Rianta Inter-
national also project managed the construction of the duty-free shops at Hong
Kong's Chek Lap Kok airport. Then, in 1998, ARI expanded into North America
for the first time by acquiring the duty-free division of Canada's United Cigar
Stores and the concession for duty-free shops at Montreal, Winnipeg, Edmon-
ton and Ottawa airports (Table 6.3).

Table 6.3   Aer Rianta's involvement in international retailing activities, 2000

Region	Location
Europe	Larnaca airport
	Paphos airport
	Greece (Hellenic duty-free shops at 15 airports, 5 seaports and 8 border crossings)
CIS	Sheremetyevo I and II airports, Moscow
	Pulkova II International airport, St Petersburg
	Borispol airport, Kiev
Middle East	Bahrain international airport
	Karachi International airport
	Kuwait International airport
	Beirut International airport
	Damascus International airport
	Qatar Airways (in-flight)
North America	Montreal airports
	Winnipeg airport
	Edmonton airport
	Ottawa airport

Source: Aer Rianta annual reports.

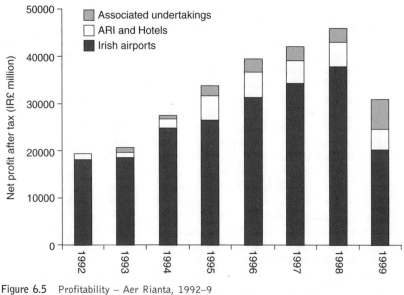

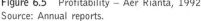

Figure 6.5   Profitability – Aer Rianta, 1992–9
Source: Annual reports.

In addition to providing duty-free retailing, ARI has also become involved with the ownership and management of international airports. In 1997, 50 per cent of the ownership of Düsseldorf airports was sold to ARI and its consortium partner Hochtief, the German construction company. In the same year a consortium of ARI and NatWest Ventures bought 40 per cent of Birmingham airport.

In 1999 the turnover of all these international activities (excluding joint venture activities) was IR£30 million compared with IR£234 million for the Aer Rianta Irish airports and £29 million for the hotel activities. In terms of profits, ARI made a profit of £7.1 million compared with £20.4 million for the Irish airports and £3.6 million for Great Southern Hotels. The airport group has become more and more dependent on these external activities over the years and by 1999, the subsidiaries and associated undertakings of Aer Rianta accounted for a third of all profits compared with just 3 per cent in 1992 (Figure 6.5). The year 1999 was a particularly problematic year for the Irish airports because of the abolition of duty free. Airport charges had not increased at these airports since 1987 and this, coupled with a widespread discount scheme to encourage more traffic, had meant that just prior to the end of EU duty-free sales, airport charges only represented 17 per cent of Irish airport revenues (Aer Rianta, 2000). Thus the profits from the international business were seen as particularly welcome. With traffic maturing on many routes in Ireland and substantial investment needed, the international activities are seen as invaluable for future success.

BAA: the development of a new retail approach

In the first few years after the privatization of BAA plc in 1987, there were a series of developments which resulted in the company undertaking a thorough review of its non-aeronautical activities. First, the airport group gained a reputation in the press of being a 'rip-off' airport in terms of the value for money of the goods on offer and the associated quality of service. Second, a regulatory review looming which would determine the level of aeronautical charges for the next five years. Moreover, costs were increasing at the airports and passenger growth was slowing down (Phythian, 1996).

This led to the launching of a new retail strategy in 1990. There were various elements to this strategy. An improved system of market research and customer satisfaction was introduced by the replacing the passenger opinion survey (POS) at the airport with the QSM. The QSM considered more effectively issues such as quality, choice, speed of service and value for money. In addition Egon Ronay, the renowned food critic, and his team of inspectors began to monitor the quality of all the catering outlets at Heathrow and Gatwick airports.

To overcome the problem of being regarded as a 'rip-off' airport, BAA plc launched its value guarantee in 1991. The key message with this was that all tax paid goods sold at the airport were guaranteed to be the same price as equivalent goods in the high street. Savings of up to 50 per cent were assured for duty-free goods such as liquor and tobacco, and 30 per cent for fragrances. The next stage of the value guarantee was introduced in 1994 after BAA plc had undertaken further extensive market research into its commercial operations. This promised a full refund on goods bought at BAA airports to passengers from any region of the world, with a freepost address in the UK and refunded postage elsewhere. BAA plc also introduced a free telephone enquiry number for shopping facilities, pre-ordering possibilities and help desks, and personal shopping consultants at its airports.

A year later at Gatwick airport the bonuspoints scheme was launched, whereby points could be earned for car parking, eating, drinking, shopping and currency exchange, and could be traded for money off certain goods and services such as car parking and shopping at the airports or points on some airlines' frequent-flyer programmes. The bonuspoint initiative was subsequently adopted at all the airports in 1996 and relaunched in 1999 as worldpoints. By 2000, this scheme had over 300 000 members, a quarter of whom were not UK residents. A credit card, BAA WorldCard was introduced. The early 1990s also saw BAA plc progressively introducing more and more international brand names to its airports and offering increased competition with many of the services on offer particularly in areas such as catering, banking, and car parking. The total floor space allocated to retail activities was increased substantially from a mere 41 000 square metres in 1990 to over 90 000 square metres ten years later (Figure 6.6).

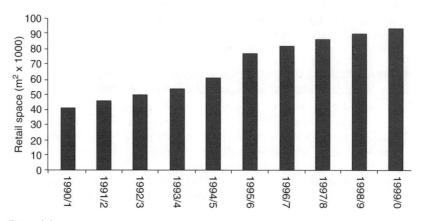

Figure 6.6 Retail space at BAA UK airports, 1990–2000
Source: Annual reports.

At Heathrow and Gatwick airport, BAA plc began undertaking a continuous departing passenger survey called a retail profiler. Around thirty thousand passengers at Heathrow and 14 000 passengers at Gatwick are annually inter-viewed and, since 1999, the survey has also included 6600 passengers at Stansted. The passengers are asked about which outlets they have visited and the amount they have spent – both landside and airside. Information about the key characteristics of the passengers, such as nationality, frequency and reason for travel is also gathered. BAA plc has also undertaken passenger-tracking surveys to understand where departing passengers spend their time in the termi-nal and how available time influences retail spend. They do this by planting a sticker on passengers at check-in and tracking their passage to the gate by recording the time at various points on the way (Maiden, 2000).

Another feature of the retail strategy in more recent years has been develop-ment of the internet as a marketing and distribution medium. A new web site was introduced in 1998 which gave information about the commercial facilities on offer and enabled the pre-ordering of retail goods, currency and car parking to take place. Links to the expendia web site were established so that travel arrangements could be made. Then in January 2000, BAA plc invested £7.7 million in lastminute.com to give BAA an extensive range of last minute products on its own web site and to give it coverage on the lastminute.com web site (BAA, 2000).

BAA plc now has more control over its duty- and tax-free shopping. Up until 1993, these facilities were provided by concessionaires using a traditional concession fee basis. In 1993 BAA plc wanted to take more responsibility and control, so they negotiated new management contracts with their concessionaires. With this system BAA plc funded the costs and kept all the sales revenue except for paying a management contract fee to the concessionaire. In addition, if targets were exceeded, the concessionaire would receive a share of the profits. Then in 1996 BAA plc launched World Duty Free, a wholly owned subsidiary of BAA, which it established to run airport duty- and tax-free shops. BAA plc claimed that this would give it complete control over the duty-free business at its airports and would enable the company to introduce more effective warehousing and distribution systems, and obtain procurement discounts. Gradually BAA plc started to replace the management contracts at its own UK airports. This process was completed in 1999.

The establishment of World Duty Free was also seen as a way to give BAA plc opportunities to expand its commercial activities to non-BAA locations, either through commercial management contracts or as part of an overall privatization package to operate the whole airport. Subsequently in 1997, BAA plc acquired the US retail chain Duty Free International which had around 200 outlets, mainly in the US at airports and border crossings. It was also involved in diplomatic and in-flight business. This subsidiary was renamed World Duty Free Americas with BAA's original duty-free company being renamed World Duty Free Europe. The acquisition was undertaken to provide greater geographical strength away from Europe, where the abolition of sales appeared imminent and to increase the company's purchasing power.

In a parallel development in the 1990s, BAA plc began to manage commercial facilities at non-BAA airports The first main contract was for Greater Pittsburgh International airport. This was a fifteen-year agreement signed in 1991. The new facilities were grouped together in what was called 'The AirMall' which had over 100 outlets and sixty companies – many of which has famous branded names – and covered an area of around 10 000 square metres. The AirMall was opened in 1992. With this arrangement the airport operator was guaranteed an index-linked US$0.40 per passenger. BAA plc received a certain share of income above this amount, and if further income were generated, the revenue was to be split. Consequently, BAA plc has been involved in the management of commercial facilities at other US airports such Harrisburg, New York Newark, and BA's Terminal 7 at New York JFK. BAA plc has also looked after the commercial facilities at airports where it has an equity share (Melbourne, Launceston, Naples) or airport management contract (Indianapolis and Harrisburg). In addition, in 1999 it took over responsibility for the commercial facilities at the terminals for the Channel tunnel at Folkstone and Calais/Coquelles on a profit-sharing based fifteen-year contract with Eurotunnel.

Another area of retail diversification has been discount designer outlet centres. BAA plc entered into a joint venture scheme with the US retail developer McArthur/Glen to develop a chain of outlets in the UK and continental Europe.

Table 6.4 Key developments in BAA's retail strategy in the 1990s

Date	Development
1990	Launch of new retail strategy; QSM introduced
1991	Value guarantee launched; Egon Ronay became catering inspector
1991	Pittsburgh airport contract awarded
1994	Worldwide guarantee launched
1995	First McArthur/Glen outlet opened
1996	BAA bonuspoints launched at all BAA airports; World Duty Free established; Indianapolis airport contract awarded
1997	Acquisition of Duty Free International (renamed World Duty Free Americas); member of consortium chosen to run Melbourne airport; acquisition of 70 per cent of Naples airport; Harrisburg airport contract awarded
1998	New website launched enabling pre-ordering; Mauritius and Newark airport contracts awarded; member of consortium chosen to run Launceston airport
1999	Abolition of EU duty/tax free; bonuspoints relaunched as worldpoints; Eurotunnel contract awarded
2000	JFK Terminal 7 and Boston airport contracts awarded. Investment in lastminute.com

Source: BAA annual reports.

The first BAA McArthur/Glen centre was opened in Cheshire Oaks in the north-west of England in 1995 followed by a second centre in Troyes in north-east France. A number of other centres have opened subsequently or are planned. From 1998 onwards BAA plc has adopted a strategy of disposing of its interests in these outlets once they have been developed in order to benefit from the value which has been created from these joint ventures.

Table 6.4 summarizes the key retail developments which have taken place in the last ten years. As a result of all these non-aeronautical activities, the share of revenue from these commercial sources has increased dramatically in the last ten years (Figure 6.7). However, the abolition of intra-EU duty- and tax-free sales

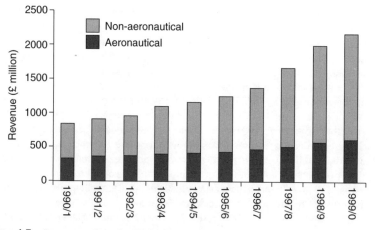

Figure 6.7 Revenue sources for BAA, 1999–2000
Source: Annual reports.

had a major impact on the financial performance of BAA plc. BAA plc estimated that it would experience a drop in revenue of £80 million (based on 1997 prices). It was predicted that £53 million of this loss would be the direct result of losing duty-free sales. A further £39 million would then be lost due to a reduced margin on duty-free sales which remained, loss of tax-free sales and advertising revenue, increases in marketing costs and the cost of paying VAT on perfume and gifts which BAA plc proposed to cover itself. A revenue gain of £12 million would be made in some areas because of a reduction in overhead charges and increased revenue from the release of duty-free space and more catering revenue because of increased dwell time. After raising landing charges by 7.5 per cent in 1999, and 2000 as was to be allowed by the regulator, the revenue shortfall was estimated to be £22 million (Monopolies and Mergers Commission, 1996; Tooke, 1999).

In July 1999, the first month after abolition, net retail income at all the UK BAA airports was down by 20 per cent. In August it was down by 16 per cent and by September by just 13 per cent. Although this downward trend showed signs that the situation was improving, it did not stop BAA plc share price falling by around 30 per cent by October 1999. BAA plc even issued a profits warning in October to alert markets that the abolition would have a more severe the impact that was previously expected – a loss of £122 million of retail sales which was over £40 million more than predicted (Skapinker, 1999).

BAA plc introduced a number of strategies to address this problem. To overcome the confusion among passengers, it reconfigured passenger flows in its major terminals so that passengers were channelled through the shops where they could still make purchases. It also launched a major advertising campaign telling consumers that they could still shop at airports – with slogans such as 'Miss you' or 'I deserve it' – and 'it still costs less at the airport'. For EU passengers, 40 per cent savings on fragrances were offered with up to 20 per cent savings on wine, champagne and a range of spirits and cigars. BAA plc added extra retail space and is planning for still more. Arrivals duty-paid shops and collection-on-arrival facilities were provided. On the aeronautical side passenger fees were raised by 58 pence per passenger – equivalent to an increase of around 12 per cent.

By the end of the 1999/2000 financial year in March 2000, retail revenue from duty- and tax-free shops had fallen by 18 per cent compared with the previous year. Retail revenue from other shops was up by 12 per cent so, overall, the loss in total retail revenue was 7 per cent. In the same year World Duty Free Americas underperformed against BAA plc's expectations, and this meant that in September 1999 BAA plc wrote down goodwill by £147 million in respect of this business in its accounts. Overall profits before tax were down by 2.6 per cent which was the first decrease since 1991/2 when the economy was in recession and the Gulf War took place (Figure 6.8).

BAA plc's strategy for recovery has been to refocus on what it sees as its core airport business by disposing of the in-flight business of World Duty Free Americas and by concentrating on airport-related property with its property company BAA Lynton. World Duty Free Americas and BAA McArthur/Glen and are not considered to be part of BAA's core business anymore – although in the shorter term development of some additional outlet centres are planned which will create additional value for BAA. It has also terminated the Eurotunnel contract which lost the company £20 million.

155

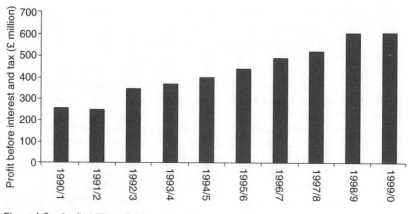

Figure 6.8   Profitability – BAA, 1999–2000
Source: Annual reports.

Dubai airport: non-aeronautical strategies for a competing airport

Many of the Gulf airports are in fierce competition for transit and transfer traffic – albeit to a lesser extent nowadays because of more non-stop long-haul flights. They are very interesting airports as regards non-aeronautical strategies as they have probably done more than any other airports in the world to attract passengers by promoting the duty-free facilities on offer. Dubai airport is the largest airport in the region. In 1999 it handled 10.7 million passengers compared with just 4.5 million in 1989 – representing an average growth rate of 9 per cent. The airport is forecast to handle 30 million passengers in 2010 – although it only has a national population of 790 000 (Bampton, 2000). It works closely with the national airline, Emirates, which is based at the airport. The airport serves Dubai, which has become the major trading base of the Gulf region as well as being used as a transit stop for intercontinental services.

The airport is owned and operated by the Dubai Department of Civil Aviation. The duty-free shop operator Dubai Duty Free (DDF) is also run by this department. This state ownership enables the prices to be kept low and very competitive compared with other airports. The DDF works very closely with the airport management and this enables it to get involved with the master planning process at a very early stage. The first DDF shop was introduced in December 1983 and then, in 1987, arrival duty-free shopping was added. Since 1984 the turnover associated with these sales has increased by 850 per cent, totalling around US$190 million in 1998 (DDF, 2000). Gold and jewellery account for around 16 per cent of these sales and liquor, and cigarettes and food represent a further 45 per cent of sales (Bampton, 2000). Another important area of diversification is the Dubai Airport Free Zone which was launched in 1997. This covers an area of over 1.2 million square metres and includes areas used for apron space, light industry and public facilities such as retailing and catering.

In November 1989, the DDF launched its 'Dubai Duty Free Finest Surprise' to mark the expansion of its shopping complex. This promotion offered a Rolls-Royce Bentley Mulsanne car to the winner of a raffle. The tickets, which were sold exclusively at the airport, were limited to 1000 per draw. The promotion was extended throughout the 1990s with a continuous high-profile display of luxury cars in the airport concourse. After 1991 two cars were offered simultaneously and, by 1999, over 800 luxury cars had been won. Other competing airports in the Middle East, such as Abu Dhabi and Bahrain, as well as airports in other areas such as Malta have also undertaken similar promotions.

In 2000 a new duty-free area was opened at the airport in the new 180 000 square metres, US$200 million five-level terminal concourse (Walters, 1999). The duty-free complex covers an area of 9000 square metres and is four times larger than the previous shop. All routes to the twenty-seven departure gates go through the retail area. To commemorate the opening of these new facilities, the airport launched another promotion called the 'Dubai Duty Free Finest Cyber Surprise'. This promotion offered US$1 million to winners of the 'Millennium Millionaire Draw'. Tickets for this draw could only be bought at the airport and, as before, were limited in number (5000 this time) to increase the chances of winning ticket. By the end of 2000, nine passengers had been made millionaires!

Singapore airport: aiming to maintain its position as a leading Asian/Pacific hub

Singapore Changi airport, which is owned by the Civil Aviation Authority of Singapore, has developed some interesting strategies in order to maintain its position as a hub in the very competitive Asia and Pacific market. The airport is facing fiercer competition with the opening of the new Hong Kong and Kualu Lumpur airports in the late 1990s and the proposed new Bangkok airport which is planned for completion in 2005. Moreover, its passenger traffic dropped by 5.4 per cent in 1998 – the first decrease ever for the airport – as a result of the Asian crisis. This meant that it had to reduce its landing fees by 10 per cent and give rebates of up to 15 per cent for rentals at commercial concessions to remain competitive (Citrinot, 1999b). By 1999, traffic had more or less recovered and a growth of 8.7 per cent in passenger numbers was experienced. In that year the airport handled just under 25 million passengers, compared to 30 million at Hong Kong and 15 million at Kuala Lumpur. This compares with 13 million passengers at Changi airport in 1989.

The airport is now building on an already relatively sophisticated commercial strategy which it has had for many years. It offers a very wide range of commercial facilities and has pre-shopping facilities and price guarantees like BAA plc and some other airports. To appeal to transfer passengers it organizes bus tours of Singapore. There is also an airport hotel situated in the transit area which has many facilities including a karaoke room, mini putting green, swimming pool, gym, sauna and jacuzzi. One of its unusual features is its gardens. In all, it has five themed gardens! It has a cactus garden located in Terminal 1, which has more than twenty varieties of cacti which are native to North and South America. It also has a bamboo garden in Terminal 1. In Terminal 2 it has an orchid garden which covers an area of over 600 square metres and has over forty different varieties of orchids. The terminal also had a fern garden and outdoor garden terrace.

The airport aims to ensure that it provides the latest technological and communication services – particularly for its business travellers. In 1996 it was one of the first airports to offer internet services to passengers. It now has an extensive internet area which includes numerous personal computer connection points and infrared internet access kiosks. It also has a science discovery area which has devices such as holograms, colour-blindness tests and other interactive exhibits. In addition it has three television thematic lounges. There is a news lounge, a 'sports arena' lounge and a 'movie theatre' lounge which shows films twenty-four hours a day and is decorated with film posters and memorabilia. In addition to all these commercial facilities for passengers, the airport is also setting up a cargo park with the aim of establishing itself as a leading air cargo centre in South East Asia.

The growing importance of non-aeronautical revenues within the airport industry is a very visible trend which can be observed by any passenger who is able to compare their visit to an airport now with an equivalent visit of ten or fifteen years ago. However, this increased emphasis on commercial facilities has not been popular with all users – even though it may be essential for the airport operators' financial well-being. This chapter has aimed to describe the market for commercial services and to assess commercial strategies and polices. The diverse collection of case studies at the end of the chapter shows that the options available to airports are vast and no doubt, in the future, airport operators will be even more imaginative in developing new ideas.

References and further reading

ACI-Europe (1999). The ACI Europe tender code. *Marketing and Commercial Strategy Handbook*, vol. 7, ACI-Europe.

Aer Rianta (2000). *Annual Report 1999*. Aer Rianta.

Air Transport Group (1997). *Airport Development Economics*. Cranfield University.

Airport Council International (ACI) (2000). *ACI Airport Economics Survey 1998*. ACI.

Amore, M. (1999). New airport, new opportunities. *Marketing and Commercial Strategy Handbook*, vol. 7, ACI-Europe.

Anderson, D. (1999). European duty free is dead: what's changed? *Airports International*, November/December, 8–9.

British Airports Authority (BAA) (2000). *Annual Report 1999/2000*. BAA

Bampton, J. (2000). Duty free challenge. *Jane's Airport Review*, December/January, 9.

Byrd, J. (2000). Retail management structures: transatlantic differences. Ninth ACI-Europe Airport Trading Conference, London, February.

Centre for Airport Studies (1998). *Airport Retail Study*, CAS.

Citrinot, L. (1999a). New commercial strategies for airports. *Travel and Tourism Analyst*, (3), 1–19.

Citrinot, L. (1999b). Asia takes a long term view. *Jane's Airport Review*, April, 9.

Conway, P. (2000). Will check-in get smart? *Airline Business*, August, 44–8.

Copenhagen Airport (2000). *Annual Report 1999*. Copenhagen Airport.

Deutsche Bank (1999). *European Airports: Privatization Ahead*. Deutsche Bank.

Doganis, R. (1992). *The Airport Business*. Routledge.

Doganis, R. (2000). Economic issues in airport management. University of Westminster/Cranfield University Airport Economics and Finance Symposium, London, March.

Dubai Duty Free (DDF) (2000). www.ddf-uae.com (24 August 2000).

European Travel Research Foundation (ETRF) (1997). *The Duty and Tax Free Industry in the European Union: The Facts*. ETRF.

Favotto, I. (2000). Benchmarking and optimising airport retail revenue. Ninth ACI-Europe Airport Trading Conference, London, February.

Freathy, P. and O'Connell, F. (1998). *European Airport Retailing*. Macmillan.

Gethin, S. (1997). Airside shopping is becoming big business. *Jane's Airport Review*, October, 11–15.

Gray, F. (1998a). Landside shopping. *Communique Airport Business*, June/July, 42.

Gray, F. (1998b). Concessions: plan early or else! *Marketing and Commercial Strategy Handbook*, vol. 6, ACI-Europe.

Gray, F. (2000). Concession contracts and tendering processes. Cranfield University Airport Management Course, Cranfield, May.

Harrison, M (2000). How BAA is surviving without cheap booze and fags. *Independent*, 23 August.

Haugaard, B. (1998). Airport retailing: problems are opportunities. *Marketing and Commercial Strategy Handbook*, vol. 6, ACI-Europe.

Herbert, L. (1995). An exclusive commercial performance analysis of 30 airports. *Commercial and Marketing Best Practices Handbook*, vol. 1, ACI-Europe.

Institute for Retail Studies (1997). *Airport Retail Economics*. University of Stirling.

Kim, H. (2000). Dynamics in Asia: Inchon International Airport and airport community development. Ninth ACI-Europe Airport Trading Conference, London, February.

Kostelitz, A. (2000). Old experiences – new challenges. Ninth ACI-Europe Airport Trading Conference, London, February.

Maiden, S. (2000). Getting to know the market at airports. University of Westminster Marketing and Market Research Seminar, London, December.

Maiden, S. (1995). Understanding the retail market. Fourth ACI-Europe Airport Trading Conference, London, February.

Meznarsic, J. (1999). Landside vs airside – a study of airport shopping centres. *Marketing and Commercial Strategy Handbook*, vol. 7, ACI-Europe.

Middecke, R. (2000). Designing the perfect airport to optimise retail revenue; a retailers point of view. Ninth ACI-Europe Airport Trading Conference, London, February.

Monopolies and Mergers Commission (1996). *A Report on the Economic Regulation of the London Airports Companies*. MMC.

Newhouse, D. (2000). Life without intra-EU duty free – adapting to the loss of the business and exploiting new opportunities. Ninth ACI-Europe Airport Trading Conference, London, February.

O'Conner, J. (1999). Optimising income from commercial operations at Asian airports. In *Airport 2000: Trends for the New Millennium* (N. Ashford, ed.), Sovereign.

Phythian, C. (1996). Innovative commercial strategies. University of Westminster/Cranfield University Airport Economics and Finance Symposium, London, March.

Savage, R. (2000). Developing commercial strategies. University of Westminster/Cranfield University Airport Economics and Finance Symposium, London, March.

Schiphol Group (2000). *Annual Report 1999*. Schiphol Group.

Schwarz, R. (1996). A further examination of European commercial activities. *Commercial and Marketing Best Practices Handbook*, vol. 3 – ACI-Europe.

Skapinker, M. (1999). End of European duty-free party gives BAA a hangover. *Financial Times*, 5 November.

Toms, M. (2000). Critique of cost benchmarking. CAA workshop on Benchmarking of airports: methodologies, problems and relevance to economic regulation, London, September.

Tooke, L. (1999). Duty free and the leisure passenger. University of Westminster Aviation and Tourism Seminar, London, January.

Walsh, S. (2000). A winning formula. *Jane's Airport Review*, December/January, 10.

Walters, B. (1999). Dubai aims for the top 20. *Jane's Airport Review*, November, 13.

7

The role of airport marketing

The birth of airport marketing

Airport marketing as a concept at most airports did not really exist until the 1980s. Prior to this, the role of the airport as a public service meant that very often airport management would merely respond to airline requests for new slots by providing published charging and use-of-facility information rather than initiating talks to attract new services. In most cases, the airports considered it was solely the role of the airline to identify opportunities for new or expanded services. It was up to the airport to provide an efficient and safe airport with good facilities for aircraft and travellers. Promoting the air services at the airport was also not considered to be a responsibility of the airport, with the view being that this should be undertaken by the airlines and travel agents which were selling the products. It was rare to find airport marketing managers and, generally, the resources allocated to marketing activities were very small. Airport promotion tended to be very basic, typically consisting of the production of a timetable and publicity leaflets, and reactive responses to press enquiries about the airport.

This passive approach has long since gone at most airports. Airports have become much more proactive in their approach and have developed a wide range of increasingly sophisticated techniques for meeting the demands of their complex mix of customers such as passengers, airlines, freight forwarders, tour operators and so on. Within any commercially run business, marketing is considered to be a core activity and one which is a vital ingredient for success. The airport sector is no longer an exception and marketing is increasingly being seen as an integral part of the airport business.

Deregulation of air transport markets has made the airport business much more competitive. Airlines in Europe, for example, are much freer to operate out of any airport they choose without being constrained by bilateral restrictions. They are thus much more susceptible to aggressive marketing by airports. New types of airlines, for example low-cost carriers such as easyJet and Ryanair, have emerged, which certain airports may wish to attract through a range of marketing techniques. The increase in demand for air transport due to deregulation and other more general factors, such as economic growth, has meant that there have been enhanced opportunities for more airports to share in this expansion of the market. This has provided airports with greater incentive to develop innovative and aggressive market strategies so that they can reap some of the benefits from this growth. Moreover, a number of airports are close to capacity and unable to offer attractive slots for new services. This means that there may be attractive prospects for other airports to promote themselves as alternative uncongested airports.

The travelling public has also become more demanding and more sophisticated in their travel-making decisions and their expectations of the airport product. Airports have had to develop more sophisticated marketing strategies and tactics to meet the needs of the traveller. In addition deregulation, privatization and globalization trends within the airline industry have increased the commercial pressures being faced by airlines which in turn has encouraged airports to recognize the need for a professional marketing-orientated approach when dealing with their airline customers.

By the late 1990s, the majority of airports were devoting considerable resources to marketing activities. It is difficult to accurately quantify this

Table 7.1 Number employed in airport marketing at selected regional airports

Airport	Total number of marketing staff		Number of passengers per marketing staff	
	1991	1997	1991	1997
Manchester	16	27	631 000	562 000
Birmingham	10	24	325 000	227 000
Newcastle	4	6	382 000	428 000
East Midlands	7	9	164 000	202 000
Bristol	7	6	392 000	248,000
Cardiff	2	6	257 000	185 000
Bournemouth	1	4	250 000	41 000
Norwich	1	5	215 ,000	54 000
Humberside	1	4	163 000	70 000

Source: Humphreys (1999).

increased emphasis on the role of marketing but some indication of this trend can be gleaned from an analysis of staff employed in the marketing area. For example, with UK regional airports the number of passengers per marketing staff decreased significantly between 1991 and 1997 (Table 7.1). If marketing is defined in its broadest sense of satisfying customer needs, there are various other activities (which have been discussed in other chapters) which also can be considered as airport marketing. These activities include quality assessment and improvement, and environmental neighbourhood communication initiatives. The development of non-aeronautical activities can also be treated as a marketing role. Up until quite recently marketing and commercial activities, especially at regional airports, were often covered by the same department at the airport (Meznarsic, 1995). Most airports have now recognized that for both activities to be effective, very different skills and management are required, and so in all but the smallest airports they are usually now considered to be separate functions.

The nature of airport competition

It used to be commonly believed that most major airports were monopolies with their precise role being determined by the passenger demand in the catchment area. Moreover, airline choice was considered to be limited to particular airports because of bilateral agreements. While this may still be true in certain markets, there are now a growing number of opportunities for airports to compete for both passengers and airlines. The modern-day airline industry which has been transformed, particularly in Europe, from a regulated and public sector controlled activity into a liberalized and commercially orientated business, has played a major role in this changing airport situation. Certain airline developments such as the formation of global alliances and other types of co-operation between airlines such as franchising have been particularly important, as have the development of the low-cost sector, in creating new views on airport competition.

There are a number of key ways in which airports can compete (ACI-Europe, 1999). Clearly if airports are physically close, their catchment areas may overlap for certain types of traffic. For short-haul routes, passengers tend to choose the most convenient, nearest airport which has suitable services. For long-haul flights passengers may be more willing to travel further distances to an airport which they regard as offering a more desirable or superior long-haul service.

In some major urban areas or cities there are a number of situations when more than one airport serves the population. Notable examples are the European cities of London and Paris, and the American cities of New York and Washington. Sometimes the airports may be under the same ownership as with the AdP which owns Charles de Gaulle, Orly and Le Bourget airports and the Port Authority of New York and New Jersey which owns JFK, La Guardia and Newark airports. Such common ownership may clearly reduce the amount of potential competition. Elsewhere in London, for instance, BAA plc airports of Heathrow, Gatwick and Stansted compete with the independently run London City and London Luton airports, while in Washington the Metropolitan Washington Airports Authority airports of Dulles and National compete to a certain degree with Baltimore airport which is owned by the State of Maryland.

In many cases when there are overlapping catchment areas, one airport tends to become the dominant player with the other airports playing a more secondary role. In the London area, for example, Heathrow airport is considered by many passengers, particularly those travelling on business, to be the 'London airport' in spite of a range of services being offered at the other London airports. The secondary airports tend to fulfil more specialized roles (Dennis, 1995). They may act as an overspill airport when the major airport has inadequate capacity, as is the case with Düsseldorf airport, which suffers from runway constraints, and the nearby secondary airport of Moenchengladbach. Alternatively centrally located secondary airports may be able to attract a certain amount of domestic or short-haul traffic, particularly business-related traffic. These types of passengers favour the convenience and generally less congested environment which a city centre airport such as London City or Belfast City may offer. Other airports may choose to specialize in charter operations (e.g. Rome Ciampino airport) or freight operations (e.g. Liège airport).

Then there are the airports that have begun to market themselves as low-cost alternatives to the major airports – having been encouraged by the rapid development of European low-cost carriers (Table 7.2). These airports offer lower fees, faster turnarounds and fewer delays, but in many cases are situated substantially further from the town or city they are serving compared with the competing airports. In some cases these airports may be owned by the same operator which has control of the competing airports, for example, BAA plc owns Stansted airport, Frankfurt airports owns Hahn airport and SEA, the Milan airport operator, owns Bergamo airport. Elsewhere separate ownership patterns exist. Some low-cost airlines, particularly Ryanair in relation to Dublin airport in Ireland, have suggested that there ought to be competing terminals at airports run by different operators. Some limited evidence of such a practice, for example at JFK airport in New York and Toronto airport in Canada, has not proved to be particularly successful but it remains an important issue (CAA, 2001).

Table 7.2 Alternative low-cost airports within Europe

Low-cost airport	Competing major airport	Under same ownership?
Beauvais	Paris – CDG/Orly	No
Belfast City	Belfast International	No
Bergamo	Milan – Linate/Malpensa	Yes
Charleroi	Brussels National	No
Carcassonne	Toulouse	No
Cergy-Pontoise	Paris – CDG/Orly	No
Hahn	Frankfurt	Yes
Liverpool	Manchester	No
London – Luton	London – Heathrow and Gatwick	No
London – Stansted	London – Heathrow and Gatwick	Yes
Prestwick	Glasgow International	No
Rome – Ciampino	Rome – Fiumicino	Yes
Sandefjord – Torp	Oslo –Gardermoen	No
Skavsta	Stockholm – Arlanda	No

Problems can occur when a new airport is built which is perceived as providing a inferior service to the old one – perhaps being in a less conveniently situated location. A notable example is Montreal Mirabel's airport, which was built in the 1970s to provide extra capacity in addition to Dorval airport but never managed to attract the volume of traffic that was forecast. Milan is a more recent case where there has been considerable reluctance for carriers to transfer from the Milan Linate airport, which is closer to the city centre, to the newly expanded Milan Malpensa airport. Unless effective regulation is introduced, the only feasible way of ensuring that traffic will transfer to the new airport is by actually closing the old one which has happened in locations such as Munich, Hong Kong, Oslo and Denver (ACI-Europe 1999; Caves and Gosling, 1999).

The other main way in which airports compete is as a hub. Key prerequisites for a hub are a central geographic position and adequate runway/terminal capacity to enable a 'wave' system of arriving and departing flights to take place. Certain airports can compete as hubs for cargo operations especially for express parcel services, particularly if they are open all night and have a good weather record. New infrastructure, notably at Asian destinations such Kuala Lumpur, Hong Kong and Macao, has provided the impetus for more intense competition for hub traffic. Hub airports are, however, very much dependent on the operating strategies of airlines. While many medium and large-sized airports have aspirations of becoming a hub, in reality there is now less opportunity for this to happen as a result of the growing concentration within the airline industry through developments such as global alliances and code-sharing.

In most cases, passengers will have a specific destination in mind when they travel. The exception may be with some intercontinental traffic when passengers might be more indifferent. For example, Americans visiting Europe may not have a strong preference as to whether they start their European tour from Paris, London or Frankfurt. Airports serving these cities can therefore compete for this traffic. The same can be true with cargo traffic. This is particularly the case within Europe where most long-haul freight is trucked to its final destination.

Marketing concepts

The market for airport services

The focal point of any marketing system is always the consumer of the services. For the airport product, demand comes from a variety of markets each with their own specific requirements. From a marketing perspective, it is useful to divide this demand into two, namely the trade such as airlines who buy the airport facilities direct and the general public or travellers who merely consume or utilize the airport product. The marketing techniques used for these two types are very different. Most airports would probably agree that both airlines and passengers are key customers, whereas airlines tend to think of passengers as their customers and themselves as customers of the airports.

In addition, there are the other market segments such as local residents and businesses whose needs must also be met. Obviously these types of demand do not impact directly on the amount of aeronautical revenue and traffic through-put at an airport but their presence at the airport can have a significant impact on the level of non-aeronautical revenue. They can also help airports in acting as a catalyst for economic development. Concessionaires, tenants and other organizations such as handling agents can also be considered customers of the airport. Table 7.3 shows some of the major market segments at an airport. Each of these need to be further subdivided into much smaller discreet segments in order that they can be targeted appropriately and so that the airport's marketing efforts can be the most effective.

Table 7.3 The airport's customers

Trade	Passengers	Others
Airlines	Scheduled (traditional and low-cost)	Tenants and concessionaires
Tour operators	Charter	Visitors
Travel agents	Business	Employees
Freight forwarders	Leisure	Local residents
General aviation	Transfer	Local businesses

A common way to segment demand is by airline product type. For example, with passenger travel this would include a full-cost traditional service, a low-cost service and a charter service. Airline alliances could well be given special consideration. In the cargo area, the market may be segmented into integrators, cargo airlines, passenger airlines and other freight companies.

Rather than considering the demand by product type or purpose of travel, it can sometimes be useful to consider it by travel behaviour in order to match more closely the needs of each market segment. For example, there are 'Agoraphobics' who have the lowest level of need, have a fear of flying and of missing the plane, and do not want to be distracted from the departure monitor. Then there are the 'Euphorics' who are the once-a-year holidaymakers who arrive early at the airport and spend money as part of the holiday experience. Next in the order of needs are the 'Confident indulgers' who are frequent leisure fliers who are familiar with the airport product and want to be pampered. Most complaints come from 'Airport controllers' who are typically frequent business passengers flying economy with their families on holiday and feel aggrieved that they do not have the privileges that they normally experience when flying business class. Then, finally, there are the 'Self-controllers' who are frequent business fliers who just want to be processed through the airport as quickly and as efficiently as possible. The amount of time which these types of passenger spend at the airport varies from considerable in the case of the Agoraphobics down to the minimum possible for the Self-controllers (Young, 1996).

For each type of customer, choosing an airport is the result of an amalgam of many decision processes (Table 7.4). For passengers, for example, clearly the

Table 7.4   Factors affecting the choice of airports

Passengers	Airlines
Destinations of flights	Catchment area and potential demand
Flight fare	Slot availability
Flight availability and timings	Competition
Frequency of service	Network compatibility
Image and reliability of airline	Airport fees and availability of discounts
Airline alliance policy and frequent-flyer programme	Other airport costs (e.g. fuel, handling)
Surface access cost to airport	Marketing support
Ease of access to airport	Range and quality of facilities
Car parking cost	Ease of transfer connections
Range and quality of shops, catering and other commercial facilities	Maintenance facilities
Image of airport and ease of use	Environmental restrictions

nature of air services on offer – in effect the airline product – will be the key factor as no one will choose to fly from an airport unless it offers the required travel opportunities. Factors such as the distance, cost and ease of surface access to a certain airport can also be very important. The quality of the airport product can have a marginal impact, but only after these other factors have been taken into account. For business passengers, facilities such as fast-track processes and airline lounges may affect choice, while for customers with special needs, for example disabled passengers, the quality of the provision of wheelchair, lifts and general assistance may be important. Then there are other factors which are more difficult to explain and quantify. For example, in many European countries there will be a preference for the established capital city airport even if there are alternative airports that offer a comparable service. This is especially the case among the business community. In some instances, this may be because of better flight availability and frequency at the main airport, but not always. It may be because of ignorance about the other airports, especially among travel agents, or because of some other factor such as the traveller's choice of a certain airline in order to add to their frequent flyer points.

For the airline and other trade customers such as tour operators, it is clearly the nature of the catchment area rather than design details of the airport facilities which are of paramount importance. Depending on the type of route being considered, key factors are business and tourist appeal of the catchment area for incoming passengers, and the characteristics and purchasing power of those residing in the catchment area (Favotto, 1998). Other important elements include the availability of attractive slot times, the presence of competitors and the marketing assistance which the airport is prepared to give, not only in terms of pricing incentives but also with the funding of activities such as market research and promotional campaigns. Other customers will take into account different factors. For example, retailers will only wish to operate at an airport if they have proof that the passenger profile is attractive enough and that the airport has a sufficient traffic throughput.

Table 7.5 gives reasons, obtained from passenger surveys, for why the three largest airports in the UK, namely London Heathrow, London Gatwick and Manchester, were chosen in 1998. As expected, the location of airport and flights on offer are the key factors determining choice. For the London airports, most important is the nature of flights on offer – at Heathrow for both local and connecting flights. Half the passengers at the regional airport of Manchester, however, chose the airport because it was close to their home, with an additional 13 per cent picking it because it was near to their business or leisure destination. Gatwick has a higher proportion of leisure passengers which may explain why passengers were more influenced by travel cost. Similarly the timing of flights appears to be a more influential factor at Heathrow, because of its higher share of business passengers, than at Gatwick or Manchester airport. Through modelling survey data, Ashford (1989) identified three key factors affecting passenger choice, namely access travel time, flight frequency and air fare. In highly regulated markets, such as Nigeria in Africa, flight frequency and air fare were found to be unimportant and surface access time to be very influential.

Table 7.5 Passengers reasons for choice of UK airport in 1998

Reason for choice	London Heathrow	London Gatwick	Manchester
Near home	12.8	20.0	49.6
Flights/package available	38.0	51.3	25.2
Connecting flights	19.0	6.8	1.6
Near business	6.1	2.4	6.7
Near leisure	4.5	2.4	6.3
Economic/cheaper	6.2	7.5	2.4
Prefer airport	2.7	2.2	3.0
Timing of flights	4.6	2.2	1.3
Local services inadequate	1.8	0.8	2.2
Prefer airline	2.8	2.4	0.2
Better surface access	0.1	0.7	0.9
Special promotion	0.5	0.3	0.1
Other	0.9	0.9	0.5
Total	100.0	100.0	100.0

Source: CAA (1999).

The airport product

The airport product consists of a supply of services, both tangible and intangible, to meet the needs of different market segments. Marketing theory often divides the product into the core, actual or physical and augmented elements. The core product is the essential benefit which the consumer is seeking, while the actual product delivers the benefit. Product features, quality level, brand name, design and packaging will all make up the physical product. The augmented product is then additional consumer services and benefits which will be built around the core and actual products, and will distinguish the product from others. Much of the competition will typically take place at the augmented level (Kotler et al., 1996). Sometimes the physical product is referred to as the 'generic' product with the 'wide' product representing the augmented elements (Jarach, 2001).

Each market segment will perceive these product levels very differently. For the airline, the core is the ability to land and take off an aircraft, while for the passenger it will be the ability to board or disembark an aircraft. For freight forwarders it will be the ability to load and unload the freight on the aircraft. In order to provide the core product for the airline, the actual product will need to consist of the runway, the terminal building, the freight warehouses, the equipment and so on – and the expertise to provide all these facilities efficiently and safely. For the passenger, the actual product will include check-in desks, baggage handling and other features such as immigration control which will enable the passenger to fulfil their need of boarding or disembarking the aircraft. The actual product will also include adequate transport services to and from airport, and the provision of outlets selling essential travel goods, as well as other facilities such as information desks and toilets. At the augmented level the airport may, for example, offer marketing support or pricing incentives to the airlines or may formalize some agreement about the exact service levels to be expected. For the passenger the range and diversity of shops, catering and other commercial facilities as well as other features such as ease of transfer between different aircraft could all be considered to be part of the augmented product.

It is difficult to apply this marketing concept to the airport sector because of the composite nature of the airport product. From a passenger viewpoint, the airport product includes the airline product as well as the product of the concessionaire, handling agent and so on. Another way of looking at the airport product is by considering its 'raw' and 'refined' features. The raw product consists of both physical tangible elements (such as the runway, buildings, apron, lighting, navigation aids, fuel, fire and rescue) and intangible service elements provided by the airport operator's own staff and those of the customs, immigration and security agencies. To produce the refined product involves adding the services provided by concessionaires and other tenants and the air travel elements, both tangible and intangible, provided by the airlines (Reantragoon, 1994).

At the broadest level, the airport product can be considered to be a large commercial centre, which meets the needs of travellers, visitors and residents. Within this context, the Schiphol Group has defined Amsterdam airport as an 'AirportCity' to get over the message that the airport, like any other city, provides services twenty-four hours a day in the form of shops and catering, hotels and recreation, and information, communication and business activities. It wants to market this concept internationally through airport alliances and partnerships, and is already applying this model to other airports where it has some management involvement (Schiphol Group, 1999).

Related to the concept of the airport product, is the idea of an airport brand. In marketing theory a brand is represented by a name, logos, design, signing, merchandising and advertising which all give the product an identity. These tangible and intangible features of the identity differentiate the product from its competitors. Within the airport sector it is certainly true that there are widespread attempts to create a corporate identity with the use of catchy publicity slogans, and eye-catching logos and designs on promotional information and within the terminal itself. For airport operators who own more that one airport, use of similar signposting, colour schemes and interior design may also be used for all its airports. For example, BAA plc has traditionally used a common and constant brand image for its seven UK airports. Whether such 'branding' actually gives an airport any competitive edge is, however, very debatable although it may make the customer feel more at ease because of the familiar surroundings. Many airports use a number of sub-brands for different areas. For instance, Manchester airport has used 'Manchester Connects' for its transfer product and 'En Route to the World' for its retail product (Teale, 1996). Too many brands may confuse passengers, however, particular as airlines and their alliance groupings are also becoming increasingly keen to have their own identity represented in the area of the terminal where their passengers are handled.

Marketers often give considerable attention to the name of the airport. Many regional airports like to be called 'international' airports to demonstrate that they serve international as well as domestic destinations – even if in some cases there may be only one international route! On the other hand, as airports become more developed and more well known for their range of services, they may choose to drop the international name as Manchester airport did in 1986. Other airports will include the name of the nearest large city or town, even if it may not be particularly close, and there may be more conveniently located airports. For example, with the London area there is now not only London Heathrow, London Gatwick and London Stansted but also London Luton, London Manston, London Southend, London Biggin Hill and London Ashford. Charleroi is known as Brussels South, Sandefjord-Torp as Oslo South and Skavsta as Stockholm South. The name EuroAirport for Basel-Mulhouse airport has been devised to reflect its central European location and bi-national ownership characteristics. Other interesting examples include Zurich airport which was rebranded as 'Unique Zürich Airport' in 2000 to reflect a new management structure, partial privatization and expanded facilities (Hill, 2000). In the same year Lyon airport in France changed its name from Lyon Satolas to Lyon-Saint-Exupery in an aim to strengthen the airport's worldwide reputation (European Regions Airline Association, 2000).

Ultimately most decisions concerning the choice of airport will be based primarily on the air services available at the airport (i.e. the airline product) and the proximity of the airport to the potential customer. It is very important for the airport to remember this and to focus its marketing on the air services on offer and the airport's convenience rather than giving every fact about the facilities on offer. Similarly when marketing to airlines, it is information about the nature of catchment area and potential demand rather than small details about the airport infrastructure which will most probably sell the airport. No amount of money spent on improving facilities will attract airlines to the airport unless they consider that there is a market for their services.

Airport marketing techniques

Successful airport marketing involves focusing on understanding and responding to the needs of the various customer segments. Clearly every airport is unique and needs to be marketed in its own specific way. At small airports, all marketing tasks may be undertaken by a couple of staff, whereas at larger airports there may be separate departments for coping with different customers such as the passengers and airlines, and different teams looking at different marketing activities such as market research, sales and public relations. Once an airport gets to a certain size, the marketing focus is likely to change. Small airports may concentrate on growing specific services which appear to offer opportunities for the airport. Larger airports, which already have a reasonably developed route network, may be more concerned with putting forward a good positive image for the airport and building on a corporate identity. The marketing of airports aiming to be hub or feeder points is totally different from marketing an airport which relies on point-to-point services such as charter or low-cost services. Airports with considerable spare capacity will adopt different strategies to congested airports. Smaller airports competing with major capital city airports will probably find that they are always faced with an uphill struggle but nevertheless a considerable amount of proactive and aggressive marketing may achieve results.

Trade

At the most basic level, airports promote themselves to airlines, tour operators, freight forwarders and so on by producing general publicity information, by placing advertisements in trade journals and by being represented at exhibitions, travel trade seminars and workshops, roadshows and other similar events. The aim here is to increase awareness among the trade. Sometimes simple messages may be used to sell the airport. Vienna airport, for instance, has promoted itself as being 'Europe's best address', while Nice airport has described itself as the 'Greatway to Europe'. With other airports the key message may be more specific. Large hub airports may focus on their size to demonstrate that the airport is popular and has connecting traffic possibilities. For instance, Atlanta airport has invited airlines to become 'Members of the busiest airport in the world' while Rome airport has used the message 'With more than 150 destinations we help half of the world to reach the other half. And vice versa'. Other airports try to emphasize different product characteristics such as uncongested facilities and quick processing times. Kansas airport told airlines not to 'Get drawn into a congested hub', while Stansted claimed that it was a 'London airport where you can call the shots'. The small Palm Beach airport's slogan was 'Touch Down 11:00, Towel Down 11:45'. Price sometimes features in such advertising. Geneva airport, for example, has sold itself as being 'The high yield airport with surprising low costs', while Macau airport advertised half price landing fees at night with the message 'Our night fall brings sweet dreams . . . 50% off at night'.

Developing regular contact with key airlines and tour operators through visits by airport sales staff, or with regular mail shots and other promotional activities, may also be effective. Airports tend, however, to deal with potential airlines customers in a much more direct and personal way. This hard-selling approach was developed in the 1980s owing to the realization that airports were actually in the good position to identify new route opportunities for airlines.

This was a task previously left solely to the airlines. The airport marketers analysed passenger and catchment area data which gave them adequate information to suggest new route opportunities to potential operators. Many of the airports had the advantage that they already kept at least some of this data for their own passenger marketing and forecasting. They also benefited from certain cost economies by being able to consider all different markets and routes simultaneously. For a small airline interested in operating just one or two new routes, the cost of undertaking such research could well have been too prohibitive.

So the airports started to take a leading role in initiating interest from airlines, tour operators and other trade users. From their databases, they would provide airlines with information about potential routes and the size of the market and perhaps other factors such as the likely requirements for frequency and aircraft size, and route cost and yield considerations.

By the 1990s, airline presentations from the marketing departments of airports to route planners in airlines had become commonplace. Typically the presentation would give a detailed analysis of the new route or routes. This would be supplemented by information about the catchment area, in terms of the characteristics of residents and its tourist and business appeal for incoming passengers. Information would also be given about the airport's facilities and also accessibility by transport links.

The airports which first adopted this more reactive approach to marketing to airlines, such as Manchester and Vienna, have claimed many success stories. Times have now moved on in the air transport industry and both the airports and airlines have developed more sophisticated marketing techniques. The airline presentation is still an important element of an airport's marketing but it has to be highly focused. The emphasis must be very much on the potential demand at the airport with the quality of facilities taking second place. Emphasis on architectural excellence and best-quality facilities could even have a negative impact, with airlines being concerned that the cost of such infrastructure may be passed on to them. The airlines themselves have become awash with route studies from numerous airports and so have become much more skilled in using this information to back-up and verify their own research.

Once an airline has shown some interest in a potential route, the airport will typically agree to provide additional support in a number of ways. For example, reduced fees may be offered for a certain period of time. These can be particularly important and can be crucial particularly for low-cost carriers. Such discounts will usually diminish as traffic grows and the service becomes sustainable, although this may develop into an area of considerable friction between the airport operator and airline (see Chapter 5). Joint advertising and promotional campaigns may be run to promote the new service both through the media and travel agents by pooling resources. The airport may also agree to share the costs of further advertising to ensure that the initial level of demand is sustained. The airport may promise to undertake further market research or help to lobby government to remove bilateral regulatory obstacles. Manchester airport was particularly active in this latter activity in the 1970s and 1980s when it frequently attempted to get gateway status, alongside the London airports, in a number of bilateral agreements. A more recent example is San Francisco airport, which successfully helped persuade the regulatory authorities to agree to non-stop services being operated to Shanghai. Such services began in 2000. Airports may also choose to give advice on scheduling decisions, particular if an airline is to benefit from connecting traffic from other airlines. A good example of this practice is again Manchester airport, which worked together with airlines to co-ordinate the arrival and departure time of air services in order to create 'Manchester Connects' – the interline hub.

Airports may be able to make themselves appear particularly attractive if they guarantee that the overall package of costs which an airline is faced with will be reasonable. In many cases, airports will be able to offer discounted airport charges but will have no control over handling or fuel charges. However, a few airports such as Abu Dhabi in the Middle East offer a one-stop approach when there is a single contract for all ground services at the airport. Since all the facilities, including aircraft fuelling are owned by the government, the airport is in a position to do this and to have complete control over what it offers to the airlines. At other airports, for example at Moenchengladbach airport near Düsseldorf, the airport operators are able to offer discounted public transport for the airline passengers. Another way in which an airport can put together an attractive deal for an airline and be cost-effective in its marketing is by pairing up and co-operating with the airport at the other end of a route which has been identified as having potential.

An interesting development as regards airline marketing has been the 'Routes' conference. This has been held annually since 1995 and is an oppor-tunity for airport marketers and airline route planners to get together to discuss future market opportunities. In prearranged, one-to-one meetings airlines explain their expansion strategies to airports, who in turn try to sell the virtues of their facilities and services. New routes, frequency increases and opportuni-ties for connecting traffic may be discussed, as well as marketing initiatives in the form of discounted fees and other incentives which the airport may be in the position to offer.

Travel agents

In spite of the increased use of the internet and other direct-booking methods, for the moment travel agents still remain highly influential when passengers go through the process of selecting and assessing possible travel options. Some of the general sales promotions directed at the airlines may be targeted at the travel agency sector as well, and may help to give exposure to the airport and the services which it offers. Regular mail shots to agents may enhance that awareness.

In many cases, however, this is not enough. Numerous airports, particularly the regional and smaller ones, have found that is particularly important to spend some time and effort in developing close and personalized links with travel agents serving the direct catchment area. This usually involves regularly sending out a sales representative who can talk to the agents about new devel-opments at the airport and explore the agents' knowledge and views of the services on offer. There are many stories of regional airports discovering that all their neighbouring travel agents are completely unaware of any local air flights. Instead, the agents will have automatically advised passengers to travel via a larger airport further away. Cardiff airport in the UK overcame this problem by buying a chain of twenty-two local travel agents in an attempt to promote flights from its airport (Humphreys, 1998). Norwich airport, also in the UK, has adopted a similar strategy.

This one-to-one contact can be supplemented with frequent, personalized mail shots giving details of routes launches, promotions, new facilities, up-to-date timetables and other information. Very often airports will also organize competitions, airport tours and other social events to encourage greater interest in the airport and to forge closer links with the agency sector.

Passengers and the local community

Generally a much more soft-sell approach is adopted for passengers. Airport timetables with details of airport services, facilities and surface access and other promotional literature is commonly distributed to travel agents, libraries, shopping centres, tourist information offices and so on. Travel brochures, produced jointly with tour operators or airlines, can be circulated. This not only has this advantage of sharing the cost but also has the benefit of having the operators' brand associated with the airport.

At the airport itself, information services are provided for passengers and visitors, as are maps and other information about the facilities and services. To increase awareness of the airport and improve relations with the community, open days, air shows, exhibitions and educational visits are also often organized. Branded giveaways to reinforce the airports image and identity, such as badges, key rings, T-shirts and stationery items are frequently distributed. Sponsorship of key events is also quite common in the airport business.

Airport information is now available on airport web sites which have been set up by most airports, with various degrees of sophistication. The type of information usually available includes airport location details, car parking and local transport details, with perhaps opportunities for pre-booking car parking space or buying public transport tickets on line. Tourist and other information about the airport's catchment area might be included. Nearly all the web sites, even the most basic ones, include terminal maps and a list of facilities, such as shops and catering, on offer. Many of the major airports have real-time flight information and flight-delay details. This is bound to become common practice.

However, the internet clearly has a much greater role to play than merely providing information for the traveller. The local community can find out about achievements, for example, in environmental protection. Shareholders can track the performance of their shares and have instant access to the airports' financial reports. Airlines should be able to retrieve traffic statistics and catchment area information, while details about customs requirements, and handling and warehousing facilities should be available to cargo customers. (Hoevel, 1999).

The internet can offer potentially numerous marketing and revenue opportunities, although as yet only a small number of major airports have taken full advantage of this. Customer profile and preference information could automatically be collected from users of the web site. Pre-ordering purchases, online shopping and advertising can increase non-aeronautical revenues. Airports are experimenting with various initiatives. For example, BAA plc in co-operation with the travel company expedia UK provides online reservations for many airlines and hotels, last minute travel details, weather updates, health advice, travel plans and destination profiles. Moreover, in 2000 BAA plc invested in lastminute.com. It also has airport upgrade packages available on the net.

Airports advertise to the public through the internet and all the other usual media channels such as television, radio, newspapers, magazines and posters. The choice of media, as with all marketing, clearly depends on the relative costs, the target audience and the message which the organization wants to put across. A basic message or idea can be successfully communicated with radio or television media (although in practice this is rare), whereas more detailed information, for example timetable or flights material, needs to be presented in the written form. As with the marketing to airlines, airports adopt various approaches to woo passenger to their airports. Most commonly airports try to increase the consumer's awareness of flights and closeness of the airport by listing the destinations on offer or by focusing on the convenience of the public transport links. More specific messages may relate to a certain service or facility at the airport – a notable example being the advertising which various airports have undertaken to recover some of their lost retail trade since the loss of EU duty- and tax-free sales. The advertising may be targeted at certain market segments, particularly business travellers. For instance, Abu Dhabi's airport marketing campaign 'Start at the Heart' was based around a heart logo designed to inform business travellers that they could check in at the 'heart' of the city and take a luxury car to the airport.

The ultimate aim of promotional and advertising activities is usually to sell a product, but the airport has a rather unique relationship with its passengers as it is not directly selling a product to them. The passenger will not go to the airport unless the required airline service is there and marketing communication techniques can usually only encourage use at the margins. Similarly, the quality of commercial facilities is unlikely to have an impact over a passenger's choice of airport unless perhaps the passenger is transferring flights or the incentives are very considerable – as with the high-value raffles at the airports serving Dubai, Bahrain and Abu Dhabi.

Airports, of course, have a major impact on the local community not only by providing local flights for the residents, but also by generating jobs and other economic benefits. On the other hand, the environmental impacts such as noise and pollution are of major concern. Generally, the aviation industry being the newest of all transport modes, still holds a fascination and wonder for some and a fear for others. For all these reasons, airports tend to receive extensive coverage, both favourable and otherwise in the press. It is worthwhile for airports to put reasonable effort into trying to capitalize on the general interest that people have with airports and to create a degree of goodwill between airports and the community, particularly should anything so wrong. Developing good links with local, regional, national and, in some cases, foreign media is crucial, and hosting events for journalists and travel writers can increase interest in the airport and stimulate press coverage. Arranging school visits and other trips will also be an essential public relations activity.

Market research

A fundamental element of marketing is market research – in order that organizations can have a thorough understanding of the characteristics and needs of their market. Most research will cover two areas, namely market characteristics in terms of market size, share, segmentation and trends, and the more subjective area of passenger satisfaction. Chapter 4 has already considered passenger satisfaction and so the emphasis of the discussion here is very much on the first area.

Information about passengers can be collected from a number of different sources. Passenger surveys at the airport are the most common but surveys or group interviews at home or at work are also possible. Views about current services and particularly any underserved destinations can be gleaned from organizations such as travel agents, local businesses and freight forwarders. Most major airports will carry out periodic surveys of their passengers to find out details such as origin and destination, age, sex, socio-economic group, flying frequency and so on. These surveys may be tied in with the quality surveys so that correlations between passenger profiles and levels of satisfaction can be made. In some countries surveys may undertaken by the national civil aviation authorities or government transport departments instead of, or in addition, to those carried out by the airport operators. For example, in the UK the CAA regularly surveys passengers at all main airports. This has the advantage in producing survey data that are directly comparable for different airports.

Market research information, supplemented with traffic data, will assist airport operators in the identification of new routes or enhanced frequency opportunities. Data which are particularly useful are the true origin and destination from global distribution systems such as Sabre and Amadeus. The cost of obtaining such information is, however, normally beyond the reach of many airport marketing department budgets. Most of the market analysis which is undertaken is based on revealed preference techniques, that is by assessing the passenger's current behaviour to determine future travel patterns. The alternative is to use stated preference techniques when passengers are asked to state their preference between a number of different scenarios. The techniques have been used to look at airport choice and also transport modal choice for surface access. For instance, passengers might be asked how they would trade-off higher journey cost to an airport compared with journey time. Such information can give airports invaluable insight into how passengers rate the factors which influence passenger choice. While stated preference techniques are widely used for other transport modes, their application within the airport industry is more limited. Manchester airport was one of the first airports to use such techniques in the mid-1980s (Swanson, 1998).

Most airports, particularly in the regions, refer to the surrounding population and economy which they serve as their catchment area. This is the area where most of the local traffic comes from and so will be where airports concentrate their marketing effort. The most basic approach to defining a catchment area is by using a certain drive time period criteria – typically one hour. Isochromes of longer times may represent weaker or secondary catchment areas. The size of the catchment area and the proportion of it which is likely to fly will depend on factors such as the quality of the road network, the

economic, business and tourist activity within the area, the demographic characteristics of the residents and the competing services at other airports. Improvements in the road infrastructure or public transport, or new or additional
services at neighbouring airports, can significantly alter the catchment size. The
catchment area is a dynamic rather than static measure, therefore, that has to
be constantly reviewed and revised. It also changes depending on the destination being assessed. Many regional airports have overlapping catchment areas.
Usually for short-haul travel to popular destinations there may be considerable
competition from other airports and so the catchment area will probably be
comparatively small. For less popular or longer-distance destinations there is
likely to be less competition and so the catchment area will be extended over
a greater area. The notion of catchment areas for large capital city airports is
not generally so applicable since in many cases these airports may offer the
only link to the destination under question in the whole country (Humphreys
and Gardner, 1995).

Southampton airport

Southampton airport's modern history began in 1961 when the airport was
bought by an aviation enthusiast from the public sector owner, Southampton
Corporation. Various subsequent changes in ownership took place until the
airport was finally purchased by BAA plc in 1990. Since then BAA plc has
invested £27 million on a total redevelopment of the airport which has included
a new terminal which was opened at the end of 1994 and a runway refurbish-
ment which was completed in 1997. The airport is situated on the south coast
of Britain around 80 miles south of London, is accessible by two motorways and
has a rail station which has direct services to London and other south-east destinations.

It is the airport's intention to become a business airport for local demand and
to attract traffic which traditionally has used the congested London airports of
Heathrow and Gatwick. Business travellers accounted for 47 per cent of the
traffic in 1994/5 compared with only 18 per cent in 1985 (CAA, 1996a) This
is also reflected in the fact than two-thirds of the travellers are males, mostly
in professional or semi-professional occupations, with 70 per cent of them travelling alone (Table 7.6). A significant proportion of the passengers (16 per cent)
appear to be relatively frequent travellers, making more than seven trips
annually. In 2000 the airport had scheduled services to a number of domestic
destinations, including the nearby Channel Islands, and the international airports
of Amsterdam, Brussels, Dublin, Frankfurt and Paris. Nearly 80 per cent of the
airport's traffic is domestic. It also has some limited summer service charters
but, overall, package holiday travellers represent just 13 per cent of total traffic
– a much lower share than at most other UK regional airports. Much of the
leisure traffic in its catchment areas uses services from the nearby airports of
Gatwick, Bristol and Bournemouth.

The airport considers that its relative small size gives it a significant advantage in terms of the level of personal attention that is provided and the relative
short check-in times. Its overall rating in BAA plc's quality of service monitor
in 1998/9 was the best out of all BAA plc UK airports. In spite of its small

Table 7.6   Passenger profile at Southampton airport 1994/5

Journey purpose	%	Sex	%	Flights in past 12 months	%
Package	13	Male	64	First	46
Other leisure	40	Female	36	1–3	26
Business	47	Total	100	4–6	11
Total	100			7+	16
				Total	100

Flight type[1]	%	Socio-economic group	%	Group size	%
Scheduled international	18	AB professional	45	Alone	70
Charter international	4	C1 semi-professional	40	2–3	26
Domestic	78	C2/DE blue-collar	15	4+	4
Total	100	Total	100	Total	100

Note: [1] Flight type data is for 1999.
Source: CAA (1996a; 2000); Southampton Airport (1998).

size, it has an airline lounge for business travellers and was the first regional airport in the UK to introduce electronic ticketing for BA passengers.

The airport has a range of marketing activities to encourage traffic growth. At the most basic level it has a request book at the information desk where travellers can fill in suggestions for new destinations. The marketing department meets with a group of frequent business travellers, the so-called 'High Flyers', at least four times a year to discuss future developments at the airport. It also has periodic meetings with the travel and aviation press, the 'Scoops' group. In addition, it regularly arranges for current and prospective airlines to meet and hear the views of local corporate travel agents named the 'Dirty Dozen' (Airline Business, 1999). The airport also aims to forge links with the local community, for example by sponsoring the region's youth games.

In 1990 when BAA plc bought the airport, the annual throughput of passengers at the airport was around 493 000 (Figure 7.1). In the early 1990s, traffic growth was slow while the new facilities were being developed. In 1995 the airport handled 516 000 passengers. This increase of just 1 per cent per annum can be partly explained by general factors such as poor economic conditions and the Gulf War, but growth was also considerably less than the average annual rate of 4.7 per cent which was experienced at all UK airports. However, in the following four years, with the new facilities in operation and with an increased emphasis on airport marketing, the airport experienced far greater growth and, by 1999, was handling 755 000 passengers. Undoubtedly a healthy economic climate and other factors such as European deregulation had a role to play with this development, but during these years the airport managed to achieve an annual growth rate of 10 per cent compared with the national average of 6.7 per cent.

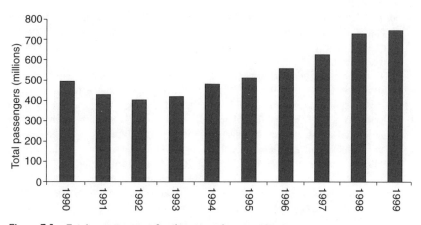

Figure 7.1 Total passengers at Southampton airport, 1990–9
Source: CAA airport statistics.

Norwich airport

Norwich airport is a regional airport situated in East Anglia in the east of Britain, around 130 miles north of London. It has been operated by the local authorities of Norwich City and Norfolk County as a commercial civil airport since 1969. The airport has one scheduled international flight to Amsterdam and four domestic services. Two-thirds of the traffic is for leisure purposes with a large proportion of the passengers taking charter services (Table 7.7). This means that compared with Southampton airport there are more travellers from the C2 and DE socio-economic groups. A higher proportion of leisure passengers would

Table 7.7   Passenger profile at Norwich airport 1994/5

Journey purpose	%	Sex	%
Leisure	66	Male	68
Business	34	Female	32
Total	100	Total	100

Flight type[1]	%	Socio-economic group	%
Scheduled international	31	AB professional	8
Charter international	47	C1 semi-professional	36
Domestic	22	C2/DE blue-collar	57
Total	100	Total	100

Note: [1] Flight type data is for 1999.
Source: CAA (1996b; 2000).

normally mean a more even split between males and females, but the dominance of North Sea oil-related business traffic at Norwich, which consists almost entirely of male travellers, means that male passengers still outnumber females by two to one.

The airport has adopted a very unusual approach to encourage passengers to use its airport. In 1988 it opened its own travel agency in the terminal building to persuade passengers to buy flights and package tours departing from Norwich. This also acted as a call centre for London City airport which brought in additional non-aeronautical revenue. The success of the agency encouraged the airport to open another five outlets in the surrounding area of the airport in 1998 to further promote the sales of flights from Norwich airport.

The other development has been the decision by the airport to operate its own charter flights. This move came about because the airport had been unable to persuade the large tour operators to operate programmes from Norwich airport. In 1995 a weekly service at a total annual cost of £400 000 was operated from the airport to Alicante. This destination was chosen because it was apparent from passenger surveys that there was considerable demand, not only for package holidays, but also because there was a large number of British-owned villas in this area. The service was a success, bringing in a profit in the region of around £150 000 directly from aeronautical charges and associated increases in non-aeronautical revenue from sources such as car parking, retail and catering. Some of the seats were sold to tour operators and some direct to passengers. The airport added summer services to Malaga and Faro in 1996 and a winter service to Malaga in 1997. By 2000, it was offering services to Malaga, Faro, Minorca, Alicante and Malta. Having its owns chain of travel agents is thought to have significantly helped in the selling of these flights and in raising the awareness of Norwich airport amongst the local population (Eady, 2000).

The airport initially took the risk of chartering its own aircraft to prove that there was a market at the airport, but has subsequently made a considerable profit from such operations in spite of increased competition from low-cost

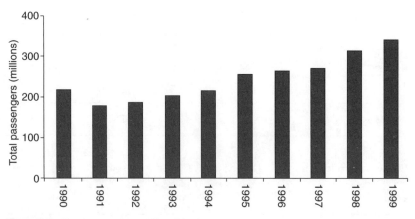

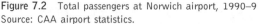

Figure 7.2   Total passengers at Norwich airport, 1990–9
Source: CAA airport statistics.

scheduled operators such as Go and easyJet at neighbouring Stansted and Luton airports. Like Southampton, its annual growth of 3.3 per cent between 1990 and 1995 was lower than the national average of 4.7 per cent. Between 1995 and 1999 when the charter flights were in operation and with the expanded travel agency business, traffic grew annually at 7.4 per cent compared with 6.7 per cent nationally (Figure 7.2). About 30 000 of the passengers, or around 10 per cent of the passenger throughput of 343 000, was associated with the airport-operated flights. Between 1991 and 1999, the proportion of traffic on international charter services increased from 18 per cent to 47 per cent of the total.

References and further reading

ACI-Europe (1999). *ACI Europe Policy Paper on Airport Competition*. ACI-Europe.

Airline Business (1999). The airport marketing awards. *Airline Business*, October, 74.

Ashford, N. (1989). Predicting the passengers' choice of airport. *Airport Forum*, **3**, 42–4.

Caves, R. and Gosling, G. (1999). *Strategic Airport Planning*. Elsevier.

Civil Aviation Authority (CAA) (1996a). *Passengers at Airports in Wales and in the South and South West of England in 1994/5*. CAP 657, CAA.

Civil Aviation Authority (CAA) (1996b). *Passengers at Airports in East of England in 1994/5*. CAP 656, CAA.

Civil Aviation Authority (CAA) (1999). *Passengers at Gatwick, Heathrow and Manchester Airports*. CAP 703, CAA.

Civil Aviation Authority (CAA) (2000). *Airport Statistics 1999*. CAA.

Civil Aviation Authority (CAA) (2001). Competitive provision of infrastructure and services within airports. Consultation paper. CAA.

Dennis, N. (1995). The competitive role of secondary airports in major conurbations. PTRC annual conference, Warwick, September.

Eady, T. (2000). Developing a travel product for regional airports. University of Westminster Regional Airport Seminar, London, May.

European Regions Airline Association (2000). Name change and airport expansion part of master plan for Lyon. *ERA Regional Report*, July, 12.

Favotto, I. (1998). Not all airports are created equal. *Airports World,* December, 17–18.

Hill, L. (2000). Unique Zürich airport. *Air Transport World*, August, 71–3.

Hoevel, M. (1999). Airports on the Net. ACI *Europe Marketing and Commercial Strategy Handbook*, vol. 7, ACI-Europe.

Humphreys, I. (1998). Commercialization and privatization: the experience of Cardiff Airport. *Department of Maritime Studies and International Transport Occasional Paper No 49*, University of Wales.

Humphreys, I. (1999). Privatization and commercialization: changes in UK airport ownership patterns. *Journal of Transport Geography*, **7**, 121–34.

Humphreys, I. and Gardner B. (1995). Airport marketing: an analysis of the use of primary catchment areas. *Department of Maritime Studies and International Transport Occasional Paper No 25*, University of Wales.

Jarach, D. (2001). The evolution of airport management practices: towards a multi-point, multi-service marketing driven firm. Fourth Air Transport Research Group conference, The Netherlands, July.

Kotler, P., Armstrong, G., Saunders, J. and Wong, V. (1996). *Principles of Marketing: The European Edition*. Prentice-Hall.

Meznarsic, J (1995). Structure of airport retail and marketing functions. *Commercial and Marketing Best Practices Handbook Volume 1 – Commercial Practices*. ACI-Europe.

Reantragoon, A. (1994). Criteria for successful airport marketing. University of Westminster Marketing and Market Research Seminar, London, December.

Schiphol Group (1999). *Creating AirportCities*. Schiphol Group.

Southampton Airport (1998). *Southampton Airport Profile*. Southampton Airport.

Swanson, J. (1998). The use of stated preference techniques. University of Westminster Demand Analysis and Capacity Management Seminar, London, October.

Teale, D. (1996). Creating the airport image. *ACI Europe Good Communication and Better Airport Marketing*, April.

Young, D. (1996). Knowing your customer. *ACI Europe Good Communication and Better Airport Marketing*, April.

8

The economic impact of airports

The wider picture

The focus of this book now shifts in the next two chapters from the internal environment within which the airport operates to considering the wider consequences of the airport business. This chapter looks at the economic impacts of airports while the next chapter discusses the environmental effects. A key issue for any airport operator is how to optimize the economic potential of an airport while providing acceptable environmental protection. This may be a particular problem when the economic benefits of airport development may be perceived as being the most relevant within a regional or national context, whereas the negative environmental impacts may be hardest felt by the local community.

An increasing number of airports are now undertaking economic impact studies. They are doing this for a number of reasons. They want to inform debates about strategic economic investment and to make the economic case for investment in new airport facilities or off-site infrastructure such as roads or rail links. Alternative expansion options may be evaluated with consideration of the relative economic benefits which they will bring. Impact studies may be used for planning purposes to assess whether there is enough land for new commercial projects in the vicinity of the airport or whether there is a sufficient supply of labour and associated housing to support such developments. Impact information may also be used for lobbying purposes, to gain regulatory approval, for example, for more direct services. Moreover such studies can have an important public relations role in educating policy-makers, airport users and the general public of the economic value of airports (Mason, 2001).

There are basically two types of economic impacts at airports. First, there is income, employment, capital investment and tax revenues which airport operations can bring by nature of the fact that they are significant generators of economic activity. Second, there are the wider catalytic or spin-off benefits, such as inward investment or the development of tourism, which can occur as the result of the presence of the airport. This can contribute to the economic development of the area surrounding the airport. Thus, within an economic context airports have role to play both by being a significant economic activity in their own right and by supporting business and tourism activity.

Economic impacts are measured in a variety of ways. A key indicator is the number of jobs generated. This is the most readily understandable measure and can easily be used to determine an airport's relative importance within an economy. In addition, there is the 'income', 'earnings' or 'value added' measure. This is the value that the airport dependent activities add to the economy in terms of wages, salaries, interest and profits. This indicator can be related to an area's total income or GDP to assess the relative contribution that the airport has on wealth generation. Then there is the economic activity or output measure which is the sum of the gross revenues of all the businesses which depend on the airport. Indicators related to capital investment and tax revenues can also be considered.

Airports as generators of economic activity

Economic effects can be classified as direct, indirect and induced impacts. The direct or primary impact is the employment and income generated by the direct operation of the airport. This is the most obvious economic impact and is the most easily measured. This impact is associated with the activities of the airport operator itself, the airlines, the concessionaires providing commercial facilities, the handling agents and other agencies which provide services such air traffic control, customs and immigration, and security. Some of these activities, such as car parking, car hire, in-flight catering, freight forwarders and hotels may actually be located off-site, in the surrounding area of the airport.

However, the economic impact of an airport is not just limited to these direct, airport-related effects – although this is the impact which is most frequently quantified and studied. The role of the suppliers to the airport industry also needs to be considered. This requires an examination of the indirect impact, which is defined as the employment and income generated in the chain of suppliers of goods and services to the direct activities that are located both at and in the vicinity of the airport. These types of activities include the utilities and fuel suppliers, construction and cleaning companies, food and retail good suppliers. In addition, the impact that these direct and indirect activities have on personal spending also needs to be taken into account. This so-called induced impact can be defined as the employment and income generated by the spending of incomes by the direct and indirect employees on local goods and services such as retail, food, transport and housing. The indirect and induced effects are together often known as the secondary effects (Figure 8.1).

These indirect and induced impacts are clearly much more difficult to measure, involving an understanding of how the airport interacts with other sectors within the economy. Their combined impact can be measured by the economic multiplier. This concept takes account of the successive rounds of spending that arise from the stimulus of the direct impacts and assumes that one individual's or organization's spending becomes another individual's or organization's income in the next round. Some of the money spent on airport-related activities will be re-spent on purchases from suppliers of goods and services – the indirect effect – with a proportion of this leaking out of the economy as imports. Much of the remainder will be spent on labour or will go to the government in the form of taxes. The suppliers will then make purchases locally, import goods and services, distribute wages and salaries, and pay government taxes. During each round of spending a certain proportion of the money will accrue to local residents in the form of wages, salaries and profits. Some of this money will then be re-spent again, producing the induced effects. The rest will be saved and not recirculated within the economy. Eventually the successive rounds of spending will become so small that they will be considered negligible. The multiplier analysis thus quantifies the economic value and jobs of the financial transactions which take place within any economy.

There will be new investment associated with these direct, indirect and induced activities in the form of airport facilities, computer systems, maintenance facilities, offices and so on. Airport activities can also have a significant impact on local, regional and national government revenues. Employees will pay income tax, and sales transactions will be subject to sales or value added taxes.

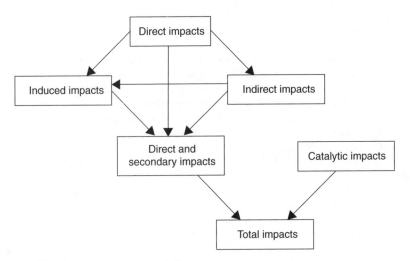

Figure 8.1 The economic impact of airports

Airports, particularly in the private sector, will probably also be subject to other taxes such as property or land taxes and business or corporation taxes. On the one hand, some airports in the public sector may be exempt from these but may, on the other hand, pass over a considerable share of their profits to their government owners. In return, of course, many government owners have traditionally allocated considerable public sector funds to aid airport development. Then there are the taxes collected through airport charges. These may be required to cover some specific airport service such as immigration and public health inspection as in the USA, to provide funds for investment such as the US transportation tax, or just to boost public sector funds as in the UK with the air passenger duty. Conversely, in the duty- and tax-free sales area of operation it can be argued that the airports and their passengers receive a direct tax subsidy.

Measuring the direct, indirect and induced impacts

There are a number of different techniques, of varying levels of sophistication, available to airports which want to measure their economic impacts. Historically it has been in the USA where these techniques have been developed and where most of the economic impact studies have been undertaken. However, in more recent years other airports have been becoming increasingly interested in assessing their overall economic value. This is particularly the case in Europe. ACI-Europe has become actively involved with promoting best practice within the industry and has published two airport impact study kits (ACI-Europe, 1993; York Consulting/ACI-Europe, 2000).

Direct impacts

Direct impacts are clearly the easiest of all the impacts to measure. Employers at the airport can be asked to provide details of their employees, how much they earn and where they live. Details concerning purchases of goods and services, location of suppliers, revenues, expenditures and capital expenditure also need to be gathered. While such a process for on-site airport activities should not pose too many difficulties, the off-site data collection may be more difficult. First, a definition of 'off site' needs to be established – a rule-of-thumb figure is an area within a twenty-minute drive time (York Consulting/ACI-Europe, 2000). Then the relevant companies within this area need to be identified by taking into account the knowledge of the airport operator and other industry bodies and, perhaps, by direct visual inspection. Many airports systematically measure the direct economic impacts – particularly the employment effects. For example, at London Heathrow airport there is an annual spring census of all airport-related employers, which produces total numbers of staff by type of employer. Then every few years BAA plc also undertakes a survey to find out details of employees characteristics such as home address, travel to work mode and whether they are engaged in functions more related to passengers, aircraft movements or cargo (Maiden, 1995).

The direct employment at an airport will vary according to a combination of factors such as the volume and structure of passenger traffic, the amount of

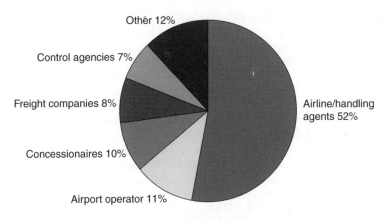

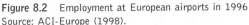

Figure 8.2 Employment at European airports in 1996
Source: ACI-Europe (1998).

freight and the actual capacity utilization of the airport. The role of the airport also has to be considered, for example, whether it is a major hub, whether it acts as a base for airline activity and whether it provides other opportunities such as office or other commercial development. A study of employment in 1996 at European airports showed that the airline and handling agents were, on average the largest employers at the airport, followed by the airport operators and concessionaires (Figure 8.2). Eighty per cent of the employees were male – although women made up 60 per cent of the part-time workforce.

For meaningful airport comparisons to be made, airport direct employment is related to the traffic throughput of an airport to produce an employment density figure. This is usually equivalent to the number of employees per million passengers per annum (jobs per mppa) or per WLU if freight is an important activity at the airport. A figure of 1000 jobs for every million passengers equal to a density figure of 1000 tends to be the rule-of-thumb figure generally accepted by the industry, although it obviously masks wide variations in employment at different airports. Globally in 1998 it has been estimated that there were 289 000 airport operator employees and a total of over 3 020 000 employed at the airport. This gave an overall employment density figure of 1531. For every person employed by an airport operator, there were another nine working for other companies at the airport. This ratio was much higher for the North American and Pacific airports since many more activities are outsourced (ACI, 2000).

Within Europe jobs per mppa figures average around 1100. Airports such as Barcelona, Malaga and Gran Canaria in Spain have much lower values – below 500 – because of limited development at the airports, dependence on incoming tourism traffic and no base airlines. They are also run by the operator, AENA, which concentrates most of its resources at Madrid. By contrast, airports such as Brussels, Cardiff and Hamburg have density values of over 1500, primarily because of higher than average involvement in freight operations at Brussels and major maintenance facilities being located at the other two airports (ACI-Europe, 1998).

It has been suggested that airports can be classified according to their economic impact characteristics. There are six main groups of airports, namely international gateway airports, national hub airports, regional airports, tourist generator airports, tourist receiver airports, and transit and interline airports. The international gateways, such as Heathrow, Paris CDG, Amsterdam and Frankfurt, have the ability to attract extensive off-airport business, particularly in the form of international company headquarters and distribution and retail centres, and to encourage long-haul tourism. The national hubs, such as Madrid, Oslo and Stockholm, can act as airline bases and encourage capital city tourism. Tourist generator airports, such as London Luton can be bases for charter airlines or low-cost carriers while tourist airports such as Dubai can be important for duty-free trade and cargo operations (Andrew and Bailey, 1996).

Very often in using economic impact studies to support proposals for future development, airport operators will have to project their employment figures into the future. This will involve some assessment of the productivity gains which are likely to occur. These should be derived from historical trends and experience elsewhere, and should also take account of the changing demands on airport employment due to more stringent security and quality requirements and technological developments. Analysis of past trends at Amsterdam airport has enabled 'elasticity' values to be produced for various types of employment. With passenger-related employment (e.g. check-in, cabin crew and commercial facilities) the elasticity value is 0.97, which indicates that a 1 per cent change in passenger numbers brings a 0.97 per cent change in related employment. Corresponding values for freight-related (e.g. handling and freight forwarders) and aircraft-related (e.g. maintenance, fuel and air traffic control) activities are 0.77 and 0.46 (York Consulting/ACI-Europe, 2000). At Heathrow (assuming that a fifth terminal is built) values of 0.83 for passenger-related employment and 0.61 for cargo have been estimated for the future (Maiden, 1995). Any economies of scale that also apply to labour productivity should be taken into account. For example, aircraft size may rise with traffic growth which will increase staff productivity in certain areas.

Indirect and induced impacts

There are two main approaches to estimating the multiplier effect and measuring the indirect and induced impacts. The first method involves using multiplier values that have been calculated by using information which has been gathered from surveys of on-site and off-site employers and by making assumptions about the tax rate and the share of purchases which are imported.

A more sophisticated approach involves using an input–output model. This model looks at the linkages which exist within any economy by considering the relationships between the different economic sectors (e.g. agriculture, manufacturing, construction and services) within a certain area. This methodology involves constructing a transaction table which shows, in money terms, the input–output relationships for the sectors in the economy. Each sector is shown as a column representing purchases from other sectors and as a row representing sales to the other sectors. From this table, coefficients or multiplier values can be obtained for each economic activity. This technique will thus allow the impact of additional spending in any one specific economic activity to be identified sector by sector as well as for the area as a whole. One country which has extensive experience of using the input–output method to measure impacts is the USA. Since the 1980s, the Bureau of Economic Analysis in the Department of Commerce has been developing their regional input–output modelling system, RIMS II. This has been used widely to estimate regional impacts in both the public and private sector, and forms the basis of many of the airport economic impact studies. The input and output structure of nearly 500 US industries is contained within the model (US Department of Commerce, 1997).

The choice of method will usually depend on the amount of data which is available and the resources which can be utilized. Clearly the data requirements will be greatest for the input–output models, and this technique tends only to be used at a national or regional level. If a more local situation is being assessed, the other approach may be more appropriate, or there may be the option, with a considerable degree of caution, of adapting the national or regional input–output model.

Globally, it has been suggested that on average the number of total jobs (i.e. direct and secondary) per mppa ranges between 2500 and 8000, with between 750 and 2000 of these jobs being direct airport-related employment (ATAG, 2000). Another estimate is 2700 total jobs per mppa, of which 1200 are direct and 1500 are secondary. With this estimation a distinction was made between international hub airports which were assumed to generate 1500 direct jobs per mppa and 2100 secondary jobs compared with lower values of 1000 and 1100 respectively at smaller regional airports (Mason, 2001). Within Europe it is estimated that, on average, in addition to 1100 direct jobs, there are the same number of indirect and induced, or secondary, jobs (ACI-Europe, 1998). In the USA average direct figures are 1270 staff per mppa and secondary are 2063 – which gives a ratio value of secondary to direct jobs of 1.62 This ratio ranges from 2.32 for the larger airports, to 1.32 for the medium-sized airports, and only 0.2 for the small airports (ACI-North America, 1998). In Canada the comparable figures are 1773 (direct) and 1951 (secondary) with a secondary:direct ratio of 1.1 (ACI-North America, 1999).

Clearly these aggregate figures will hide significant variations which exist between different airports. Individual values will depend on many factors such as the nature of the traffic at the airport, propensity to travel characteristics, employment sector mixes and the role of the airport. They will also be related to the size of the economy under consideration, depending on whether the national, regional or local situation is being assessed. The indirect impacts tend to increase with the size of the study area as this increases the likelihood of goods and services required by airport-related companies being supplied within the area, rather than being imported from outside. The choice of study area will depend primarily on the role and size of the airport and the reason for measuring the impact. Large capital city and main international airports tend to have such an important impact on the overall economy, that it makes sense to assess their impact within a national context. Specific issues, however, particularly related to the employment market, may be more appropriately considered at a regional or local level. The impacts of smaller airports clearly need to be considered within a narrower context.

Estimates for airports may vary quite widely because of the use of different terminology and methodology or the adoption of models of varying levels of sophistication. Even, in the USA where the FAA recommends procedures for identifying and quantifying the economic impacts of airports there are substantial differences in the detailed methodologies used. Studies adopt different definitions of multipliers and interpret direct and indirect impacts in a number of ways. For example, sometimes all off-site impacts are considered as indirect impacts, irrespective of whether the activities are directly airport related. This makes it very difficult to compare multiplier values. Then there is the problem of how to treat any activities which are based at the airport but not actually related to airport operations. Very often the split of activities on and off-site will depend on whether the actual site is constrained or not.

One of the major areas of discrepancy is in the treatment of jobs associated with leisure and business tourists who arrive via the airport. These jobs are thus in tourism industry activities such as hotels, restaurants, attractions, conferences and exhibitions. Some airports, particularly in the USA, treat these as indirect jobs, which can have a dramatic effect on the overall magnitude of indirect impacts. Other studies separately identify the visitor impacts, or adopt a more qualitative approach to assessing this effect. Another area of inconsistency between airports occurs with the treatment of construction activities. Sometimes the temporary staff employed in the construction industry will be included in the impact figures and sometimes they will not. When there is a major capital investment programme, such as a new runway or terminal, airports tend to identify the impacts separately to add additional support to the case for new capacity.

These differences largely will be responsible for the spread of employment density figures which have been estimated for a number of European and North American airports (Table 8.1). Direct jobs per mppa range from as little as 395 at Malaga airport to 1980 at Brussels airport. Munich, Phoenix and Vancouver airports have been estimated to generate over 2000 secondary jobs per mppa, whereas Newcastle airport only has 245. This means that the secondary: direct jobs ratio is very varied – ranging from as little as 0.3 at the airports of Cardiff and Newcastle to over 2.5 at Phoenix and Milan airports. At Gatwick airport the secondary:direct ratio was also estimated to be around 0.3 with the bulk of the secondary employment coming from induced effects. About 15 per cent of direct employment was off-site (Figure 8.3). When income generation is considered, just as wide-ranging impact values are obtained. For example, the secondary:direct income ratio has been estimated to be below 0.5 for Brussels, Birmingham, Manchester, Barcelona and Cardiff airports, and between 1 but less than 2 for airports such as Düsseldorf and Glasgow. The Paris and Milan airports are thought to have a value of around 2.

At a national level in various countries, studies are undertaken to assess the overall economic impact of aviation, including airport operations. For example, in the USA the Department of Transportation's databases and the RIMS II model are used to assess the overall impact. Figures for 1998 estimate that the aviation industry generated US$911 billion in economic activity, US$259 billion in annual earnings and 10.3 million jobs (Wilbur Smith Associates, 2000). Aviation's contribution to GDP was estimated to be 4.7 per cent. In the UK, in the absence of any equivalent of RIMS II, an input–output model of Oxford

Table 8.1 Employment impacts at European and North American airports

Airport	Year	Passengers (millions)	Direct jobs per mppa[1]	Secondary jobs per mppa[1]	Direct and secondary jobs per mppa[1]	Secondary jobs / Direct jobs
Europe:						
Amsterdam	1997	31.0	1581	806	2387	0.5
Barcelona	1994	10.7	458	463	921	1.0
Birmingham	1994	4.9	1008	479	1487	0.5
Brussels	1993	10.0	1980	1011	2991	0.5
Cardiff	1997	1.2	1570	483	2053	0.3
Düsseldorf	1997	15.5	774	966	1740	1.2
Glasgow	1995	5.5	953	1325	2278	1.4
London Gatwick	1997	27.3	1147	354	1501	0.3
Malaga	1995	6.3	395	772	1167	2.0
Manchester	1993	13.1	1457	886	2343	0.6
Milan	1994	13.0	649	1984	2633	3.1
Munich	1996	15.7	1075	2131	3206	2.0
Newcastle	1994	2.5	867	245	1112	0.3
Oslo	1996	11.1	854	1195	2049	1.4
Paris CDG	1996	31.7	1560	1910	3470	1.2
Paris Orly	1996	27.4	1068	828	1896	0.8
Vienna	1996	9.1	1142	1082	2224	0.9
North America:						
Ottawa	1997	3.0	951	1202	2153	1.3
Phoenix	1996	30.4	1213	2998	4211	2.5
Vancouver	1997	14.8	1546	2005	3551	1.3
Victoria	1997	1.1	812	733	1545	0.9
Washington Dulles	1998	15.6	992	796	1788	0.8
Washington National	1998	15.8	646	402	1048	0.6
Winnipeg	1997	3.0	1621	796	2407	0.5

Note: [1] mppa = million passengers per annum.
Source: Individual airport economic studies as reported by the airports themselves and ACI-Europe (1998) and ACI-North America (1998; 1999).

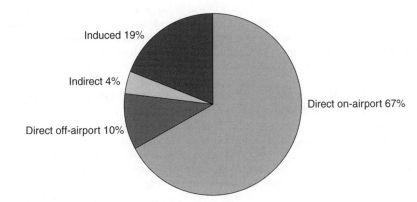

Figure 8.3 Employment at Gatwick airport in 1997
Source: BAA Gatwick (2000).

Economic Forecasting has been expanded to include the aviation rather than just the transport sector in order to assess the overall economic impact of aviation. The industry is thought to contribute £10.2 billion to UK GDP which is 1.4 per cent of total GDP and at least £2.5 billion goes to the government in the form of taxes (Oxford Economic Forecasting, 1999). National estimates for just the airport sector are more difficult to obtain. ACI-North America has calculated values for both Canada and the USA by using the individual airport studies in both countries. Overall US airports are estimated to generate 1.6 million direct jobs and 5.8 million jobs in total. They are estimated to generate US$380 million in economic activity, US$155 billion in income and US$31.2 billion in taxes. In Canada, it is estimated that there are 292 000 jobs in total – with 139 000 of these being direct. Economic activity is estimated to be Canadian $30.8 billion with Canadian $4.5 billion tax revenue generated.

Airports and economic development

As well as being a generator of economic activities in its own right, an airport can also play a role in attracting and sustaining wider economic activity in the surrounding area – both in terms of business and tourism development. This is the catalytic, magnetic or spin-off impact. This impact can be defined as the employment, income, investment and tax revenues generated by the wider role which an airport can play by being an economic magnet for the region it serves. Airports can give a company easy assess to other parts of the company as well as to suppliers and customers, and can offer speed and security for goods being transported. Hence airports can play an important role in influencing company location decisions. They can encourage inward investment and the relocations of businesses by attracting industries which rely on quick and convenient access to air services for both people and goods. These businesses will not rely directly on the airport for their operation, but they will have a preference for a location near an airport because of the accessibility benefits which can be gained. Airports can also help retain current businesses or encourage them to expand. Moreover, by providing access to a wide range of both passenger and freight services, an airport can enhance the competitiveness of the economy and can contribute to the export success of the businesses located in the vicinity of the airport. In some cases the airport can be the lifeline to local economies, as has been the situation in some developing countries in Africa and Latin America where air travel has enabled the export of fresh and perishable fruit and flowers to western economies.

The trend towards globalization, both in terms of multinational companies and also in terms of increased reliance on imported components and products, has increased the importance of locating in the vicinity of an international airport. Some of the fastest growing knowledge-based industrial sectors such as computing, electronics, communications and pharmaceuticals are the most international, and are heavily reliant on air travel for the transportation of their high-value/low-weight products. The increasing reliance on just-in-time inventory systems for these expanding industries and more traditional sectors, such as car manufacturing, has meant that air travel has become a critical element for a quick and efficient distribution system and rapid delivery times. In short, airports have become increasingly more important for businesses operating in global marketplace.

In economically disadvantaged areas, where unemployment is high and there is a narrow declining economic base, airport development is often seen as a way of generating new employment, creating wealth and regenerating the area. These arguments are frequently used to gain approval for airport expansion or development. A good illustration of this was the recent planning enquiry for Manchester airport's second runway. Manchester airport claimed there would be some much needed economic development as the result of the second runway, whereas neighbouring Liverpool airport, which opposed the plans, claimed that there would substantial economic benefits for the Liverpool area if the runway was not built and Liverpool airport expanded instead.

Airports undoubtedly play an integral part in economic development, and areas which are relatively inaccessible by air will be at a distinct economic drawback. Certain regions will find it difficult to attract inward investment if their airports have not reached the critical mass needed to provide an adequate range of services. Thus airports are often considered as a vital component of a regional development policy and can be viewed as giving a real advantage to competing regions. However, it is very difficult to formally establish the causality between the expansion of an airport and wider economic development (Caves and Gosling, 1999). In many cases it is impossible to establish whether it is the nature of the surrounding economy of an airport, in terms of wealth and population size and distribution, which has encouraged airlines to operate from the airport, rather than the development of air services influencing the economy. In the USA, for example, evidence suggests that the links between air transport and economic growth are largely historical (Graham, 1995).

It is certainly true that investment in airport infrastructure is not usually sufficient in itself to generate sustained increases in economic growth. The ability of airports to generate jobs and attract new business should never be used as the main justification for new airport construction. The wider economic benefits will depend very much on the scale of the airport and, very critically, its ability to attract air services. In the end, it will be the airlines that will determine the success of an airport and broader economic impacts, in choosing whether to operate from the airport or not. Their primary concerns will be whether sufficient passenger demand exists and the airport's strategic and geographic location, not the quality of the infrastructure (Graham and Guyer, 2000).

It is extremely difficult to isolate and quantify the economic effects which are due to the presence of the airport from the wide range of other factors which will affect a company's location decision. The exact location of any business activity will be only partially related to the existence of any nearby airport services, with other factors being the availability, quality and cost of any potential development sites, the nature of the local labour market, tax incentives, trade policy and the supporting communications and transport infrastructure. The situation is also made more complex by the fact that many economic regions are served by a number of airports, with either complementary or competing roles.

Airports can play a role in encouraging both business and leisure visitors to the surrounding area. There are many examples of countries, particularly in developing areas such as the Caribbean, Asia and Pacific, where the tourism potential of a destination has only been realized after direct services and suitable airport infrastructure have been provided. The increase in visitor numbers may then have a spin-off effect on the income and employment generation in tourism industry activities such hotels, restaurants, attractions, conferences and exhibitions. Tourism markets which are particularly dependent on air travel include package holiday travel, city break tourism, long-haul travel and conference business. Causality between airport growth and tourism development, as with business development, is very difficult to prove. For example, is it new air services at a resort which encourage new hotel development, or do more bedspaces encourage more frequent flights? Some impact studies, particularly in the USA, have a separate visitor impact category. An estimate of spending is often calculated by multiplying the visitor numbers by average daily spend and length of stay. Other airports choose to categorize the visitors' impact as indirect. Admittedly many of these tourism businesses will be reliant on air services for their tourism demand, but it unlikely, except in an isolated island situation, that this tourism industry would not exist if a certain airport was not present. It thus seems rather inappropriate to include these tourism impacts as indirect impacts. Instead, it is more preferable to consider them alongside the catalytic impacts causing business development.

Since it is very difficult to prove any direct causality between airports and broader business and tourism development, it is not usually feasible or suitable to identify with any certainty the exact number of jobs, or the amount of income which is generated from these catalytic or spin-off impacts. Some studies have made some estimates by usually assuming that a certain proportion of jobs within the business and tourism industries in the vicinity of the airport exists because of the airport. Within Europe such estimates have ranged from below 1000 jobs per mppa for airports such as Amsterdam, Birmingham, Brussels and Oslo to above 2000 at Barcelona, Düsseldorf and Newcastle in the UK. An average figure is 1800 jobs per mppa (ACI-Europe, 1998). There is a danger, however, that by including crude estimates for these catalytic impacts that these have the effect of reducing the credibility of the more accurate direct, indirect and induced impact measurements (York Consulting/ACI-Europe, 2000).

A more qualitative approach is often adopted which will involve investigating factors such as the significance of the airport to location decision, competitiveness and business performance by surveying and holding discussions with relevant businesses. This will be in order to gain a closer understanding of the nature of the interaction between the airport and the wider elements in the local economy. For example, a survey of US corporate executives found over 50 per cent of the sample felt that the road infrastructure, and the skills, wage rate and trade union profile of the local labour market were very important locational decision factors. Other factors mentioned included financial incentives, environmental regulations, proximity of markets, telecommunications, property costs, the school system, unskilled labour, raw materials, housing and the health system. Eighteen per cent identified the presence of major airport as being important (Mason, 2001). In another survey in Europe, the top five cities for transport links with other cities, namely London, Paris, Frankfurt, Amsterdam and Brussels, were also rated as the top five cities in which to locate a business (ACI-Europe, 1998). Similarly trends in business and leisure tourism can be investigated and the importance of the role of the airport discussed among industry experts. A difficulty with this interview approach is to ensure that respondents give genuine comments. They will often have a very positive but perhaps not totally realistic view of the value of new air services, for example, since the respondents will bear no direct costs associated with the new services but may benefit from the gains.

Alternatively the impact of opening up new routes can be considered in order to see how air services directly impact on business or tourism development (Button and Taylor, 2000). For instance, in 1996 at Phoenix Sky Harbor International, three major non-stop international routes to London, Düsseldorf and Toronto were opened. It was calculated that in the first year of operation the routes generated US$39 million direct income and 366 jobs, with indirect/induced income of US$97 million and 915 jobs. It was also estimated that the routes created US$351 million air exports income, 3323 jobs, and US$52.7 new annual tax revenues (ACI-North America, 1998). Other interesting examples include an assessment of the impact of the four long-haul routes, namely Manchester–Atlanta, Manchester–Hong Kong, Manchester – Dubai and Birmingham – New York, which was undertaken by the UK CAA (CAA, 1994).

In assessing the impact that airports have on the wider economy, it is the net benefits which should be considered (Caves and Gosling, 1999). For example, airports cannot only encourage visitors to the local region but can also enable local residents to holiday abroad rather than staying in the local region. Similarly, the availability of nearby direct air services may increase the use of imported goods and services at the expense of local products. The impacts should also ideally be compared with possible alternative, non-airport related, economic activities with an assessment being made of the comparative economic benefits and opportunity costs. Alternative developments could have a better overall impact on the economy. The crossover effects on other industries, for example the impact on other modes of transport, all need to be considered. Increased industrial and economic activity around an airport may merely be draining resources from other areas, such as city centres. The negative or adverse potential impacts of airport development, such as extensive urbanization and industrialization, overheating of the economy and consequences of local labour shortages, also need to be taken into account. The overall impact on the local community of tourism development related to aviation activity also needs to be assessed. The positive effects may not be very substantial if the tourism industry has to be supported by a substantial level of imports and foreign investment (Wheatcroft, 1994).

By way of illustration, Table 8.2 presents a selection of economic impact measures for the Washington, Brisbane, Geneva and Vienna airports to give an example of the range and type of measures which are available in different areas of the world. These airports are all medium-sized airports with passenger throughput varying from 6.4 million at Geneva airport to 15.8 million at Washington National. Each of the studies have been undertaken separately so there is no consistency in the method used – which may explain some of the differences. For comparative purposes, the measure have been divided by passenger throughput, although many of the wider economic benefits are likely to be less linked to passenger volume. Washington National airport has the least

Table 8.2   Economic impacts at Washington, Brisbane, Geneva and Vienna airports

	Jobs	Income (US$ millions)	Output (US$ millions)	Taxes (US$ millions)	Jobs per mppa[3]	Income per ppa[4] (US$)	Output per ppa[4] (US$)	Taxes per ppa[4] (US$)
Washington Dulles (1998) 15.6 million passengers								
Direct	15 481	548	4 125	440	992	35	264	28
Total[1]	27 888	992	n/a	n/a	1 788	64	n/a	n/a
Visitors	47 981	998	1 989	277	3 076	64	128	18
Construction:								
Direct	778	31	n/a	7	50	2	n/a	0
Total[1]	1 281	56	n/a	n/a	82	4	n/a	n/a
Washington National (1998) 15.8 million passengers								
Direct	10 211	384	2 414	295	646	24	153	19
Total[1]	16 562	664	n/a	n/a	1 048	42	n/a	n/a
Visitors	69 805	1 347	2 909	425	4 418	85	184	27
Construction:								
Direct	417	17	n/a	4	26	1	n/a	0
Total[1]	650	32	n/a	n/a	41	2	n/a	n/a
Brisbane (1996/7)								
Direct	16 400	n/a	n/a	n/a	1 547	n/a	n/a	n/a
Total[1]	83 600	1 596	8 685	67	7 887	151	819	6
Geneva (1998) 6.4 million passengers								
Direct	6 587	n/a	1 458	n/a	1 029	n/a	226	n/a
Total[1]	13 174	n/a	n/a	n/a	2 058	n/a	n/a	n/a
Catalytic	10 779	n/a	4 404	n/a	1 684	n/a	684	n/a
Visitors	[2]	n/a	1 488	n/a	[2]	n/a	231	n/a
Vienna (1996) 9.8 million passengers								
Direct	10 394	1 058	n/a	255	1 142	116	n/a	28
Total[1]	20 234	2 361	n/a	462	2 224	259	n/a	51
Visitors	n/a	n/a	2 361	n/a	n/a	n/a	262	n/a

Notes: [1] Direct and secondary impacts.
[2] Included in 'total'.
[3] mppa = million passengers per annum.
[4] ppa = passengers per annum.
Sources: Brisbane Airport Corporation (1998), Geneva Airport (2000), Metropolitan Washington Airports Authority (1999) and Vienna International Airport (1998). Geneva Airport (2000)

jobs per mppa primarily because of the domestic nature of the passengers and less involvement in other activities such as freight. The total jobs and output at Brisbane is very high, and it is likely that this is reflecting the impact of aviation on the neighbouring Australia TradeCoast economic development area. The total employment is estimated to represent 5.2 per cent of employment in Queensland, with the income accounting for 6.8 per cent of the gross state product. With some of the airports visitors activities are identified separately and so the impact of including them in the economic assessment can be seen. At Geneva airport the catalytic impacts associated with business development, in addition to the tourism activities, have been identified. The Washington airports also estimate the impacts of the US$31 million capital expenditure programme at National airport and the US$57 million capital programme at Dulles airport.

In conclusion, there is little doubt that airports have a substantial economic effect on the region in which they are located. This chapter has discussed these various economic impacts. While concepts such as the multiplier or the catalytic effects are reasonably straightforward to understand, they are very difficult to actually quantify with any degree of confidence. More and more airports are showing interest in measuring their economic impact but still there are considerable inconsistencies in the terminologies and methodologies used. As research into this area continues, it is likely that in the future more consistent and accurate approaches to measuring economic impacts will be developed.

References and further reading

ACI-Europe (1993). *The Economic Impact Study Kit*. ACI-Europe.

ACI-Europe (1998). *Creating Employment and Prosperity in Europe*. ACI-Europe.

ACI-North America (1998). *The Economic Impact of US Airports*. ACI-North America.

ACI-North America (1999). *The Economic Impact of Canadian Airports*. ACI-North America.

Air Transport Action Group (ATAG) (2000). *The Economic Benefits of Air Transport*. ATAG.

Airports Council International (ACI) (2000). *ACI Airport Economics Survey 1998*. ACI.

Andrew, H. R. and Bailey, R. (1996).The contribution of airports to regional economic development. PTRC European Transport Forum, Brunel University, September.

BAA Gatwick (2000). *Gatwick Airport Sustainable Development Strategy*. BAA Gatwick.

Brisbane Airport Corporation (1998). *Master Plan – Executive Summary*. BAC.

Button, K. and Taylor, S. (2000). International air transportation and economic development. *Journal of Air Transport Management*, **6**, 209–22.

Caves, R. and Gosling, G. (1999). *Strategic Airport Planning*. Pergamon.

Civil Aviation Authority (CAA) (1994). *The Economic Impact of New Air Services*. CAP 638, CAA.

Geneva Airport (2000). *The Economic Impact of Geneva International Airport – Summary*. Geneva Airport.

Graham, B. (1995). *Geography and Air Transport*. Wiley.

Graham, B. and Guyer, C. (2000). The role of regional airports and air services in the United Kingdom. *Journal of Transport Geography*, (8), 249–62.

Maiden, S. (1995). *Proof of Evidence: Forecasting – Heathrow Terminal 5 Enquiry*. BAA/31, BAA.

Mason, N. (2001). The economic impact of airports. University of Westminster/Cranfield University Airport Economics and Finance Symposium, London, March.

Metropolitan Washington Airports Authority (1999). *Regional Economic Impact*. MWAA.

Oxford Economic Forecasting (1999). *The Contribution of the Aviation Industry to the UK Economy*. OEF.

US Department of Commerce (1997). *A User Handbook for the Regional Input-Output Modelling System (RIMS II)*. 3rd edn, DOC.

Vienna International Airport (1998). *Introducing our Airport and its Economic Potential*. Vienna International Airport.

Wheatcroft, S. (1994). *Aviation and Tourism Policies: Balancing the Benefits*. Routledge.

Wilbur Smith Associates (2000). *The Economic Impact of Civil Aviation on the US Economy – 2000*. Wilbur Smith Associates.

York Consulting/ACI-Europe (2000). *Europe's Airports: Creating Employment and Prosperity – an Economic Impact Study Kit*, ACI-Europe.

9

The environmental impacts of airports

Growing concerns for the environment

In the 1990s the airport industry, like all other industries, faced the effects of increasing environmental pressure. The level of environmental concern varies from country to country or indeed from one airport to another, depending on views about aviation and other social and political attitudes. In many countries increased prosperity has led to greater expectation for the quality of life and more sensitivity to the environmental impacts of airports. For this reason it has become increasingly difficult to substantially expand airport operations or to build new airports. All indications are that this will become even more difficult in the future as concern for the environment grows. At the same time continual growth in demand is putting greater commercial pressures on airports to develop activities. The problems are particularly acute for airports which are popular because of their proximity to local population centres but which means that a significant proportion of the community is affected by airport operators. In short, environmental issues must be seen as one of the greatest challenges to, and possible constraints upon, the future activities of the air transport industry.

The environmental impacts have to be considered at two levels, namely global and local. Within a global context, the role that aviation plays in contributing to world problems such as global warming and ozone depletion is increasingly coming under scrutiny. These are long-term issues which society as a whole has to address. The meeting of governments in Kyoto in 1997 was one of the first attempts to introduce constraints upon environmental impacts at a global level although aviation currently is excluded from this. At a local level, impacts due, for example, to aircraft noise and air quality have to be considered. In some areas of operation airport operators may be legally required to minimize the adverse effects, whereas elsewhere many airport operators are increasingly voluntarily introducing measures to mitigate the impacts. Public concern at a local level, for example concerning airport noise, can be accurately assessed by monitoring noise levels at airports. Pressures from the environmentalist lobby for a reduction in air transport because of overall environmental needs, at the expense of economic growth, is a very different and in some ways much more difficult challenge facing the aviation industry. It is the more local problems which airport operators mostly have to address on a day-to-day basis. The focus of this chapter, therefore, is very much at the local level, although some investigation of the global developments has also been made to put the local issues into a broader context.

Consideration of the environmental impacts at airports is made that much more difficult because of the many different bodies involved in, or affected by, airport operations. These include the airport operator, the airlines, governments and statutory organizations, amenity and conservation groups and local residents. These will have a complexity of different, and often conflicting, interests. Issues such as resident safety, or loss of wildlife habitat can cause anxiety among certain sectors of society and generate considerable emotive concern. Other impacts may require complex technical data to be assessed, which may be difficult for all interested parties to fully understand. Some impacts cannot adequately be measured. Then, when mitigation measures are considered, most standard procedures have to be adapted to suit each airport's individual circumstances because of variation in aircraft use, night flights, land-use rules, closeness to residential areas and overall environmental sensitivity of the community.

The main impacts

The main environmental impacts can be divided into five categories:

1 Noise.
2 Emissions.
3 Water pollution and use.
4 Waste and energy management.
5 Wildlife, heritage and landscape.

Noise

Aircraft noise has traditionally been considered the most important environmental problem at airports and, in many cases, public tolerance of aircraft noise has been diminishing. This is in spite of the fact that over the years the noise levels associated with aircraft movements has been declining. This reduction has been primarily due to the development of less noisy aircraft and the pressure of more stringent requirements for noise certification of new aircraft types. Current aircraft types are typically 20 dB quieter than aircraft of thirty years ago – reducing noise annoyance by around 75 per cent (ATAG, 2000). Noise certification was first introduced in 1969 by the USA in the Federal Aviation Regulations Part 36 (FAR Part 36). ICAO adopted similar international standards in 1971. These standards were included in the Environmental Protection Annex 16 of the Chicago Convention. The initial standards for jet aircraft, based on the maximum noise level given a certain flight procedure, became known as 'chapter' 2 or 'stage' 2 in the USA. In 1977 more stringent standards, known as chapter or stage 3, to be applied to all new aircraft designs, were adopted by the ICAO. Chapter 2 aircraft include the Boeing, 727, DC-9 and older types of Boeing 737 and 747. Newer aircraft certificated under chapter 3 include the Boeing 757, 767, 777 and all the airbus family of aircraft.

Since 1990, the first generation of noisy aircraft (i.e. chapter/stage 1), such as the Boeing 707, have been prohibited. Since that time the second generation chapter 2 aircraft have become the noisiest types. They were phased out completely in the USA at the end of 1999 and internationally ICAO requires these aircraft to be phased out by 2002. In 1998 in the EU it was estimated that there were two chapter 1 aircraft, 224 chapter 2 aircraft, 2448 chapter 3 and 13 supersonic in the world's fleet (European Commission, 1999). For some time ICAO explored the scope for a new chapter 4 noise standard but reaching agreement between all ICAO member states proved very difficult. A standard was finally agreed in 2001 but not decision was reached about further phasing out of noisy aircraft (Feldman, 2001).

An issue which has complicated this noise certification process is the treatment of hushkitted or re-engined jets. These are chapter 2 jets which have been modified to comply with the chapter 3 rules. They are, however, the noisiest of the chapter 3 aircraft and so there are pressures, particularly in Europe, for phasing them out. This has been the cause of a very major dispute between European and American authorities. The absence of an agreed standard from ICAO meant that the EU in the interim introduced its own regulation. This banned the addition of new hushkitted aircraft to European registers from 2000 and excluded all this type of aircraft entirely after 2002. The first measure was originally to become effective from 1999 but was delayed in the hope that an agreement with the Americans could be reached.

The Americans were strongly opposed to this unilateral action by the EU, claiming that it discriminates against the US aviation industry. This is because the US is the sole supplier of hushkit technology and US airlines have a higher proportion of hushkitted equipment than any others. For example, with all single-aisle aircraft in January 2000, globally 15 per cent was certified chapter 1 or 2, 19 per cent was hushkitted or re-engined, and the remaining 66 per cent were chapter 3 compliant. By far the greatest proportion of chapter 2 aircraft is in Latin America and Africa where they account for over half the total. In the USA 31 per cent of aircraft are hushkitted and 60 per cent are chapter 3 compliant, compared with corresponding global figures of 9 and 86 per cent. This largely explains the difference of opinion over this issue (Baker and George, 2000; George, 2000; Gill and George, 1999).

Undoubtedly international certification has an impact on reducing aircraft noise levels but these take a considerable length of time to achieve – given the heavy investment needed by both aircraft manufacturers and airlines, and the long lifetime of an aircraft. Individual airports can, however, introduce unilateral noise abatement operating measures which can more immediately reduce the annoyance caused by aircraft noise. For example many airports have introduced preferred noise routes (PNRs) to minimize the noise impact on the surrounding population. This is usually done by directing aircraft away from the most densely populated areas. Airports may also choose to place restrictions on flight procedures by requiring, for example, reduced power and flap settings for take-off or approach.

Flight-track monitoring equipment when combined with airport surveillance radar is used to improve airline departure and arrival procedures and to monitor the adherence to the PNRs. In some cases, airport operators may impose financial penalties on airlines that deviate from their required flight track. There may be difficulties with this, however, because airlines quite legitimately may be required to depart from their preferred route for ATC reasons. Money from penalties may be used for soundproofing or other community projects. Many airports also use noise-monitoring equipment. This can be used to measure local noise levels and calculate noise contours, or to enforce noise limits. The information gathered from the noise- and track-monitoring procedures can be provided for the airlines, local community, governments and other interested parties, and a growing number of airports actually publish the results.

Airports can also impose other operational measures to reduce the noise impact. A common restriction is a night curfew or limitations on night flights. This may involve a blanket ban on all aircraft, or a limit on the noisier aircraft eg. Such constraints may significantly impact on the development of freight or charter traffic which often rely on night movements, and make scheduling long-haul services more difficult. In most cases restrictions on noisier aircraft only apply at night but in some case they have been imposed during the day as well. Salzburg was one of the first European airports to ban all chapter 2 aircraft as early as 1991. The government of Belgium proposed a total night-time ban at Brussels airport in 2003, but due to pressure from the airport and DHL which has its European base there, this blanket ban has been replaced by night noise quotas. Airports may also choose to use the runways in a such a way as to minimize the number of people being affected by take-off or landing-related noise. Many airports also impose noise surcharges for noisier aircraft and an incentive to use quieter aircraft. These charging policies are, however, unlikely to influence an airline's choice of aircraft unless the fee differential is very large. Frankfurt airport was one of the first airports to introduce such charges in 1974. In the 1980s and 1990s, these became increasingly popular – particularly in Europe (see Chapter 5).

Düsseldorf airport, which is situated relatively close to the city of Düsseldorf, is an interesting example of an airport which has had its operations restricted by noise concerns. A second runway was completed in 1992 but because of environmental pressures, has a very restrictive upper limit on movements. On both runways, the airport was restricted to 91 000 aircraft movements of over 5.7 tonnes MTOW in the busiest six months of the year. The airport also has daily movement limits and a night ban between 2300 and 0600. In December 1997 a so-called 'noise budget' was approved which made an allowance for a gradual increase in the number of flight movements because of the use of quieter aircraft. This allowed a maximum of 120 000 movements in the six-month period. However, due to political and environmental pressures, the budget was repealed in 1999. The airport consequently applied to fully utilize the single runway capacity of 120 650 movements and was granted approval in 2000 (Düsseldorf Airport, 2000a; 2000b). These limitations over the years have placed restraints on the growth of both passenger and freight traffic at the airport. In order to provide capacity for smaller aircraft operating regional services, the airport had invested in the nearby small airport of Moenchengladbach.

There is also the noise from airline engines running, especially during maintenance. To reduce the noise emission levels a number of airports have introduced mufflers or noise attenuating walls and special noise attenuating hangars. Restrictions have been placed on when and how engine tests can be undertaken. Restrictions have also been placed on the use of reverse thrust by airlines. However, the noise problem is not just limited to the aircraft landing, taking-off, taxiing or engine testing. There is the noise from ground vehicles and auxiliary power units. Noise has been reduced at a number of US airports which have mostly fixed rather than auxiliary power units, as is the case of a few European airports such as Zürich and Copenhagen.

In 1992 a survey was undertaken of 104 European airports concerning noise-related operational restrictions. The survey findings give a good indication of the relative acceptance of the different noise measures, although more airports have introduced new measures in more recent years. Around three-quarters of the airports used PNRs and restrictions on engine testing. Half the airports had noise preferential runway use while a quarter had night-time restrictions on chapter 2 aircraft. Twenty-nine per cent of the airports had noise charges – with this proportion rising to 57 per cent at large airports. Thirty-five per cent of airports had a noise-monitoring system and 30 per cent had track-monitoring systems. For some of these airports, this monitoring system was a legal requirement (ACI-Europe, 1995).

The appropriate control of land use near the airport is vital when the mitigation of the noise impacts is being considered. This is in order to prevent the gains which have be achieved by using quieter aircraft being offset by people living closer to the airport. To overcome this problem noise zoning is often applied to airports. This involves defining a certain area, or noise buffer, around an airport where the construction of new houses and other noise-sensitive buildings is not allowed. However, there will always be some residents who will be subject to noise annoyance, and for this reason many airport operators will fund or assist in the funding of noise insulation for properties in the vicinity of the airport – either voluntarily or because it is a legal requirement. Housing and also buildings such as schools and hospitals may be insulated. Sometimes the funds may come from airport noise charges or noise taxes as it the case with the Paris airports where, for example in 1999, FF37.75 million grant money was allocated to 624 sound insulation projects from tax income (Aeroports de Paris, 2000).

Noise abatement procedures have existed at most major airports for some time, although technology is increasing the sophistication of such practices. Zürich airport was one of the first airports to address noise issues seriously. In 1964 it employed its first noise abatement employee and in 1966 a simple noise-monitoring system was introduced. In 1984 a flight-track monitoring system was added. Since 1972 there have been night-time restrictions and in 1980 noise-related surcharges to the landing charges were introduced. For some time the airport has had three noise zones. Zone A is in the centre of all airport activities where only airport-related buildings are allowed and residential property is prohibited. Surrounding this area is zone B where industrial buildings are permitted. Then there is zone C where housing with special noise insulation is allowed – but the cost must be borne by the house owner or developer (Meyer, 1996). By contrast, federal law in Germany requires airports to provide and pay for sound insulation within a noise zone around the airports.

Emissions

Through the combination of the development of quieter aircraft and noise abatement operating procedures, most airports have managed to contain many of the problems arising from aircraft noise. However, there is a 'new' environmental threat which has been growing in recent years – that of aircraft emissions. The present fleet of subsonic aircraft globally consumed around 130 million tonnes of fuel in 1992. This is expected to reach 300 million tonnes in 2015 and 450 million tonnes in 2050 (Intergovernmental Panel on Climate Change, 1999). By consuming fuel the aircraft are producing emissions of carbon dioxide, water vapour, nitrogen oxides, particles (mainly soot) of sulphur oxides, carbon monoxide and various hydrocarbons.

Some of these gases, primarily carbon dioxide (CO_2) and water vapour are greenhouse gases which contribute to global warming and climate change. Globally aviation's contribution to the world total of human-made CO_2, which is the most important of all the greenhouse gases, is considered to be fairly small, at around 2 per cent. The radiative forcing or global warming effect of all aircraft emissions is estimated to be around 3.5 per cent.). By 2050, this global share may have risen to around four to 15 per cent, depending on different growth scenarios and other assumptions (Intergovernmental Panel on Climate Change, 1999) Within the EU, CO_2 emissions from all forms of transport account for around 26 per cent of all CO_2 emissions. By far the greatest proportion comes from road transport with air accounting for 12 per cent of the total transport impacts (AEA, 1999).

Although the absolute amount of emissions is relatively small, they directly occur in the upper troposphere and lower stratosphere, when the aircraft are flying at altitudes of between 9 and 13 kilometres. As yet, the effect of these emissions at high altitudes is not fully understood. As well as the greenhouse gases, nitrogen oxides (NO_x) are also thought to have a significant impact on the ozone layer but, again, the exact effect is unclear. Of more certainty is that future global air traffic will increase at growth rates which will outperform the impact of any technology improvements which will reduce engine emissions. Aircraft in the 1990s were 70 per cent more fuel efficient than forty years ago. It is projected that there will be a 20 per cent improvement in fuel efficiency by 2015 and a 40–50 per cent improvement by 2050 (Intergovernmental Panel on Climate Change, 1999). In Europe the AEA fleet is predicted to be 22 per cent more fuel efficient by 2012 (AEA, 2000). However, the scale of these developments will only be sufficient to partially offset the growth effect. In addition, while greater fuel efficient aircraft will may produce less emissions such as CO_2, the higher combustion temperatures needed for greater efficient may actually produce more NO_x emissions. All this also has to be viewed within the global context where major CO_2 reduction efforts are taking place in other industrial sectors.

At present there does not appear to be a viable alternative to jet fuel. Thus the aviation industry is looking at other ways to mitigate aviation emissions. Improved operational procedures, such as more efficient air traffic management, could bring about a further reduction in fuel burn of around 8–18 per cent in the next twenty years – but still these developments by the themselves are not likely to reduce emissions to an acceptable level (Intergovernmental Panel on Climate Change, 1999).

Market-based options are another alternative. These include a kerosene tax. In the late 1990s the European Commission expressed significant interest in the introduction of an EU-wide fuel tax. It considered two options, first, just taxing EU carriers on intra-EU flights and, second, taxing all flights of all carriers operating within the EU. It was estimated that, if such a tax was introduced in 1998, the first option would reduce fuel consumption by 0.5 per cent between 1992 and 2005. The second option would bring a greater saving of 2.5 per cent. The subsequent effect on the operating result of the airlines with the first option was predicted to be a reduction of 12 per cent for EU carriers and a 4 per cent increase for other carriers. The alternative of taxing all flights was estimated to bring down the results of EU carriers by 15 per cent and other carriers by 4 per cent. The taxing of EU carriers would therefore give them a distinct competitive disadvantage and produce fairly marginal emission savings. This was not considered to be acceptable. The environmental effectiveness of taxing all routes would be far greater but this option would be very difficult to implement since international air service agreements explicitly exclude foreign operators from local taxation. This would involve complicated reworking of bilateral agreements or amending global policies – most probably through agreement with ICAO. It was concluded that this it was not a feasible option in the short term (European Commission, 1999).

An alternative to a tax is an emission charge which could be levied as part of the airport or ATC charge. Initially in 1989, the Swedish government levied an emission tax on Swedish domestic flights at a rate of 12 Swedish Crowns per kilogram of nitrogen oxides and hydrocarbons and 0.25 per kilogram of carbon dioxide (Alamdari and Brewer, 1994). However, according to EU directives, this type of tax was not allowed in Europe and was also seen as discriminatory towards Swedish carriers once full European liberalization has occurred. Therefore the Swedish government abandoned this tax in 1997 and replaced it with

Table 9.1 Emission charges at Swedish Airports in 2000

Class of aircraft	Average value of emissions during LTO[1] cycle	Increase in landing charge (%)
0	> 19 g/kN HC or > 80 g/kN NO_x	30
1	< 19 g/kN HC and > 80 g/kN NO_x	25
2	< 19 g/kN HC and > 70 g/kN NO_x	20
3	< 19 g/kN HC and > 60 g/kN NO_x	15
4	< 19 g/kN HC and > 50 g/kN NO_x	10
5	< 19 g/kN HC and > 40 g/kN NO_x	5
6	< 19 g/kN HC and > 30 g/kN NO_x	0

Note: [1] LTO = landing and take-off.
Source: IATA (2000).

an emission charge (Table 9.1). Geneva and Zürich also introduced an emissions charge in 1997. The Swiss and Swedish authorities are working together towards a harmonized system with the aim of making it easier for users and for other countries to adopt. The impact of such unilateral policies on fleet choice seems to have been rather limited – which, as with the noise surcharges, is the result of the relative price inelastic demand at airports. A survey of airlines of the European Regions Airline Association found that 91 per cent had not yet altered their fleet mix as a result of the charges in Switzerland and Sweden, and 67 per cent would not consider doing so despite the fact that 73 per cent were now paying high charges as a result of the schemes (McNamara, 2000).

Other options, other than emission taxes or charges include voluntary or regulatory agreements to reduce the level of emissions. Since 1981 ICAO has laid down standards for four categories of engine emissions, namely smoke, hydrocarbons, carbon monoxide and nitrogen oxides. These standards are aimed at local air pollution problems, since they are based on the aircraft landing and take-off (LTO) cycle and do not cover emissions during the cruise phase. They are also not legally binding and it is up to member states to include these standards into their law. It is conceivable that these standards could be extended to include greenhouse gases. In short, there are a range of options available to the air transport industry to reduce the impact of aviation emissions – but the feasibility or effectiveness of each measure is still not entirely clear (Baker, 2000).

While the global impacts of aircraft emissions have attracted a great deal of attention in recent years, clearly they are not the only impacts which need to be considered. At a regional level the emissions from aviation are thought to contribute to acid rain. At a local level the air quality of the area in the immediate vicinity of the airport can be affected – primarily due to emissions of hydrocarbons, carbon monoxide and nitrogen oxides. An increasing number of airports monitor local air quality at airports – sometimes because they are legally required to do so by law. Very often independent companies will undertake the monitoring. The monitoring systems vary considerably in their level of sophistication and accuracy. Some airports use these systems to help them model predicted air quality in the future.

While the ICAO emission standards can have an influence over aircraft emissions at airports, the actual airport operators have very little control over this matter. Encouraging more fuel efficient operating procedures such as continuous descent approach may help a little. The operator can also seek to reduce the impact of running engines while the aircraft are on the ground. As with the noise issue, the problem at airports is not just limited to aircraft operations since the local air quality may also be affected by the ground service vehicles, which tend to be fuel powered. At some airports, electric vehicles which are more economically and environmentally favourable, have been considered and used in a few instances. Then there are emissions from maintenance and cleaning processes, auxiliary power units and from the cars and other surface transport modes. The targets for the Los Angeles airports are an example of policies to reduce emission from ground vehicles. Currently 33 per cent of the 600-vehicle fleet is burning clean fuel but this is targeted to increase to 50 per cent in 2003. By 2001 a fleet of fifty-two natural-gas buses will be operating, replacing the current fuel fleet of forty-three, and twenty additional recharging stations for electric vehicles will be installed. Already 134 gates operate with fixed ground power and also a fully electric pushback tug is due to be tested (Jane's Airport Review, 1999).

Another impact, not directly related to emissions but to the trail of turbulent air left behind by an aircraft, is wake vortices which can damage the tiles and windows of property under flight paths. Responsibility for this sometimes rests with the airport operator or property owner, but more often with the airline. However, it is very difficult to identify the specific airline involved and so the airport operators often provide a repair service and introduce measures to minimize the likelihood of this happening.

Water pollution and use

Water pollution at airports can occur for a number of different reasons. Surface water discharge or run-off which goes into local watercourses from runways, aprons, car parks and other land development may be contaminated by anti-icing and de-icing fluids such as glycol which are used during the winter months. The chemicals used in maintaining and washing aircraft and vehicles, as well as fire training activities and fuel spillages, can also contribute to this pollution. Leakages from underground tanks and pipes, and grass fertilizers used in landscaping activities can contaminate the soil. Then there is the normal wastewater from buildings and facilities such as domestic sewerage. An increasing number of airports now monitor water quality as well as air quality and have adopted various measures to minimize this water pollution. These include revised operational practices to reduce the use of the harmful chemicals, to improve cleaning processes and to minimize the spillage and leakages. Balancing reservoir treatment may be undertaken before the surface water joins local watercourses.

Waste and energy management

Waste pollution is also an issue, as it is with most other industrial activities. In many cases there may be general legislation related to waste management.

However, airports are also faced with specific operating restrictions because of the nature of the aviation business. For example, airports need to incinerate or send to a controlled landfill site all 'international' food waste from aircraft. In addition, the transfer of waste from airside to landsite at airports is problematic because of security, customs and insurance restrictions.

The waste at airports is generated by airlines, airport operators and other airport-related companies. While most of the waste comes from the airlines, it is usually the airport operators who have overall responsibility for waste management for the entire airport activities. Most of the individual companies, especially the airlines, do not have enough space for waste management facilities and there are cost economies of scale to be gained by having communal recycling and other waste management procedures. Improvements can usually be brought about by an assessment of on-airport treatment methods and the scope for reducing, reusing or recycling waste. In-flight catering waste, with the disposable nature of most of the packaging, is considered to be a particular problem. Off-airport disposal methods which typically involve incineration and landfill also need to be considered.

Energy management, associated with the provision of heating, ventilation, air conditioning and lighting, is also very important. It has been estimated that energy costs account for about 5 per cent of the operating costs of an airport. Energy conservation techniques can reduce this by between 5 and 20 per cent (ACI-Europe, 1995). Some airports undertake energy audits. With energy conservation, as with waste and water management, there are good financial reasons for why airports should address these issues since environmental improvements may bring about considerable cost savings.

Wildlife, heritage and landscape

The major impacts of noise and emission clearly can have a significant affect on the population living in the vicinity of the airport. However, it is not just the effects on the daily life of people that the airport operator has to consider. The need to protect the wildlife, heritage and the landscape of the local environment also needs to be addressed.

There are many examples of how specific airport operators have tackled the disturbance of certain wildlife habitats – particularly during the construction of a new airport or during airport expansion. While the new Chek Lap Kok airport in Hong Kong was being built, a 1-kilometre exclusion zone for dolphins was set up to ensure that their sensitive hearing was not harmed during blasting work. At Indianapolis airport 3000 new bat homes for the Indiana bat had to be installed due to a new maintenance building which displaced the bats. At Perth airport, development was halted when a rare western swamp tortoise colony was discovered. At Miami airport the death of four manatees beneath the runway forced the airport operator to take action to protect this endangered species. At Manchester airport, badger setts had to be relocated, and a rare breed of newt had to be protected when the second runway was being built. At Oslo Gardermoen airport, a bridge had to be built to prevent the 1000 moose who annually migrate across the region from wandering onto the airport approach roads (Anker, 1997).

Heritage may also be affected by airport development. For example, historic buildings may be situated within the area which has been allocated for airport expansion. In the case of Manchester and Copenhagen airports, this has meant that such buildings have been moved, to other locations. Landscapes can be radically changed by airport development, which can disturb the ecosystem and can be visually intrusive. When Stansted airport in London was developed, for example, a considerable amount of time and effort was expended in attempting to integrate the airport as much as possible into the local landscape. An unusual example is San Francisco airport. Here environmental lobbyists were actually in favour of airport development, rather than being opposed to it, because it involved the restoration of 55 acres of wetlands in the San Francisco Bay area (Gethin, 1998).

The role of other transport modes

There are two ways in which the use of other transport modes can affect the direct and indirect environmental impacts of airports. First, there may be some opportunity for passengers on short and medium distance flights to be diverted on to high-speed rail services. In Europe it is estimated that around 10 per cent of passengers could be transferred from aircraft to high-speed trains (International Panel on Climate Change, 1999). In the 1980s and 1990s there was a continuing growth in the number of high-speed rail services notably in France and Germany. Various studies have shown that a quick city centre to city centre rail service have been quite successful in attracting a certain share of the population away from competing air services. For example, it was estimated that the rail share of traffic on the Frankfurt–Munich route increased from 30 to 37 per cent in the first year of operation with a drop in airline share from 27 to 23 per cent. On the Stockholm–Gothenburg route the rail share was estimated to have increased from 40 to 55 per cent in the first four years of operation and the first TGV route in France between Paris and Lyons was claimed to have gained an 90 per cent market share (CAA, 1998a).

An interesting development occurred in Germany when, in 1998, Lufthansa and the railway company, Deutsche Bahn, signed a memorandum of understanding. This relates to short routes from air to rail once the high-speed network in Germany has been completed. It is Lufthansa's aim to gain more slots for longer-haul services. Elsewhere an agreement between the French and Americans has been reached which allows the airlines to offer passenger services which include a rail connection or other surface mode of transport (DETR, 2000).

However, switching from air to rail is only feasible when dense routes are being considered. Such rail links also require huge capital investment. Moreover, they are clearly not usually an attractive option for transfer traffic unless the high-speed network is linked to airports, as at Frankfurt for instance. The appeal of the rail alternative will also depend very much on the comparable level of fares and the quality of service on offer. For example, the diversion rate of air to rail on the Eurotunnel London–Paris route has been far greater than that for the London–Brussels routes. There is some evidence to suggest that this has been partly due to the availability of much cheaper air fares on the London–Brussels route (Dennis, 1999).

The individual airport operator has far greater control in influencing the mode of surface travel used by passengers and employees to reach the airport – which is the other aspect of surface transport that needs to be considered. Ground transport makes a major contribution to the overall noise levels and air pollution at an airport, with the impacts rising as the transport system becomes congested. Many airports are trying to develop more effective public transport alternatives to the car for accessing the airport. They have also introduced many initiatives to encourage passengers and airport employees to use public transport.

Historically, most passengers arrived at airports by private car or taxi, with only a small proportion using bus or coach transport. With airport growth in the 1970s and 1980s, some existing suburban rail services (e.g. underground or light rail services) were extended to reach the airport. They are still the most common form of rail link today, with many examples being found in North America and other airports such as Düsseldorf, Munich, Stuttgart, Barcelona, Changi Singapore and Shanghai. In 2000, there still remained no rail links to any of the three New York airports. However, a monorail extension was due to be completed to Newark in 2001, an AirTran light rail system at JFK was planned for opening in 2003 and LaGuardia airport was considering a subway extension (Ashworth, 2000).

Many of these services are relatively slow, with a rather basic quality of service, and are not dedicated links to the airport. They may popular with employees but less attractive to passengers. This has meant that a number of airports, particularly those with large traffic volumes or a long journey away from the city centre, have instead developed high-speed dedicated links. Such links bring environmental benefits and alleviate road congestion as well as bringing extra convenience for passengers. Indeed, Arlanda, Stockholm airport's third runway was only approved subject to a rail link being built. Other dedicated airport rail link examples include Gardermoen in Oslo, Heathrow in London, Chek Lap Kok in Hong Kong and Sepang in Kuala Lumpur. A number of airports have also developed high-speed links connecting airport terminals to international routes such as Charles de Gaulle in Paris, Lyon, Frankfurt, Zürich and Amsterdam.

Some airports also have integrated regional and high-speed rail links – Paris Charles de Gaulle being a good example. Frankfurt airport has three railway interfaces. There is a regional train station below Terminal 1, an AIRail terminal for long distance services and a rail connection to Cargo City South. Other airports as well are looking at rail links for the carriage of freight. This is a relatively new idea since, historically, the only freight transported has been aviation fuel. Airports particularly interested in developing rail freight include Liege, Leipzig/Hall Amsterdam, Paris Charles de Gaulle, Milan and London Heathrow (IARO/ATAG/ACI, 1998).

Figure 9.1 shows the total number of rail links to airports – both currently in existence and planned. There are many more rail links in Europe than in North America as they are considered to be a much more acceptable and attractive surface access option in Europe. Few of the North American links integrate effectively with other rail services as is the case with a growing number of links in Europe. Remote baggage services are also frequently available in Europe but not in North America. The most developed service of this

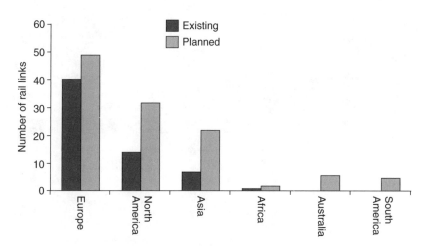

Figure 9.1 Existing and planned rail links to airports
Source: IARO/ATAG/ACI (1998).

type is the Fly Rail Baggage system in Switzerland which provides two-way check-in for Zürich, Basel and Geneva at 116 rail stations. At twenty-three rail stations complete check-in can be made for flights of Swissair and partner airlines. These factors plus the greater car dependency in North America explains why rail modal share and the actual number of rail links is far less common there than in Europe.

A growing number of airport operators have recognized that encouraging passengers onto public transport is very much more than just consideration of journey time. It also includes looking at the accessibility of the surface modes, ease of transfer to the airport and arrangements for baggage. Some airports are designing better interchange processes between public transport and the airport, and offering more remote check-in. Others have tried making improvements in marketing, signage and the availability of information.

A study of eighteen European airports found that passenger public transport use varied from 1 per cent at Lelystad to 41 per cent at Munich airport. The average was around 21 per cent – 9 per cent for rail and 12 per cent for buses (Navarre, 1996). More recent studies show that Zürich airport, which was not included in the original study, has a very high share of 59 per cent of passengers accessing the airport by public transport (Grossenbacher, 1999). Figure 9.2 shows the public transport share for some other European airports.

Many airports now set targets for public transport use. For example, Heathrow has set a target for passenger public transport trips of 40 per cent by 2000, and Gatwick has an identical target for 2008. Manchester airport has a target of 25 per cent for all public transport journeys by 2005. Amsterdam has a target of 40 per cent of collective transport passenger journeys by 2003. This airport nearly achieved this target in 1999 with 39 per cent. The most popular reasons for car use at the major UK airports have been identified as cost and convenience, and because a friend or relative was available to offer a

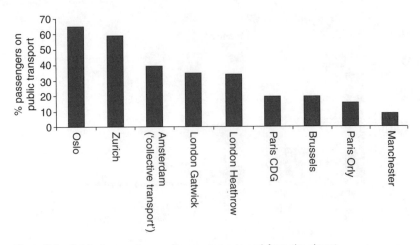

Figure 9.2 Public transport usage by passengers to and from the airport
Source: Compiled by the author from various sources for years 1997–9.

lift (CAA, 1998b). For Zürich the key reasons for using rail transport were comfortable access (46 per cent), rail ticket included in package (17 per cent), rail being the quickest way of getting to the airport (17 per cent) and parking costs at the airport being too high (20 per cent) (Grossenbacher, 1999).

Airport operators have also been trying to encourage more airport employees to use public transport. Inherently there are a number of characteristics of airport employment which encourage the use of private car. Many of the jobs tend to be on a shift basis, often at unsociable times when public transport services are inadequate. Employees' residences tend to be dispersed around the vicinity of the airport which makes it much more difficult to provide an effective public transport system. Moreover, airport employees have traditionally been provided with free parking spaces at airports – thus increasing the attractiveness of car transport. As a result of these factors, car use tends to be even higher for employees than for passengers. For example, at Manchester airport in 1996, 80 per cent of passengers used private cars or taxis, while the equivalent figure for employees was 92 per cent (Manchester Airport, 1997). Surveys at other airports also show this greater dependence on car transport (Niblett, 1996). Staff initiatives to encourage public transport use include discount bus and rail travel, dedicated airport workers buses, the development of cycling networks, and park and ride schemes. When car use is still necessary, car sharing has been encouraged at some airports. Restrictions on car use within the airport area have also been introduced. Some airports have also set targets for public transport use for staff. For example, Amsterdam airport had a target of 40 of per cent of employees using 'environmental-friendly' (i.e. public transport plus cycling, carpooling etc). It reached this target in 1998 with a share of 42 per cent (Schiphol Group, 2000).

From 1998 in the UK all airports with scheduled services were required to form airport transport forums (ATFs) and prepare airport surface access strategies (ASASs) as part of a national policy framework for integrated transport (DETR, 1998). The ATFs have three specific objectives (DETR, 1999):

1 To agree short- and long-term targets for decreasing the private car usage to and from airports.
2 To devise a strategy for achieving these targets.
3 To oversee implementation of the strategy.

The ATF consists of the airport operator and representatives from local businesses, local government, transport operators, the local community and other interested parties. In preparing the ASASs the forum has to ensure that the proposals are consistent with the broader integrated transport plans for the area. London Heathrow airport was the first UK airport to establish an ATF, in 1995 – before this became official government policy. It was followed by London Gatwick airport in 1997, London Stansted in 1999 and Manchester in 2000.

The Heathrow ATF is served by a steering group of ten members which oversees the composition of ten working groups and sets them work programmes (Figure 9.3). At Heathrow over 75 per cent of staff arrive by car and 66 per cent of the passengers also use this means of transport (Figures 9.4 and 9.5). In 1999 Heathrow was the first UK airport to launch its five-year

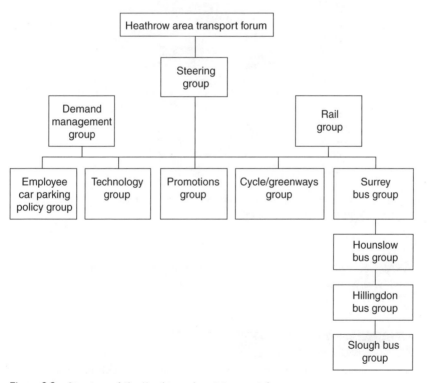

Figure 9.3 Structure of the Heathrow airport transport forum
Source: BAA Heathrow.

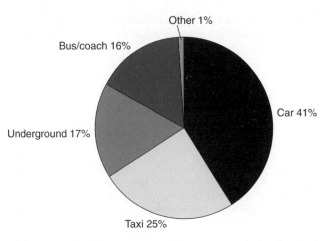

Figure 9.4 Mode of surface transport used by passengers at London Heathrow airport
Source: CAA airport survey, 1997.

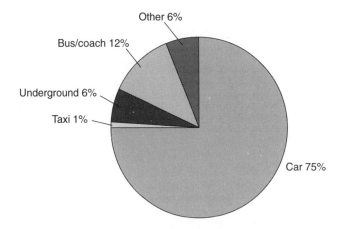

Figure 9.5 Mode of surface transport used by employees at London Heathrow airport
Source: Heathrow airport survey, 1999.

ASAS setting out nineteen targets and commitments (Table 9.2). The six targets to be delivered before the end of 1999 (targets 6, 9, 10, 11, 15 and 17) have already been met (BAA Heathrow, 2000a).

The social consequences

So far consideration has been given to the economic and environmental impacts of airports. Aviation can clearly have a multitude of impacts on society as well. In the broadest context, it is often claimed that air travel brings wider benefits

Table 9.2 Targets and commitments: Heathrow airport surface access strategy, 1999

Travelling to and from Heathrow Rail	1. 40% of air passengers by public transport by 2000 2. Long-term target of 50% 3. BAA to work with Railtrack to introduce an interim stopping service between Heathrow and Central London by end of 2000 4. BAA to work with Railtrack for approval of Heathrow express service to London St Pancras with first phase operational by end of 2002 5. BAA and Railtrack to work with promoters group to prepare a Transport and Works Act application for Airtrack scheme (i.e. to seek approval for new this additional rail service)
Bus and coach	6. Prepare a strategy for the provision of on-airport bus priority by the end of 1999 7. The ATF (through the bus working groups) to work to develop performance indicators by end of 2000
Cycling and walking	8. Double the number of employees cycling to work by end of 2002 9. Produce a cycle implementation plan by end of 1999
Road	10. To introduce road traffic monitoring at all airport entrances and exits by 1999
Accessibility and interchange	11. BAA to continue to consult with transport operators, business partners and user groups on design of public transport interchange at Terminal 5 and Hatton Cross, and improvements to existing Central Terminal Area interchange
Parking	12. To introduce a pilot scheme that relates car parking availability to staff need and public transport availability by end of 2000 (subject to detailed discussions with stakeholders) 13. To introduce limit the number of parking spaces under BAA control to 46 000 if Terminal 5 receives planning permission
Managing demand	14. The ATF to continue to operate for at least five years 15. Journey planner to be available to all Heathrow and off-airport employees by end of 1999 16. BAA to work with on-airport employers, encouraging ten of them to produce their own travel plans by end of 2000
Monitoring	17. To develop a computerized surface access database by end of 1999 18. To publish each year a report on progress against the targets in the surface access strategy 19. To include in the first annual report a comprehensive analysis of effectiveness of public transport initiatives in changing Heathrow employee travel behaviour

Source: BAA Heathrow, 1999.

to society in the form of strengthening ethnic and cultural links between countries, enhancing opportunities for travel and increasing consumer choices for foodstuffs and other products. These are all very general impacts, which are extremely difficult to quantify or contribute to any one airport.

In acting as a catalyst for economic development, airports will also have a major social impact on the surrounding area. Employment and living patterns will change with implications for housing, health, education and other social needs. An overheated economy associated with a successful airport development may bring problems of labour shortages, insufficient housing and rising prices. Another very obvious social role played by certain airports is that of providing lifeline links to remote areas which might otherwise remain isolated.

Clearly airport environmental impacts can have a detrimental impact on the quality of life of residents in the vicinity of the airport. The major areas of concern are aircraft noise, air pollution, fuel odour, ecological damage and the safety of aircraft. While the exact relationship between human health and well-being and these factors is still not entirely clear, an area which has received particular attention is the problem of sleep disturbance due to night flying. It is for this reason that many airports restrict aircraft movements at nights or ban noisier aircraft types. The rising number of aircraft movements has also increased concerns about aircraft safety and has resulted in some airports establishing risk contours around airports associated with third party death and injury.

Many airports address some of the social issues raised by airport operations within the framework of a broader environmental or sustainability strategy. For airport employees this may involve consideration of issues such as equal opportunities, ethics policies, skills training and workplace safety and security. Moreover forging strong links with the community and ensuring continual public dialogue with all interested parties is often considered an important role. Most airports get involved in community relations such as the provision of information about environmental and other developments, offering a complaints-handling service, supporting and sponsoring local events, and developing educational links. Some airports set up residents' forums. Many airports also have consultative committees with representatives from local government, amenity groups, local commerce and industry, and airport users. These may be a legal requirement.

Environmental management

For many airports operators, environmental policies increasingly are becoming a core component of their overall business strategy. Environmental pressures from governments, users and other bodies have made it essential for airports to address environmental issues very seriously. In some areas, such as air or water quality, airports often have to comply with environmental legislation. Airports have recognized, though, that sound environmental practice can also bring financial benefits through the effective management of resources such as energy, waste and water. As a result, most major airports in the western world now have well-established environmental strategies and relatively sophisticated policies which typically seek to reduce noise and emissions, control pollution, reduce waste and energy use, and encourage the use of renewables and public transport. Increased technology and new mitigation methods are constantly enabling improvements in the efficiencies of such policies. Smaller airports and airports in the developing world have more basic approaches – but few have managed to escape the whole issue of environmental management entirely. Since airport operators themselves produce relative little of the direct environmental impacts, a key to any successful environmental strategy is a partnership approach between all the different interests on the airport site.

Many airports have seen their environmental control processes develop into comprehensive environment management systems. These provide the framework for airport operators to develop an effective and co-ordinated response to all the environmental issues. Within any system, clearly defined objectives and targets are set for reducing the impacts and the most appropriate mitigation methods are identified. Through adopting such an approach the airport operator also sends messages to the outside world that it is tackling the environmental issues in a responsible manner. In Australia, the Airports Act of 1997 actually requires airport operators to prepare airport environmental strategies for government approval.

Some airports choose to formalize their environmental management system by conforming to the International Environmental Management system standards ISO 14001 This is equivalent to ISO 9000 standard for quality management (see Chapter 4). To meet the requirements of ISO14001, airports need to review their environmental impacts, formulate an environmental policy, ensure that their practices comply with all relevance legislation, set objectives and targets to improve environment performance and demonstrate that appropriate measures have been introduced so that environmental practice can be monitored and targets can be reached. Dublin airport became one of the first European airports to receive ISO 14001 certification, in 1999, and Toronto Lester B. Pearson was the first airport in North America to achieve this standard, in 1998.

Within the EU, there is an additional system called the Eco Management and Audit Scheme (EMAS) which is based on 1993 European regulation. The EMAS takes the ISO 14001 standard that much further by requiring companies to report to the public about their environmental performance. This report, as well as the implementation of the management system, is subject to external scrutiny. A number of airports were involved in the piloting of this standard and by 2000 some airports, such as Brussels, were hoping to achieve certification (Brussels International Airport Company, 2000; European Commission, 1999).

One of the key elements of any environmental management system is the identification of suitable environmental indicators which can be used to monitor performance and set targets. The indicators should provide a representative picture of the issue under consideration and it must be possible to obtain relatively easily and accurately the data required for such indicators. The indicators need to be fairly simple, easy to interpret and able to show trends over time. The results should be available to everybody who has an interest in the airport, including the local community.

The exact number and range of objectives and targets will vary considerably. For example, in 2000 BAA had eighty-five environmental targets and for the first time these targets played a part of the senior management salary incentive scheme – just as with the financial and surface quality targets. In 1999, Amsterdam airport adopted twenty-nine key targets and Geneva airport's environmental action plan had twenty-seven key measures which needed to be addressed. In 2000, Nice airport adopted an environmental charter which identified a total of fifteen objectives and these were broken down into forty-six detailed actions. Table 9.3 shows some common key environmental performance indicators used by airports. Many of these tend to be further disaggregated when detailed targets are being set.

Table 9.3   Key environmental performance indicators at airports

Impact	Performance indicator
Noise	Proportion of chapter 3 aircraft
	Population within specified noise contour
	Number of noise limit infringements
	Number of engine testing rules infringements
	Proportion of aircraft on track
Emissions	CO_2 and NO_x emissions per passenger (and other emissions)
	Fixed electrical power usage
Water	Number of spillages per 1000 ATMs
	Water consumption per passenger
Waste	Waste per passenger
	Proportion of waste recycled
	Proportion of waste going to landfill sites
Energy	Energy consumption (gas, electricity, fuel) per passenger
Transport	Proportion of passengers using surface transport
	Proportion of staff using surface transport
Social policy	Ethnic origin of staff
	Gender split of staff
Community relations	Number of complaints
	Response time for complaints

It should possible, as part of the environmental management system, to identify the expenditure and savings related to their environmental, economic and social management policies. Table 9.4 shows these for Heathrow airport. The greatest expenditure was for capital projects and infrastructure which included investment in noise mitigation measures, transport infrastructure projects and water treatment schemes. The savings were in waste management and energy conservation.

Table 9.4   Environmental, economic and social expenditure and savings at Heathrow airport, 1999/2000

	Expenditure (£000s)
Environmental communications/public relations	146.7
Staff	786.5
Revenue/consultancy/research projects	1 062.7
On-going management and maintenance	1 812.2
Regulatory charges	5.0
Capital projects/infrastructure	6 296.5
Monitoring	50.6
TOTAL	10 160.2
Savings	−792.7

Source: BAA Heathrow (2000b).

When an airport is planning a major extension of its facilities, it is usually required by law to undertake an environmental impact assessment (EIA) as part of the planning approval process. This will examine the potential impacts of the proposed development during the construction and operational stages. The results of this assessment are summarized in an environmental impact statement (EIS).

EIA for the new Oslo airport at Gardermoen

Since 1939 Oslo has been served by Fornebu airport. However, by the 1980s this airport, situated close to Oslo city centre was beginning to reach capacity but could not be expanded because of physical constraints and environmental pressures. A number of new airport sites were assessed and, in 1991, the existing military airport site of Gardemoen was chosen.

The EIA for Gardermoen considered the following impacts (Luftfartsverket, 1991):

1   Pollution factors
    (a)   noise
    (b)   air pollution
    (c)   climate.

2   Impact on natural resources and natural conditions
    (a)   land and forest resources
    (b)   water resources
    (c)   outdoor recreational areas
    (d)   landscape
    (e)   minerals
    (f)   flora and fauna.

3   Impact on cultural heritage
    (a)   pre-Reformation heritage
    (b)   post-Reformation heritage.

4   Social factors
    (a)   impact on the employment market
    (b)   social impacts
    (c)   impacts on municipal economy
    (d)   impacts on land utilization.

At this stage there were two options with a runway, either to the east or to west of the existing runway. For each impact an investigation of the current situation was made, along with an impact assessment of the two alternative options. In addition evaluation of possible mitigation measures and proposals for monitoring programmes were made. While the CAA, which operates airports in Norway was responsible for assessing the environmental impact of the airport itself, the Public Roads Administration and Norwegian State Railways analysed the impact of the access system. The Department of Environment and Department of Agriculture were involved in the investigation of the regional and social impacts. The decision to build the new airport was made in 1992 and it was opened in 1998 (Gaustad, 1996).

Environmental issues and a new runway at Manchester airport

Manchester airport which is owned by Manchester Airport plc (MA) handled 17 million passengers, 112 000 tonnes of freight and 170 900 air transport movements (ATMs) in 1999. Its runway had a declared hourly capacity of forty-seven movements. By the early 1990s this runway was becoming full at peak hours and so the draft development strategy published in 1991 identified the need for a second runway.

For this reason, sixteen groups of environmental experts were appointed to look at the whole range of possible impacts associated with the second runway scheme and to provide input into the environmental impact assessment. Specialist engineering consultants were also appointed at this time. The airport operator, the environmental team and the engineering design team worked together in developing the runway scheme. This enabled the environmental effects of engineering solutions to be assessed, and mitigation measures to be considered, at an early stage.

Public consultation also took place at this time. This ranged from private meetings with individuals to large scale public gatherings. Continual dialogue also had to be maintained with airport users, government agencies, local authorities and other interested parties. The feedback from the initial assessment of the environmental impacts and key areas of public concern were used to influence the design details of the runway scheme. Primarily as a result of environmental considerations, the idea of a full-length parallel taxiway was abandoned and the runway site was modified to reduce the length of river tunnel that would

Table 9.5   Key events in the development of Manchester airport's second runway

Date	Event
August 1991	Draft development strategy to 2005 published, identifying the need for the second runway
September–November 1991	Public consultation period and eight public meetings held
December 1991–March 1993	Results from public consultation were considered and environment impacts of development options were assessed. Further consultation and public exhibitions took place
March 1993	Final development option was selected
June 1993	Final development strategy was published and the EIA completed
July 1993	Planning application submitted to local authorities
July–August 1993	Public exhibitions held over twenty-two days at nine locations
June 1994	Public inquiry opened
March 1995	Public inquiry closed
January 1997	Planning permission granted
Summer 1997	Commencement of development
February 2001	Runway opened

Source: Twigg (2001).

have been required. Further consultation and assessment of the impacts took place until a final development option was selected in 1993. The proposals were subsequently developed into a planning application which was subject to a planning inquiry which lasted from June 1994 to March 1995. Planning permission was granted in January 1997 (Table 9.5).

Before the decision had been made, MA entered into a legal agreement with the local planning authorities concerning its proposed package of environmental mitigation measures, to show its commitment to the environmental issues. This package contained over 100 different measures of targets and guarantees covering noise control and night flying, environmental works, highway improvements and public transport, community relations and social policy, and the ultimate capacity of the airport. This formed the basis of Manchester airport's 'green charter' (Table 9.6). The points of agreement were related to various stages during construction and operation of the airport up until 2011 when the agreement will be reviewed. This approach to the environmental effects was costly, amounting to over £20 million, but MA viewed it as an investment and considered such an approach fundamental to gaining permission to build the additional runway (Thomas, 1996; Twigg, 2000).

Environmental practice at Copenhagen airport

Copenhagen Airport A/S (CPH) is a good example of an airport operator which has developed a comprehensive environmental policy. This company manages the two Copenhagen airports, namely Kastrup and Roskilde. In 1999 these two airports handled 17.3 million passenger numbers, 389 000 tonnes of freight and 295 000 air transport movements.

The general goal of CPH's environmental policy is that the environmental impacts and resource use should not increase at the same rate as traffic growth. The stated aims of the environmental policy are as follows (CPH, 1999):

1 To protect the environment through initiatives to prevent negative impact and improve conditions.
2 To safeguard the working environment of employees.
3 To use cleaner technology in the operation and expansion of CPH's airports.
4 To increase environmental awareness among CPH's employees and other users of the airport.
5 To provide information on CPH's environmental performance.

Table 9.7 summarizes the main environmental indicators used, how the data is collected and the indicator value for 1999. As regards noise, over 98 per cent of all movements at Kastrup take place on the two main runways. There is a third runway which involves aircraft passing over more built-up residential areas, and so it is only used when special weather and wind conditions make it necessary for safety reasons. There are rules related to noise levels, and engine testing and airline performance in these areas is monitored. Between 1996 and 1999, the overall noise impact declined by 2.7 dB although the number of air transport movement increased by 10 per cent during the same period. This was due to greater use of newer, quieter aircraft and less use of the noisier, older aircraft.

Table 9.6 Manchester airport's 'green charter'

Environmental topic	Main measures
Noise control	The noise impact will be controlled up to at least 2011 and will be no worse than in 1992 A noise and aircraft track monitoring system will be maintained Monthly monitoring reports will be produced and an annual external audit undertaken 100 % of scheduled night movements to be by the quieter chapter 3 aircraft 92% of total scheduled operations to be by chapter 3 aircraft by 1998 and 96% by 2000 A preferential charging system for quieter aircraft will be developed MA will continue to seek powers to penalize aircraft that deviate from the set departure routes A ground noise policy will limit night ground engine tests to 20 per year; require the use of the engine test bay; and encourage use of fixed electrical power
Night flying	The night noise level will be controlled up to at least 2011 and will be no worse than in 1992 Night movements will not exceed 7% of total movements Chapter 2 aircraft will not operate at night Financial noise penalties will apply at night The use of reverse thrust will be restricted at night The second runway will not normally be used at night

Environmental works	More than twice as many ponds will be created or restored than those lost
	Landscape and ecological mitigation works proposal will be submitted to the local authority for agreement
	A fifteen-year landscape and management plan will be developed
	Ecologists and landscape architects will oversee and implement the environmental works
	MA, local authorities, statutory bodies and local wildlife groups will form a nature conservation steering group
	The MA will financially support the Bollin Valley project and upgrade the River Bollin channel to encourage the migration of fish
	Where possible, permission will be sought to relocate two of the four affected listed buildings
	The aviation viewing park will be relocated
Highway improvements	MA will fund a number of road improvements
	Restrictions will be placed on operation times and routes taken on construction traffic, and construction material is to be brought by rail
Public transport	25% of all trips to the airport will be made by public transport
	MA will promote the extension of Metrolink and development of heavy rail services
	A ground transport group will promote and develop enhanced public transport services and a ground transport strategy will be introduced
	10% of the annual marketing budget will be used to promote public transport services
Community relations	The sound insulation grant scheme will be maintained
	Local environmental projects will be supported by a community trust fund with an annual budget of at least £100 000
Social policy	MA's recruitment policy will offer a fair and equal opportunity to applicants by advertising jobs in the airport job centre and local media; by operating a crèche; and by striving to achieve a representative ethnic mix of employees
Ultimate capacity	There will be no consideration of a third runway until at least 2011
	MA will oppose inappropriate development in the area other than that related to the airport's technical efficiency

Source: Twigg (2000).

Table 9.7 Main environmental indicators used by Copenhagen Airport A/S

Impact	Means of data collection	Main indicators	1999 indicator value
Traffic and noise	Traffic statistics system: ATMs by aircraft type, take-off weight, use of runway and time	Total-day-evening-night-level (TDENL) method (decibel dB)	150
Night-time noise	Noise monitoring system	Infringement of 85 dB (A) noise limit (number)	16
Engine testing	Engine test monitoring	Infringement of engine testing rules (number)	31
Waste water	Discharged volume by means of metres Water quality assessed by monthly water samples made by third party laboratory	Waste water discharged per 1000 passengers (litres) Discharged waste water quality: Substances (000 kgs) Heavy metal (kgs)	18 000 Biological oxygen 230, nitrogen 20 Zinc 90, copper 12
Surface water	Discharged volume on the basis of the pump effect of CPH's pumps or volume of participation reported by Danish Meteorological Institute. Water quality assessed by monthly water samples made by third party laboratory	Discharged surface water quality: Substances (000 kgs) Heavy metal (kgs)	Biological oxygen 142, nitrogen 11 Zinc 90, copper 24
Oil and fuel spills	Reports filed by CPH's safety service, fire services and other in-house and third party-sources	Number of spills Volume of spills (litres)	272 15 652

De-icing	Volume of glycol used calculated by companies handling de-icing	Consumption of glycol (cubic metres)	590
	Contents of collected glycol are registered for each truckload moved away	Collection of glycol (cubic metres)	330
Resources and energy	Consumption based on volumes purchased less quantities sold to other companies at the airport	Electricity consumption (Tera Joule, TJ)	170
		Heating consumption (Tera Joule, TJ)	110
		Fuel consumption (000 litres)	750
		Water consumption (cubic metres)	150
Weed control	Consumption of herbicides based on volumes purchased	Consumption of herbicides (litres)	80
Waste	Weighing slips or monthly statements from recipients of the waste	Waste per 1000 passengers (kg)	160
Working environment	Reported number of industrial accidents	Industrial accidents per 1 million working hours	18

Source: CPH (2000).

In other areas CPH, like many other airports, has made improvements to its impact monitoring process and has been developing new techniques which could reduce the detrimental environmental effects. For example, in 1999 new facilities to monitor air quality and surface water quality were introduced. A waste-handling plan to enhance waste sorting and increase recycling was prepared and CPH and the airlines investigated ways in which the environmental impact from aircraft washing could be reduced. From 1999, all new purchasing contracts between CPH and suppliers stipulate that the supplier's business is to be operated in an environmentally responsible manner. Copenhagen Airport A/S has also prepared a manual on environmentally sound design and planning, which can be used to ensure that any expansion conforms to the objectives defined in the environmental policy. CPH annually produces an environmental report which is now externally audited.

The largest single environmental investment that CPH has made took place in 1999 when the old terminal building, which was designed in 1939, was relocated. In 1997 this building had been listed as a protected building by the Historic Buildings Council. However, it was taking up valuable space for future terminal expansion – hence the need for relocation. This process took place over one weekend and involved shifting the airport terminal, which weighed more than 2600 tonnes and covered more than 4000 square metres in area, a distance of 3.8 kilometres from the east to the west of the airport.

Sustainability and environmental capacity

Fundamental to the discussions of the environmental and other impacts, is the concept of sustainability and sustainable development. Following various developments such as the publication of the Brandtland report in 1987 and the Earth Summit in Rio de Janeiro in 1992 there has been an increasing awareness and commitment to the principles of sustainable development in many industries – the aviation sector being no exception. Most definitions of sustainability tend to be rather vague and imprecise, sharing the theme of meeting today's needs without sacrificing tomorrow. Thus the benefits of any development must be carefully weighed against the resources to be consumed. Most definitions also identify the need for a balance between social, environmental and economic impacts of any activity.

No overall consensus has yet been reached as to exactly how sustainability can be defined in the context of the aviation industry. For airports, the environmental aspect of sustainable development is all about effective environmental protection and prudent use of natural resources. Many of the measures described in this chapter, for example noise and emission mitigation initiatives and water, waste and energy management programmes, can be considered as helping to encourage a more sustainable industry. Complementary social policies include active involvement by the airport operator in the local community and an effective community relations programme. The responsible management of employee health, safety and security issues at the airport and equal opportunities employment policies is also seen as promoting sustainability.

Social equity and improvements in the quality of life are often cited as key aims of sustainable development. From an economic viewpoint, sustainability is to do with the maintenance of high and stable levels of economic growth and employment, and adequate investment in infrastructure. The concept of sustainable development recognizes that economic growth, social benefits and environmental quality are not mutually exclusive events. They should not be treated as being in conflict.

Central to the notion of sustainability is the idea of environmental capacity. In a purely physical sense, an airport's capacity can be defined in a variety of ways, such as the number of runway slots, or capacity of terminals, gates or apron areas. However, increasingly it is the environmental capacity, which is set by consideration of the impacts of an airport's operation upon the local environment and the lives of residents of local communities, which will determine the ultimate overall capacity of an airport. It is the environmental capacity of airports which is likely to constrain growth, rather than any physical or financial considerations (Coleman, 1999). In many cases, airports will reach their environmental capacity before making full use of existing infrastructure. Airports may also not be able to make changes to the physical infrastructure if this involves exceeding the environmental capacity limits. In effect, airports will only be able to grow if they minimize the impact of these expanding activities on the environment and the community.

The environmental capacity can de defined as 'the extent to which the environment and the local community is able to tolerate, assimilate or process outputs derived from airport activities' (London Luton Airport, 2000). The capacity limits can be set using environmental criteria related to noise, air and water quality, surface transport and so on, rather than assessing the physical capacity of the infrastructure. If growth has to be regulated, many in the industry consider that such environmental controls are more appropriate than placing an overall limit, for example on passenger throughput. These environmental threshold values ideally should be based on scientific research and sociological research on the tolerance of local communities to environmental impacts. They can also be adjusted to take account of new mitigation measures. Within these predetermined threshold capacity values, airport operators and airlines are free to expand or modify their services (Graham, 1999).

While environmental capacity as a concept is relatively easy to understand, it is clearly very much more difficult to put the idea into practice. This can be done by looking at all the individual impacts at airports and ways to reduce them. However, many of these are separate and uncoordinated and, so, it has been suggested that in order to take on fully the ideas of sustainability, the approach to environmental capacity must go further (Gillingwater, 2000). For example, should there be some trade-off between costs and benefits associated with all the different environmental impacts and also consideration of their effects throughout time? For instance, aircraft noise is a short-term quality of life issue rather than being related, like emissions, to the long-term use of the environment. Another area of consideration is where to draw the boundary between global and local impacts when determining environmental capacity.

Environmental capacity consideration at Amsterdam airport

Amsterdam airport, which is owned by the Schiphol Group, handled 36 million passengers, 1 181 000 tonnes of freight and 393 600 aircraft movements in 1999. Throughout the early 1990s traffic was forecast to grow steadily, so in 1995 a decision was made by the government about the future development of the airport. It gave approval for a fifth runway which was aimed, not at increasing capacity, but instead at diverting traffic to a less noise-sensitive approach. A number of environmental limits were also established:

1   The acceptable noise contour was to be no larger than 15 000 houses until completion of the fifth runway in 2003, and then no larger than 10 000.
2   Passenger numbers could not exceed 44 million in any year.
3   Cargo tonnes could not exceed 3.3 million in any year.

However, healthy growth in 1997 and 1998 meant that in both these years the noise contour limitation was exceeded, although the houses affected still remained under 15 000. The airport also became slot co-ordinated in 1998. The government granted Schiphol an exemption from the noise limits, but instead imposed a limit of 380 000 movements in 1998 and then annual growth limits of 20 000 movements. At the end of 1999, the government stated its views for the long-term development of the airport. The environmental limits were still to be applied but further growth could be possible until 2010 by optimizing the environmental capacity. In the longer term, after 2010, a redesign of Schiphol might be possible or beyond 2020 the development of a new offshore airport might be considered.

The options for the short-term optimization of the capacity have been considered by the Dutch civil aviation department to assess which measures are the most efficient and lead to a minimum of economic costs and a maximum of environmental benefits. The model used assumed that passenger numbers would grow unconstrained to 65 million passengers in 2010. Various measures were then tested such as a regulatory limit on passenger numbers, a 7 Euro surcharge on all passengers and a noise surcharge related to different levels of noise. Slot trading to achieve a maximum of 600 000 annual movements was also considered. These options were assessed by analysing the impact on traffic, noise, in terms of the house affected, and airline cost or passenger fare. The impact on jobs was also considered.

The results of the analysis are shown in Table 9.8. A simple levy to reduce passenger numbers to 44 million proved to be very costly for the airlines. The airline cost fell when the option of a 600 000 movement limit and slot trading was considered, but still the economic costs were comparatively high compared with the environmental benefits. The noise surcharge provided a more optimal balance between economic costs and environmental benefits. Some combination of these measures may have to be introduced at Amsterdam and other airports in the future to enable airports to grow within the boundaries of environmental limits (Veldhuis, 2000). Another airport facing considerable environmental pressure but close to its physical capacity is Frankfurt airport. A fourth runway at Frankfurt has been allowed for landings only and this may include a voluntary ban on scheduled operations between the hours of 2300

Table 9.8   The impacts of different options for optimizing noise capacity at Amsterdam airport

		Impact of option (% change 1996–2010)			
	Unconstrained growth	44 million passenger limit	7 Euro passenger levy	1–4 Euro noise surcharge	Slot trading with 600 000 movements limit
Movements	128	−31	−15	−8	−18
Passengers	141	−32	−11	−3	−10
Fares	0	+20	+7	+2	+6
Noise	43	−35	−39	−32	−40
Jobs	43	−18	−24	−18	−21

Source: Veldhuis, 2000.

and 0500. As a result the airport may shift Deutschepost, which has domestic overnight hub operations to neighbouring Hahn airport, which it also owns. Some charter services have already been transferred there (Airport Business Communique, 2000).

In conclusion, this chapter has identified the major environmental impacts associated with airport operations and has described various environmental management approaches designed to reduce these effects. Environmental issues are beginning to affect most aspects of airport operations – even the EU proposal on slot allocations suggests that environmental as well as physical capacity should be considered. The chapter has also discussed how environmental concerns can be viewed within the context of sustainable development, which aims to balance the social, environmental and economic impacts of any activity. In spite of technological, operational and other mitigation measures to minimize the environmental impacts, the growth rates being predicted for air transport, if allowed to take place, will mean that the environmental impacts will increase. Therefore, the aviation industry clearly faces a major challenge in the future. In essence this challenge is how to maintain economic and social benefits from air transport, encourage economic development through mobility and yet respond to the increasing environmental pressures being placed on the industry. There is still a great deal of uncertainty as to how this can be achieved.

References and further reading

ACI-Europe (1995). *Environmental Handbook*. ACI-Europe.

Aeroports de la Cote d'Azur (2000). *Annual Report 1999*. Aeroports de la Cote d'Azur.

Aeroports de Paris (2000). *Annual Report 1999*. Aeroports de Paris.

Air Transport Action Group (2000). *Aviation and the environment*, Geneva: ATAG.

Airport Business Communique (2000). Europe's airports could face a 30% reduction in operations. *Airport Business Communique*, December/January, 6.

Airports Policy Consortium (1997). *On the Path of Environmental Limits*. Policy paper 6, APC.

Alamdara, F. and Brewer, D. (1994). Taxation policy for aircraft emissions. *Transport Policy*, **1** (3), 149–59.

Anker, R. (1997). Airports and the environment. University of Westminster Airport Policy and Planning Seminar, London, May.

Ashworth, J. (2000). New York's answer to Heathrow. *The Times*, 12 August, p. 26.

Association of European Airlines (1999). *Yearbook 1999*. AEA.

Association of European Airlines (2000). *Yearbook 2000*. AEA.

BAA Heathrow (1999). *A Surface Access Strategy for Heathrow: The Next Five Years*. BAA Heathrow.

BAA Heathrow (2000a). *A Surface Access Strategy for Heathrow – Interim Update February 2000*. BAA Heathrow.

BAA Heathrow (2000b). *BAA Heathrow towards Sustainability*. BAA Heathrow.

Baker, C. (2000). Emission impossible. *Airline Business*, May, 36–7.

Baker, C. and George, A. (2000). The next chapter. *Airline Business*, March, 54–7.

Brussels International Airport Company (2000). *Annual Report 1999*. Brussels International Airport Company.

Civil Aviation Authority (CAA) (1998a). *The Single European Aviation Market: The First Five Years*. CAP 685, CAA.

Civil Aviation Authority (CAA) (1998b). *Passengers at Gatwick, Heathrow and Manchester Airports in 1997*. CAP 690, CAA.

Coleman, R (1999). Environmentally sustainable capacity. ECAC/EU dialogue with the European air transport industry: aviation capacity – challenges for the future. Salzburg, April.

Communique Airport Business (1998). Good neighbour project ensures local environmental voice. *Communique Airport Business*, winter, 21.

Copenhagen Airport A/S (CPH) (2000). *Environmental Report 2000*. CPH.

Dennis, N. (1999). Low cost carriers and scheduled airline operations. University of Westminster Aviation and Tourism Seminar, London, January.

Department of the Environment, Transport and the Regions (DETR) (1998). *A New Deal for Transport*. White Paper. The Stationery Office.

Department of the Environment, Transport and the Regions (DETR) (1999). *Guidance on Airport Transport Forums and Airport Surface Access*. DETR.

Department of the Environment, Transport and the Regions (DETR) (2000). *The Future of Aviation*. Consultation document, DETR.

Düsseldorf Airport (2000a). *Annual Report 1999*. Dusseldorf Airport.

Düsseldorf Airport (2000b). Düsseldorf International granted permission to increase number of aircraft movements. Press release, 22 September.

European Commission (1999). *Air Transport and the Environment: Towards Meeting the Challenges of Sustainable Development*. COM (1999) 640 final, EC.

Feldman, J. (2001). A user-friendly decision. *Air Transport World*, March, 51–3.

Frankfurt Airport (2000). *Annual Report 1999*. Frankfurt Airport.

Gaustad, A. (1996). Environmental impact assessment: the Norwegian experience. In *Environmental Management at Airports* (N. Pedoe, D. Raper and J. Holden, eds), Thomas Telford.

George, A. (2000). EU challengers ICAO in hushkit case. *Airline Business*, October, 26.

Gethin, S. (1998). An environmental lead. *Jane's Airport Review*, October, 10.

Gill, T. and George, A. (1999). Europe breaks ranks on noise. *Airline Business*, April, 32–3.

Gillingwater, D. (2000). Environmental capacity – the challenge for the aviation industry. Sustainable cities and aviation network UK workshop conference, London, June.

Graham, B (1999). Environmental sustainability, airport capacity and European air transport liberalisation: irreconcilable goals? *Journal of Transport Geography*, **7**, 165–80.

Grossenbacher, G. (1999). Zürich flughafen as a model number 1 in Europe regarding integration of the rail and air modes. ECAC/EU dialogue with the European air transport industry: aviation capacity – challenges for the future, Salzburg, April.

IARO/ATAG/ACI (1998). *Air Rail Links: Guide to Best Practice*. IARO/ATAG/ACI.

Intergovernmental Panel on Climate Change (1999). *Aviation and the Global Atmosphere: Summary for Policymakers*. IPCC.

International Air Transport Association (IATA) (2000). *Airport and En-route Charges Manual*. IATA.

Jane's Airport Review (1999). Los Angeles airports on environment fast track. *Jane's Airport Review*, June, 23.

London Luton Airport (2000). *Development Brief*. LLA.

Luftfartsverket (1991). *New Oslo Airport Gardermoen Master Plan*. Luftfartsverket.

Manchester Airport (1997). *Ground Transport Policy*. Manchester Airport.

McNamara, S. (2000). Continuous descent approach trials reveal significant improvements in emissions and fuel consumption. *ERA Regional Report*, November, 9.

Meyer, A. (1996). Noise abatement at Zürich airport. In *Environmental Management at Airports* (N. Pedoe, D. Raper and J. Holden, eds), Thomas Telford.

Navarre, D. (1996). Comparison of airport accessibility by land transport. Second Airport Regions Conference, Vantaa, November.

Newcastle Airport (1999). *Annual Report 1998/9*, Newcastle Airport.

Niblett, R. (1996). Long distance rail services to airports. PTRC annual conference, Brunel University, September.

Schiphol Group (2000). *Environmental Report 1999*. Schiphol Group.

Thomas, C. (1996). Noise related to airport operations – community impacts. In *Environmental Management at Airports* (N. Pedoe, D. Raper and J. Holden, eds), Thomas Telford.

Twigg, J. (2000). The true cost of environmental issues. University of Westminster/Cranfield University Airport Economics and Finance Symposium, London, March.

Veldhuis, J. (2000). Determining environmental capacity at Amsterdam airport Schiphol. University of Westminster Demand Analysis and Capacity Seminar, London, October.

10
Future prospects

A dominant theme running through this book is that airports are going through a period of unprecedented change. The more competitive environment brought about by the deregulation of the airline industry, first in the USA, then Europe and to a lesser extent Asia, has had a major impact on airport operations. Airports are functioning in an increasingly commercial marketplace and are having to modify their product to meet the needs of new airline customers, such as alliances and low-cost carriers. As the airline industry evolves and as further deregulation occurs, airports will need to continue to adapt to new demands.

The introduction of new aircraft types, such the A380, will have major infrastructure and capacity implications for the airports. Technological improvements to airfield and airspace infrastructure and aircraft may improve efficiency and reduce some of the undesirable environmental impacts of airports. Technology will also enable passengers to be more informed and to be processed more efficiently through airports, as ticketless travel, machine-readable travel documents and better security scanning systems become more widely accepted. The new e-economy will also have a major impact on the nature of freight operations at airports. Furthermore, e-procurement policies, which offer substantial cost savings, are bound to increase in popularity at airports.

One of the most important changes that has occurred within the airport industry is privatization. While a number of significant airport privatizations have taken place, currently the degree of concentration and private sector involvement within the airport industry is fairly small – much less than in the airline industry. However, all indications are that many more privatizations are planned for the early years of the twenty-first century. This is in spite of the fact that the popularity of airports as investment opportunities seems to be dwindling slightly in reaction to uncertainties over regulation constraints, environmental restrictions and, within Europe, the loss of intra-EU duty- and tax-free revenues.

Therefore, there are new markets available for airport management companies who, faced with limited possibilities for expansion at home, are eager to expand. There are also now a significant number of non-airport organizations hoping to use these opportunities to become global airport players. It appears that those most likely to achieve success will be the companies who already have had both the ability and the foresight to establish themselves as international companies. The airport industry, like the airline industry, seems set to become more consolidated and more airport alliances and co-operation seems likely in the future. There probably will eventually be only space for a limited number of players.

There has been considerable debate as to whether the traditional airport companies with a long track record of operating airports, albeit often in protected quasi-monopolistic markets, are better equipped to run airports than newly established airport management companies such as TBI. Indeed, this raises the fundamental question, are airports really any different from any other business once the technical and operations know-how has been acquired? It is too early in the evolutionary stage of airport globalization to answer this question with any degree of certainty or to identify the factors which will determine the most successful type of airport management in this new global environment, or which will bring the greatest value added.

The impact of such fundamental changes within the airport industry cannot be assessed without considering the parallel airline developments towards deregulation, privatization and global alliances. The post-deregulation environment means that airlines are trying hard to control costs to improve their operating margins and are consequently putting greater pressure on the airports to control their costs. Moreover, the creation of airline alliances has meant that airlines are no longer automatically linked to the national airport of the country. Airline alliances could potentially become very powerful partners in the airport–airline relationship, but increasing globalization within the airport industry might help to balance out this. It is very difficult to predict the exact impact that globalization will have on both industries – particularly whether it will lead to greater co-operation or conflict between the two. Such developments will, however, irreversibly change the traditional airline–airport roles and interactions which have existed for many years. Some industry commentators have argued that ultimately the air transport industry will be dominated by a few powerful airport global players, each teamed up with a large airline alliance. It is difficult to see how such a system would work, if permitted on fair competition grounds, given the apparent lack of synergy between the current airline and airport groupings. Greater co-operation

Table 10.1   Long-term forecasts of global passenger traffic growth

Organization	Time period	Traffic measure	Average annual growth rate (%)
Boeing	2000–19	Passenger-miles	4.8
Airbus	2000–19	Passenger-kms	4.9
Rolls-Royce	2000–19	Passenger-kms	5.0
ICAO	1997–2020	Scheduled passenger-kms	4.5
ACI	1997–2010	Passengers	4.0

Sources: Boeing, Airbus, Rolls-Royce, ICAO, ACI.

between airports, particularly those serving the same airline alliance, may, of course, change this.

A key reason for the accelerating pace towards airport privatization is the need to find new funding for investment. Many funds traditionally came from public sources, but increasingly this sector is unable or unwilling to provide such support. All indications are that air transport demand is set to continue to grow – putting pressure on airports to expand their capacity (Table 10.1). Boeing, for example, is predicting an overall passenger growth rate of 4.8 per cent per annum until 2019. The relatively mature North Atlantic market is forecast to grow by only 3.6 per cent compared with the higher growth rates for the more rapidly developing markets of intra-Asia/Pacific and intra-Latin America – 6.7 per cent and 7.7 per cent respectively. Intra-European traffic is expected to grow at 5.0 per cent per annum. Other forecasts by Airbus, Rolls-Royce and ICAO are of similar magnitude. The units of these forecasts are passenger-miles or kilometres, which are more relevant to airlines than airports. They tend to push up passenger forecasts by up to 1 per cent per annum as the average distance flown is predicted to increase. These forecasts also do not take into account any physical or environmental constraints which may occur.

Then there are the ACI global forecasts, which are based on the passenger forecasts of its individual members, which predict an overall annual average growth rate of 4.0 per cent. The lowest growth of 2.9 per cent is expected in North America with Europe having a growth rate of 4.8 per cent. Taking all these forecasts into account, there seems to be a broad consensus of view that global passenger numbers will grow at around 4 per cent per annum.

Economic growth, which reflects business activity and personal wealth, and the cost of travel, will continue to play a major role in shaping the growth of passenger demand. For certain markets, particularly within the USA and Europe, the responsiveness of demand to changes to income may be weakening as demand maturity sets in. Elsewhere, particularly in developing areas of the world, the relative immature market and higher than average predicted economic growth will ensure high growth rates. Deregulation and particularly the introduction of low fares may stimulate new growth, as has been experienced in Europe with the new breed of low-cost airlines. More sophisticated telecommunication links may facilitate more effective teleconferencing and could reduce the demand for business travel. Such links, however, may actually

Table 10.2   Long-term forecasts of global freight traffic growth

Organization	Time period	Traffic measure	Average annual growth rate (%)
Boeing	2000–19	Freight tonne-miles	6.4
Airbus	2000–19	Freight tonne-kms	5.7
Rolls-Royce	2000–19	Freight tonne-kms	6.5
ACI	1997–2010	Freight tonnes	6.4

Sources: Boeing, Airbus, Rolls-Royce, ICAO, ACI.

encourage more global trade and act as a complement to air travel rather than as a substitute.

Freight traffic is generally expected to increase at a faster rate than passenger traffic (Table 10.2). Air freight demand is, likewise, primarily driven by economic growth and travel cost – as well as international trade. Higher growth is generally expected because of globalization trends which have led to increased reliance on global components and products that need to be transported around the world. The rapidly expanding knowledge-based industrial sectors such as computing, electronics, communications and pharmaceuticals are the most international and are heavily reliant on air travel for the transportation of their high-value/low-weight products. Increasing reliance on just-in-time inventory systems favours air freight. E-commerce has also brought substantial reductions in the distribution costs of air freight and increased demand for the integrators and the express mail sector. The proportion of freight carried on all-freight flights is likely to increase, partly due to the high growth of the express sector and partly because the current bellyhold capacity of passenger aircraft is insufficient. These freighter aircraft are increasingly likely to use uncongested hubs with no environmental restrictions – particularly at night – but such hubs may be more difficult to find in the future!

In most cases it is passenger growth which drives airport development. Even if there is a gradual slow-down in the rate of growth in certain passengers markets, the sheer volume of traffic at many airports means that even relatively small growth rates still produce large increases in the absolute number of air passengers. Airlines are much more capable than airports of adapting to market growth by redistributing capacity across the networks, increasingly by sharing capacity with alliance members, or even by adding extra aircraft to the fleet. Airports lack this flexibility. It can take years for airports to gain approval and then to build new infrastructure. The London Heathrow Terminal 5 inquiry in the late 1990s in the UK lasted more than four years and was one of the longest planning enquiries in UK history.

Very few new airports or fully expanded airports have been built in the USA or Europe in 1990s. Denver, Munich, Oslo and Milan are the only examples. The new Athens airport opened in 2001 with plans for other new airports being limited to Berlin and Lisbon. Manchester, Paris Charles de Gaulle, Stockholm Arlanda and Amsterdam are among the few European airports having or planning new runways in the early years of the twenty-first century but some of these have environmental restrictions imposed on them. The shortage of airport capacity in Asia is currently not such as a serious issue, owing to traffic growth having been delayed slightly by the Asian economic crisis of the late 1990s and the opening of several new airports such as in Hong Kong, Macau, Shanghai and Kuala Lumpur. Other new airports will open at Seoul in 2001 and in Bangkok possibly in 2005. In India new capacity will be provided at Hyderabad and Banga-lore. A number of privatizations in South America should enable greater invest-ment in this region. In the remaining areas of the world, such as Africa and Middle East, lack of sufficient airport capacity is nor usually a major problem.

The capacity problems are, therefore, most acute in Europe and North America. In Europe they are seen as a major hurdle to achieving the full benefits of a deregulated market. In spite of this, competitive pressures and the rapid growth of low-cost carriers, typically using relatively small aircraft types, has meant that in the average aircraft size has not increased substantially since the early 1980s. This has put further pressures on the already congested runways at many airports. The consequences are growing congestion and delays although, admittedly, some of these difficulties could potentially be reduced through greater ATC co-ordination and harmonization. Technical improve-ments at the airport, for example advanced wake vortex technologies and arrivals and departure management systems, could optimize traffic flow in and out of the airport.

In the short term a more effective slot allocation process might alleviate some of the capacity bottlenecks. Secondary and regional airports could also take some of the growth away from major airports as could high-speed rail. In the long term, however, the problem of capacity shortages at major airports is not going to disappear. Growing pressures for greater sustainability and environ-mental capacity constraints, as experienced at Amsterdam, will make it more and more difficult to provide additional airport capacity. The more extreme environmentalists will argue that there is no way that the potential demand for air transport in the future should be met, and that the solution is to constrain growth. It is a difficult problem balancing out the needs for quality and sustain-ability of life against desires for greater mobility.

In conclusion, airport operators have a challenging time ahead. They are confronted with conflicting demands from their different stakeholders. The scheduled airlines seek greater capacity and have evolving needs as they continue to restructure themselves into global alliances. Low-cost airlines and freight operators have other requirements. The environmentalists want greater protection of the environment and society. Passenger expectations in terms of service quality is rising. Regional authorities want to ensure that airports gener-ate maximum economic benefits. Governments want to guarantee, perhaps through regulation, that airports are not abusing their considerable market power. Then, of course, there are the financial demands from the airport owners or shareholders, which are increasingly being driven by private sector concerns. This book has considered all these important interrelated issues and has aimed to provide some insight into how airport operators might address the challenges of the future.

Index